Women in 1900

Gateway to the Political Economy of the 20th Century

In the series

WOMEN IN THE POLITICAL ECONOMY
edited by Ronnie J. Steinberg

Women in 1900

*Gateway to the
Political Economy
of the 20th Century*

Christine E. Bose

Temple University Press
Philadelphia

Temple University Press, Philadelphia 19122
Copyright © 2001 by Temple University
All rights reserved
Published 2001
Printed in the United States of America

Library of Congress Cataloging-in-Publication Data

Bose, Christine E.
  Women in 1900 : gateway to the political economy of the 20th century /
  Christine E. Bose.
      p.   cm. — (Women in the political economy)
  Includes bibliographical references and index.
  ISBN 1-56639-837-1 (cloth : alk. paper) — ISBN 1-56639-838-X (pbk. :
  alk. paper)
    1. Women—United States—Economic conditions—20th century.
  2. Women—Employment—United States—History—20th century.
  3. Sexual division of labor—United States—History—20th century.
  4. Households—United States—History—20th century.   I. Title.
  II. Series.

HQ1419 .B69 2001
331.4'0973–dc21   00-032567

*To Henry Peter Bose, Dora Wacker Bose,
Henry Frederick Christensen,
and Elmina Carlson Christensen,
whose experiences inspired this volume*

Contents

Preface and Acknowledgments

MY INTELLECTUAL CURIOSITY about women's roles at the beginning of the twentieth century was engaged by several experiences. First, my early investigation into the status of contemporary housewives and the effects of technological change on housework made me consider how and if the industrial revolution had actually "revolutionized" women's home and work roles or had modified the links between them in any way. Later, at the University of Washington, my attention was captured again by the opportunity to watch the manuscript census being coded and computerized, creating the 1900 Public Use Sample of data on individuals and their households. Reading the original census forms I could observe the variety of household structures that families created, notice the range of old and new occupations that household members entered (including interesting job titles such as "capitalist" and "typewriter"), and envision people's history as immigrants and migrants. On a personal level, the manuscript census concretized and brought to life the experiences of my grandparents, most of whom immigrated to the United States shortly after 1900. On an academic level, I was drawn to consider the obvious differences and some surprising similarities between social patterns at the beginning and end of the twentieth century.

As a result of these observations, I used the 1900 data as the source for two published pieces of research, one on how household resources predicted women's employment (Bose 1984) and the other on the undercount of women's work (Bose 1987). Still, I felt there was a larger and more detailed story about women's roles in the political economy that remained untold. Yet I needed to reach an end-of-the-century perspective myself before I could recount that tale in a manner that would do it justice.

As with every research project that has extended over a long period of time, there are many people and funding sources to thank. I am grateful for support from the National Science

Foundation (SBR-9320663) and from the University at Albany, State University of New York (SUNY) Center for Social and Demographic Analysis, especially for their Center Associates Award (1991–92) and for other aid provided through their grants from the NICHD (P30-HD32041) and NSF (SBR-9512290). At an early stage, this research also was partially funded by a grant from the State University of New York Research Foundation (320-7519A) and by the original NSF grant to Samuel Preston, then at the University of Washington, that supported the creation of the 1900 census Public Use Sample. The opinions in this book are my own and do not represent those of the funding agencies.

The data analysis for this volume involved considerable reformatting of the original census data sample and the efforts of many skilled people at both the University of Washington and the University at Albany, SUNY. Stephen N. Graham initiated this work at the University of Washington by rectangularizing the data set and calculating a series of variables that summarized information on households. Later, at the University at Albany, Ruby Wang translated my guidelines for "hidden headship" into a database of single mothers living as subfamilies. Her work also was invaluable in changing my data formatting each time the university changed computer systems. Patty J. Glynn calculated several measures that gave me the contemporary comparisons I needed for my 1900 findings. Last, but probably most important over the years, has been the expert research assistance of Rachel Bridges Whaley, the only person besides me who knows all the census recoded measures that were created for this project. As a testimony to both the time it took to write this book and her own skills, she has evolved from a research assistant to an excellent researcher in her own right and a valued co-author on other projects. She gave unstintingly of her time to merge the county- and state-level ICPSR data with the census data, to run most of the data analyses, and to catch mistakes in any of my computer programming ideas.

Many other people have given me important feedback on drafts of each chapter. I especially wish to thank members of the Women and Work Research Group, who read and commented on innumerable versions of most of the chapters when we met twice a year. They suggested helpful readings, encouraged me to avoid the passive voice, helped unpack complicated ideas that were squashed into too few sentences, and generally cheered me on. Most important among this group, especially for strengthening this book, have been Myra Marx Ferree, Carole Turbin, Natalie Sokoloff, and Frances Rothstein. Other friends and colleagues deserve thanks for their comments and suggestions on individual chapters, including Lisa Brush, Eric Sager, Matthew Sobek, and Stewart Tolnay.

Finally, I would like to thank several people for nourishing this project. At Temple University Press, Michael Ames and series editor Ronnie Steinberg encouraged me to write this book, putting faith in it from the beginning. At the University at Albany, Edna Acosta-Belén has given me many years of her personal support to finish this volume. Not only did she read chapters, suggest improvements, and urge me to move faster, but she also believed in my vision of this book and changed many of her plans to accommodate my drive to complete it. I doubt that I can ever thank her and all my friends, both those named and unnamed, quite enough.

Women in 1900

*Gateway to the Political Economy
of the 20th Century*

1   Introduction

Understanding the Past
to Interpret the Present

THE PERIOD around the year 1900 has always interested me, perhaps because it was around this time that my grandparents emigrated from Europe to the United States. But historical information from this era really caught my attention when the 1900 census data first became publicly accessible. As these data were being entered into computer files, my eye was drawn to the case of a husband and wife in California who both worked as raisin pickers. I found this situation odd, since one could not possibly pick raisins—you pick grapes, which are dried to make raisins. But after I understood their job actually was to pick through or sort raisins, I noticed that their household included the wife's twenty-year-old sister as well as the couple's three young children. I realized that having another adult woman in a household was a major way for working-class wives to make some provision for child care so they could hold a job outside the home. Even more common in other households were co-resident relatives who held jobs and supplemented the household's income so that wives could stay home with their children. I was struck by the constancy of women's problems ensuring child care, by the insufficiency of one wage for many households in that period, and by the different solutions they chose to similar problems we still have today.

These observations were the inspiration for my writing this comprehensive, national-level study of women's work and the general place of women in the U.S. political economy during the key transition period around the turn to the twentieth century. Although the study is rooted in data from the year 1900, my primary goal is to examine the forms some of our contemporary issues and concerns took then, revealing both enduring patterns as well as some of the changes that have taken place subsequently, thus deepening our understanding of women's evolving economic situation over the course of the twentieth century.

The relatively short time span around 1900, between 1890 and the end of World War I, set the stage for much of the twentieth century. It was a crucial historical period in which a wide array of changes occurred that affected many facets of women's (and men's) employment. The major economic transformation in the United States was the transition from an agricultural and industrial employment base to an industrial and white-collar one. As new jobs were created and existing jobs underwent modifications in their technology base or their work organization, the skills workers needed began to change. Less obviously, the shift in occupational structure created changes in the sex composition and sex segregation of jobs.

During this same interval a major social and cultural transformation took place in the United States, driven by the rapid growth in immigration, which peaked in 1909. New groups of workers, especially from Europe, constantly were entering the labor force, and many first- or second-generation immigrant women were visible among the ranks of domestic and factory workers.

Finally, the turn of the century was a time of geographic mobility, with many people moving into cities. About half of the population still lived in towns or rural areas of less than a thousand people, but the urban job market was growing, drawing rural residents to cities large and small. Turn-of-the-century immigrants, who had little access to farm ownership, also arrived in cities and often remained there. The year 1900 is a key time to explore, since it falls in the middle of a period of economic, social, and demographic change that both ushered in and laid the groundwork for the twentieth century.

In addition to marking a pivotal historical moment, the year 1900 is often used as a baseline against which to gauge the economic changes of the next one hundred years, since it is the gateway to the twentieth century. Unfortunately, sociological research on women's work often picks up later, examining the changes that became visible during World War II. Meanwhile students tend to think that the history of women's work began relatively recently, in the early 1960s, with the civil rights and feminist movements. Such foreshortened views leave us with misconceptions of the past and make it easy to assume that the turn of the century was a time far different from our own, when women's employment was an embattled issue. When we use the phrases "traditional family division of labor" or "traditional women's work" to depict women's tasks during this period, we invoke a past that is only imagined (Coontz 2000). These expressions conjure a model of the full-time housewife that was defined as conventional only in the late nineteenth century. Indeed, U.S. women had important economic roles in both agricultural and early industrial households. Nevertheless, the power of this imagined past has meant that most historical studies have focused on the increase in women's recorded labor force participation rates over the twentieth century, leaving the false impression that women had few economic roles in 1900. Consequently, many of us retain narrow preconceptions about this period, while ignoring many other connections with women's current positions.

ISSUES LINKING THE PRESENT AND THE PAST

By focusing on 1900, I supplement, challenge, and expand the prevailing understanding of current concerns surrounding women's economic roles. This book is intended to provide a historical perspective on contemporary issues that all too often are analyzed only in terms of the present.

When comparing the beginning and end of the twentieth century, we must keep in mind that change is not necessarily linear. Significant alterations in the U.S. political economy during the twentieth century occurred in three distinct periods: from 1890 through World War I, again in the 1940s (including both World War II and postwar years), and once more beginning in the 1970s. Of course, we have come to expect vast differences between the beginning and the end of the twentieth century. Yet there were both continuities and discontinuities in the major factors shaping, and social concerns surrounding, women's work in this century.

I begin my analysis in Chapter 2 by challenging a fundamental assumption: the popular but limited understanding of work as paid employment outside the home. This mistaken notion has been called into question by the contemporary growth of home-based small businesses in the United States and by the growth of microenterprises in the developing world. Thus, home-based work is now sometimes recognized as work. However, we often ignore women's early twentieth century income-generating work taking in boarders or in tenement sweatshops, on the family farm, or in the family business as a forerunner of current home-based work. Even though home-based employment often went unrecorded by the census in 1900, especially when done by women, it is not a new phenomenon. Indeed, some of this hidden work, such as renting out a room, selling home-made goods, or providing child care in the home, still exists in what we now call the "informal economy," whose workers remain for the most part uncounted. Finding such work and counting the workers changes prevalent images of women's employment status in 1900 and tempers perceptions of the improvements in women's employment opportunities over the century. Other unpaid work, including caring for the elderly at home or doing volunteer work outside of the home, also contributes to the political economy. Such work is beyond the scope of this book, since it would be impossible to recognize as work using either 1900 or 2000 census data.

We have preconceptions not only about the nature of work, but also about the factors that determine which jobs people hold. The significance of individual achievement in U.S. culture leads us to think that an individual's success or failure in the labor market is largely due to that person's own skills and characteristics. In fact, an entire school of economic thought, called human capital theory, is organized around this basic tenet. This belief obscures the role of other factors, such as family composition or available local economic opportunities, that have influenced individual employment decisions throughout the twentieth century. In Chapter 3, I develop a model for predicting which women were employed in 1900 that improves upon the human capital approach by incorporating features of a person's household and the local economic geography. In a further innovation, my model illustrates how a woman's individual, household, and regional experiences are each shaped by her gender, race, and social class. This new model can be applied to twenty-first century women as well. What has changed over the past one hundred years is the relative importance of specific predictors of women's work, not the general model itself. For example, among a woman's individual characteristics, education is more important to increasing the probability of her employment than it once was, while being married is less of a hindrance to paid work. After considering the conditions leading to women's employment in Chapter 3, in the next two chapters I investigate the specific occupations in which women were employed. Before looking briefly at the content of those chapters, however, I want to spend a bit more time delineating the household structure and geographic components of my analytical model.

Household structure is not entirely ignored in discussions of contemporary economic problems. Salient issues right now are the increased rate of single motherhood and of female-headed households, both associated with high rates of women's poverty and the consequent need for women's employment. We correctly see this trend as an income problem for the people involved. However, we incorrectly think of it as a recent phenomenon and compare it with the "traditional family structure" of the past, when divorce was difficult to get and husbands supposedly provided most of the financial support for their families. These are false assumptions. Although divorce was rare in 1900, desertion by men was fairly common, leaving women to survive on their own. Industrial accidents also created a plentiful supply of widows, who frequently had young children to support and no life insurance. In reality, about 10 percent of all women were heads of households in 1900, and still others were single mothers with children living in someone else's household. The plight of these women was as much a social concern early in the twentieth century as it is now, although the cause of their household headship and the social construction of their problems were sometimes different. There is much to be learned that is useful in the present from studying how these women subsisted in 1900 without welfare, as I describe in Chapter 6.

Geography entered our current economic discussions during the 1970s, when there were large waves of regionally concentrated plant layoffs associated with U.S.-based corporations moving their production operations overseas. The process, now labeled "de-industrialization," changed the industrial Northeast and Midwest into regions then nicknamed the "rust belt," while there was considerable job growth in the southern and western sun-belt states. Ironically, it was those same rust-belt states that had driven the economy earlier in the century. In Chapter 7, I show that economic geography and regional differences in employment patterns have been important throughout the twentieth century. Indeed, some of the seeds of later change were already apparent in 1900.

Not only do job opportunities vary according to geographic area but, in 1900 as now, in most locations the labor markets for women and men rarely overlapped. This phenomenon, known as occupational sex segregation, was firmly established by the early twentieth century. Occupational segregation is probably the most broad-ranging contemporary work issue as well. It is widely recognized as a major source of gender inequality in the labor market and is largely responsible for the current male-female wage gap. And because employed women earn less than men and often work fewer years than men, their social security and retirement benefits are lower. This difference is accentuated because women often work in less profitable industries, which may not provide pensions at all (Reskin and Hartmann 1986). Occupational segregation hinders women's economic mobility, insofar as there is a "sticky floor" in women's traditional work (Berheide 1992) in addition to the "glass ceiling" most women reach in male-dominated occupations. Furthermore, in sex-atypical jobs, sexual harassment appears to be a major consequence for women, and being treated as tokens is a problem for both men and women.

Occupational segregation according to race was also fairly extensive in 1900. Yet because occupational race segregation declined significantly over the twentieth century, while sex segregation remained relatively high, some think that sex segregation in the workplace was always stronger than racial segregation. In Chapter 4, I show that the interaction between the two was much more complex. Furthermore, the waves of immigration that crested in the early twentieth century added the element of ethnic segregation. The combined result of these two trends was considerable racial-ethnic specialization in the labor force, even among women whose job options were already limited by gender. In mid-century, immigration rates were low, but they are now approaching peak levels again, suggesting that we should still look for ethnic as well as racial specialization in women's work.

Notwithstanding labor market segregation, one job was most common among practically every racial-ethnic group of women in 1900—domestic work. In fact, many immigrant women today still end up as domestics or in sweatshops or doing factory out-work as their predecessors did, even though the immigrants now come from different countries and the industrial structure they encounter in the United States has changed since the early twentieth century. Perhaps because discussions of immigrant communities have shifted their focus to issues of diversity and concepts like ethnic enclaves, and away from assimilation and terms like ghettos, we do not see some of the occupational similarities. Although the current ethnic enclaves have been described as helping immigrant men obtain jobs, it is little remarked how the more negatively stereotyped ghettos that preceded them helped women as well as men locate employment. In Chapter 5, I consider how women who were segregated into domestic work in 1900 labored in a type of ethnic enclave, and I compare their situation with that of immigrant women today.

This book is organized thematically, and there are important if subtle links among the different topics addressed. Work in the informal economy, the determinants of formal employment, and the occupational segregation of women and men are issues that virtually define women's role in the labor force. They are tied to our fundamental understanding of work, and as such they have been recognized in one way or another as abiding concerns of the twentieth century.

In contrast, the topics of (sometimes undocumented) immigrants' employment in domestic work, the high rates of female household headship or single motherhood, and regional diversity in job opportunities are more likely to be regarded as current social problems than as work issues. However, they are key examples of the relationship between a woman's work opportunities and her individual, household, and geographic characteristics, and as such they reveal the nature of women's place in the broader political economy. Without doubt, they are important contemporary issues, but at the same time, each had its counterpart at the beginning of the twentieth century.

"WOMEN'S WORK" VERSUS "WOMEN IN THE POLITICAL ECONOMY"

Why do I emphasize women in the political economy, and not simply women's work? Aren't they the same thing? Although studying women in the political economy includes looking at women's work, it entails a lot more. It shows us how such work is shaped by changes in the wider economy and by institutional forces such as government social welfare policies, labor law, and labor activism (Frader 1998). An examination of work may cover some of the "economy" portion, but it entirely excludes the political component.

As a field of study, political economy places employment in a broad socioeconomic and historical context. Its primary concern is usually with the effects of the U.S. economy's transformation from an agricultural base to an industrial one, and then to a service society. Political economists have been most interested in the comparative economic and political fortunes of working-class people. Indeed, their approach is frequently synonymous with social class–oriented analyses of employment, worker organizations, and social policy. Unfortunately, social class studies often concentrate on men and their social mobility. Although political economists have examined women's labor activism and the increase in married women's employment, they often ignore other gendered components of industrial transformations, such as the changing availability of part-time work or shifts in household structure.

To counterbalance this single focus on social class, two other historical and macroeconomic models have emerged to interpret the effects of twentieth-century economic changes in the United States. Immigration-focused studies developed an ethnicity- and class-oriented model. Meanwhile, feminist research on women's waged and unwaged work developed a gendered class model.

My broad vision of political economy places all three features at the center of this analysis, melding contemporary feminist visions with those focused on race and ethnicity and the more usually considered social class structures. This standpoint is inherently multidisciplinary, drawing primarily on sociology, history, economics, and social policy studies. In addition, a racial-ethnic-, class-, and gender-sensitive approach to political economy reveals previously hidden aspects of women's work, such as work's role in creating purported social problems like female-headed households.

Fortunately, the year 1900 is ideal for studying simultaneous transformations in all three of these stratifying components of the U.S. political economy. Shifts in social class position were in full swing as the economy moved from a predominantly agricultural one to an industrial economy. Women's entry into waged work was clearly evident, reshaping their family lives. And ethnicity was increasingly visible as immigration reached its peak in 1909, producing a population that was 15 percent foreign born. Although that figure subsequently declined to a low of 5 percent in 1970, the foreign-born U.S. population rose again to 9.3 percent by 1998. Late nineteenth century racial patterns did not change considerably until the northward migration of blacks after World War I; however, substantial populations of other racial groups were regionally distributed across the country, with Asians predominantly on the West Coast and Latinos in the Southwest.

Combining all the elements of my model, *Women in 1900: Gateway to the Political Economy of the 20th Century* presents a multilevel, national framework from which to understand women's economic conditions. It interweaves two sets of characteristics, somewhat like the vertical and horizontal patterns in the potholders children create. The horizontal threads symbolize the characteristics that situate women as individuals located simultaneously within their households, counties, and regions. The vertical threads represent their simultaneous experience of race, ethnicity, class, and gender. The interwoven design suggests my conceptualization of gender, class, and race or ethnicity as both structural properties of the political economy and as characteristics of individual women and the households they live in. As an example of this construction (which is explained further in Chapter 3), we can consider that while ethnicity is usually regarded as an individual trait, the ethnic mix of a county's residents is a geographic or structural aspect of the same characteristic. Thus, gender, race, and ethnicity are not merely biological categories or individual traits, they are also embedded in social institutions and in the household or geographic context of everyday life.

RECONCEPTUALIZING THE GATEWAY TO THE TWENTIETH CENTURY: A NATIONAL VIEW

Most socio-historical studies of women in the U.S. political economy do not use national-level data. I do so in order to situate particular regional or ethnic-group patterns of women's work in a broad context and to inquire how representative these experiences might have been. Most of the important books on early twentieth-century women's work have focused either on a few industrial cities, or on specific ethnic groups (or immigrants more generally), or on a single racial group, most commonly white or African-American women. Some (for example, Cohen 1992; DeVault 1990; Dublin 1994; Ewen 1985; Friedman-Kasaba 1996; Glenn 1990; Lamphere 1987) provide considerable detail on a small geographic area and generate intriguing hypotheses about the intersection of work, gender, class, and ethnicity, especially in the Northeast (for a West Coast exception, see Mason and Laslett 1983). Others (Glenn 1986; Jones 1985; Yung 1995) do the same for race-related employment issues. Numerous authors cover the history of a single female-dominated occupation, such as waitressing (Cobble 1991), sales (Benson 1986), the collar industry (Turbin 1992), or domestic servant work (Katzman 1978). The research presented in this book can be used to evaluate whether the employment patterns these authors have found for specific cities and regions, racial-ethnic groups, or occupations are replicated at a national level. Used this way, national-level data reduce the chance of inadvertently creating stereotypes through extrapolation from case studies.

At the same time, this approach develops a mutually supportive relationship between qualitative local studies and this more quantitative national one. National data reveal the range of women's work experiences and thus provide a context for single case studies. For example, national data show that what was reported as the "typical" job of Italian or Russian women actually depended on whether they resided in rural or urban areas, and that women's "typical" nonfarm occupations were different in northeastern, midwestern, and southern cities.

This is not the first book to examine women's turn-of-the-century work at a national level. For example, Watkins (1994) briefly examines gender and industry in 1910. Yet she primarily focuses on demographic issues such as fertility, mortality, and household structure. There have been other economic histories of women's employment that were nationwide and encompassed several decades of the twentieth century. However, they have tended to focus on the most easily measured concerns, such as the transformation of women's endeavors into waged work (Kessler-Harris 1982) and the increase in employment rates among married women (Goldin 1990), rather than on more contemporary concerns. Furthermore, many have relied on a variety of regional or state reports (Kessler-Harris 1982) or on published national census data (Amott and Matthaei 1991; Matthaei 1982). I reanalyze the original 1900 census data both because of inaccuracies in published figures, which I describe later, and because my analytical framework combines information on individuals, their households, and geographic area that must be constructed out of the census's original format.

Because my approach to women's roles in the political economy is national, information on geographic and economic differences must be incorporated. Simple location measures, such as the region or the size of a town or city a woman lived in, are included in the census data. However, I created additional contextual indicators to clarify how women's employment decisions were structured by the opportunities available in their local economies. This information provides the context or background against which each person lived their life. For example, a woman could escape employment in domestic work—the predominant

women's job of the period—only if there were alternative workplaces, such as manufacturing firms, especially those paying
higher wages. Or an immigrant woman might have a better
chance of finding work if she lived in a community with other
immigrants, especially of the same nationality, who would help
each other out, creating what we now call an ethnic enclave.
Measures I added, such as the county average for women's wages
in manufacturing, the average firm size, or the county's ethnic
mix, tap into these issues.

Such contextual data reduce the risk of ignoring regional variation during the search for national trends. At the same time, they
help us determine when race or ethnic-group patterns that
seemed unique or a cultural feature actually were the result of a
connection between the distribution of each group across the
country and the economic opportunities available to them in
each place.

RECONCEPTUALIZING THE DATA: THE CENSUS OF 1900

What kind of data is available with which to construct a national
portrait of women's economic activities at the gateway to the
twentieth century? And how have I reconceptualized and transformed these data to answer the complex questions I have posed
about the past as a gateway to the present?

The manuscripts for the U.S. census of 1900, which provide
much more detail than the published summary tabulations, were
closed to non-census personnel for seventy years because of con-
fidentiality issues. When they were opened to the public, in the
1970s, a set of the original data, known as a Public Use Sample,
was drawn from this source, coded, computerized, documented,
and made available by the University of Washington Center for
Studies in Demography and Ecology. This data set is a nationally
representative sample that includes one in every 760 individuals,
for a total of 100,438 people recorded in the 27,069 households
in which they lived. All the information on each individual and
household available from the original enumerator sheets was
incorporated into this data sample. I began my study using this
data set, but I also had to transform it.

First, the data had to be reformatted so that each individual woman's "record" or file included statistics on her household as well. Then, in order to include geographically based contextual measures, I matched each individual in the Public Use Sample with economic data on their county of residence—information I drew from the Inter-University Consortium for Political and Social Research's county and state data for the same period. In this way I created a data set that includes measures on individual men and women and their households, and relevant geographic contextual measures.

Unfortunately, the data gathered by the U.S. Census Bureau, like other public records, are not as free from ideological influences as one might think. This problem does not reduce the usefulness of the data, but it does mean one should understand how 1900 terminology relates (or does not relate) to that used a century later. The census definition of gainful employment used from 1870 through 1930 tended to undercount women's work in each of those decades, with the possible exception of 1910 (see also Abel and Folbre 1990; Bose 1987; Ciancanelli 1983; Goldin 1990; Sobek 1997). Furthermore, the verification procedures instituted in 1890, when the census introduced machine tabulation procedures, consistently undercounted women's nontraditional employment (Conk 1981). In 1900 the Census Bureau began systematically checking the accuracy of its new coding and data card–punching procedures by reexamining information cards for blacks in the North, foreign-born persons in the South, women in "men's jobs," and men in "women's jobs." When such "unusual" cases were encountered during the verification procedures, there was undoubtedly pressure to change some occupational codes. As Conk (1981, 68) indicates, "The punching clerks were aware that their work would be rejected if they coded men into 'female' occupations and women into 'male' occupations, even if they were true to the schedules. . . . From the clerk's point of view, it would perhaps be better to use a non-controversial occupation code in the first place and avoid having one's work scrutinized." Paradoxically, this accuracy check resulted in less precise data.

In addition, the new census occupational classifications of 1910, which loosely defined jobs according to levels of skill, created divisions between categories that were social as well as technical. Skilled workers were employed in the crafts, semi-skilled workers used machinery (operatives), and laborers found themselves in the residual category of unskilled. Women and minorities were presumed never to be skilled; and, under Alba Edwards's leadership at the Census Bureau, coders who classified individuals' occupations were advised to take into account cultural information about people. As a result, the status of some occupations was lowered from skilled to semiskilled merely because women and children held those jobs (Conk 1978). Thus, in its methods of assigning individuals to occupational categories and occupational categories to levels of skill, the Census Bureau reinforced prevailing ideologies about the sexual and racial division of labor by determining that certain occupations were "wrong."

Obviously, the social and economic purposes of the Census Bureau were rather entangled at the turn of the century (Conk 1978). Many of these problems were inadvertently alleviated when the U.S. entry into World War II instigated modifications in the 1940 census procedures that affected the verification system. As part of the war effort, the government encouraged women to enter jobs previously nontraditional for them, and it needed information on the success rate of these efforts. In order to speed up tabulations, and because of the new questions and procedures, the Census Bureau hired many new statisticians who were not well schooled in the prior verification methods that checked for white women and persons of color in "wrong" occupations. As a result, detailed census statistics published in the fall of 1941 counted many women and youths in occupations that were "unusual" for them and from which they had been excluded in previous censuses. The figures were already published, and it was too late to go back and check the occupational codes against the original reports. Thus, the sex-typed verification procedures initiated at the beginning of the century were not carried out in 1940. When the final statistics appeared in 1942, newspaper and government reports expressed delight with the success of the war effort, which had drawn so many women into traditional male occupations. However, we should recall that some of these women had been in those jobs all along but had been counted in another place. Because of these and other problems in census methods in the early part of the century, government-published national data from that period are not as reliable as they might be, which is why my study goes back to the original data on the enumerator forms. In so doing, I had the opportunity to recode women's occupations into the "correct" categories, as well as to reshape definitions of race and ethnicity, of social class, and even of gender.

Defining Race and Ethnicity

Race and ethnicity are socially defined constructs that, like definitions of work, are heavily influenced by the ideologies of dominant segments of society. When and how they are measured by the census reflects the concerns and conceptualizations of an era. Because the early twentieth century was marked by high immigration rates, the census of 1900 inquired about a person's place of birth and the birthplace of his or her parents. Such questions are not explicitly about ethnicity, but a person's ethnic origins can be constructed from this information. The 1900 census also recognized five races—white, black ("Negro or of Negro descent"), Chinese, Japanese, and Native American ("Indian"), although relatively few individuals from the last three groups are represented in the Public Use Sample. Between 1850 and 1920 the census separated the categories "mulatto" and "Negro," but in 1900 both were combined into black ("Negro"), which Washington (1996) suggests reflected fears of finding a large percentage of mixed-race people and a preference for labeling all mixtures as black. Indeed, throughout much of the twentieth century, race has been socially defined dichotomously as black and white, and only recently, owing to increasing political pressure from multiracial people, has the census considered using a mixed-race category.

Obviously, race and ethnicity are not separate dimensions. For example, in 1900, many white people were also immigrants, as were virtually all Chinese and Japanese residents. Meanwhile, people from Latin America and the Caribbean were considered by the 1900 census to be immigrants like any others, but today they are also asked to self-identify as Latino or Hispanic from a list that is composed primarily of racial groups. Some immigrant groups, such as Jews or the Irish, were popularly considered to be racial minorities around 1900, but this is not true now, and at no time did the census record them as racial groups. Nonetheless, there has been considerable historical discussion of "whiteness" and how some immigrant groups "became" white (for example, Brodkin 1998; Ignatiev 1995). Because of this complex interrelationship between race and ethnicity, I divide men and women into fourteen different "racial ethnic" (or racial-ethnic) categories that combine race and national origin, or ethnicity, in a continuum. The set of groups is defined by a combination of a person's birthplace and immigrant status. I describe each below in order of their generations in the United States.

Native Americans constitute a single category, although only 0.2 percent of all adult women fall within it. The census defines them by race, but the group also has the greatest proportion of people born in the United States of U.S.-born parents. Native Americans constitute the only truly native-born group.

Eleven other groups are each composed of immigrants and second-generation immigrants, that is, people who were born in the United States but had at least one foreign-born parent. I organize the ethnicities represented in these groups by continent of origin rather than size of the group. From Europe there were Irish, British, Scandinavians, Germans, Eastern Europeans, Russians, and Italians (as well as an assorted mixture of "other Europeans," which is the residual category and is excluded from most of the analysis). From the Americas there were French Canadians, English Canadians, and Latin Americans, the latter including men and women from the Caribbean. Japanese, Chinese, Koreans, and other nationalities from Asia are combined in an additional category, "Asians," because there were too few in the sample to study each group separately. These immigrant and second-generation immigrant groups formed the eleven largest ethnic categories in terms of representation in U.S. society at that time, and in total, 38 percent of all adult women had their roots in these countries.

Combining first- and second-generation immigrants of the same ethnic background was both practical, because the 1900 census gives place of birth for an individual and her or his parents, and sensible, because national origin characteristics, if any, are not lost to the second generation. Indeed, both immigrants and their U.S.-born children tended to be employed in the same types of jobs. Members of these eleven groups may be of any race but, except for Asian and Latin American women, would now be considered predominantly white. Asians and Latin Americans had experiences as immigrants that were somewhat different from those of African Americans, although both were, and still are, often treated as racial minorities within U.S. society.

The remaining two groups are black and white women who were at least third-generation U.S. residents, that is, born in the United States to native-born parents. For simplicity, I variously refer to these groups as blacks or whites, and sometimes as third-generation residents, even though many families had resided in the United States for many more than three generations at the time of the census. In 1900, about 11 percent of adult women were black, and most blacks were African Americans and at least third-generation U.S. residents. Only a few were first- or second-generation immigrants, usually from the Caribbean. In contrast, "white" is a residual category for those whose race is coded as white and for whom ethnic heritage cannot be determined from the census, which provides only a respondent's and her or his parents' place of birth. They may have identified themselves with some ethnic group, but the census will not reveal that information. Nonetheless, this is the group assumed by many to be the baseline for "American" family behavior. Ironically, such women barely constituted a majority, at 51 percent, of all women age 15 or older.

Although race and ethnicity are usually considered individual attributes, I also created two geographically based measures of racial-ethnic diversity. One is the county's ethnic mix, or the percentage of women who were (white) immigrants or had foreign-born parents, and the second is the percentage of women in a county who were black. Occasionally I also include a third measure of the percentage of nonblack women of color.

Defining Gender

Much has been written about the differences between *sex* and *gender*. The labels male/female (or man/woman) refer to biological sex. Thus, I appropriately might say that *Gateway to the Political Economy of the 20th Century* focuses on women's experiences in the political economy. On the other hand, the terms masculine and feminine refer to gender. Gender, like race, is socially constructed. Indeed, we now commonly talk about "doing gender" in our day-to-day lives (West and Zimmerman 1987). Consequently, we observe that men and women often have different roles in the political economy because of gender constraints. Gender can be created by social expectations, such as the notion that women should be employed only before they marry. Gender can also be shaped by social institutions. For instance, there were few women bartenders in 1900 because most states had laws that prohibited women from tending bar. In this study on the social shaping of women's employment options, I try to focus on the aspects of individual and household life, as well as of geographic location, that could be considered gendered.

As I indicated earlier, adopting a gendered standpoint on the political economy extends the very definition of work. Work is no longer limited to formal participation in the labor force but incorporates unpaid work in the informal economy or other home-based work. Indeed, this approach applies a global perspective to work in the United States, since research on developing countries has shown that work should be conceptualized as occurring on a continuum from unpaid subsistence labor through paid labor in the formal sector (Ward and Pyle 1995).

Defining Social Class

Social class can be defined in numerous ways. The most intuitive approach for many people is to divide the U.S. population into between three and six classes, such as the upper, upper-middle, lower-middle, and working classes, and the poor. In general, we use a multiplicity of indicators to know who fits into each of these categories, most commonly considering a person's occupation, income, and education. Unfortunately, this approach does not always work for historical studies such as mine because the U.S. census never collected some of the relevant information. In 1900 the census enumerators were supposed to inquire about the ability to read and write rather than about years of formal education, and they were not supposed to ask about income at all. Information on occupations is available but was not counted in categories that are comparable to current ones. The occupational structure at the turn of the century was much more heavily agricultural and industrial, with fewer white-collar and service jobs. Thus the categories of white-collar work were not as diversified then as now. In addition, the class position of some occupations has changed. For example, as "office clerk" gradually ceased to refer to an office manager and more often referred to filers and typists, the status of that occupation declined over the century.

Even though some of the information we typically use to discern social class is either missing or different, it is possible to make judgments about a person's class in 1900 using either of two methods. First, instead of using categories labeled by class, I use seven occupational categories: professional-managerial, clerical and sales, craft occupations, machine operatives and laborers, service workers, agricultural workers, and the unemployed. This approach reflects the white-collar/blue-collar/agricultural social and economic hierarchy in place at the turn of the century and follows the major occupational categories that the census used for several decades. A household head or an individual household member can be recorded in these categories.

The second approach uses a continuous prestige scale that rates occupations from 0 (low) through 100 (high). The scale was developed to measure the social standing of occupations in 1950, when the U.S. occupational distribution was closer to what it was at the beginning of the twentieth century than it is now. Staff at the University of Washington appended this information to each occupation when they created the Census Public Use data set. Of course, using these scores for 1900 is not ideal. However, the two approaches validate each other. In 1900, women achieved the highest prestige scores in professional (69) and managerial jobs (54), while attaining slightly lower scores in white-collar clerical

(51) and sales (47) work. In the elite blue-collar craft or artisan jobs, women averaged 32 prestige points. However, in factory operative jobs their status dropped to 19 points. Agricultural (13) and service work (11) had fairly equivalent, low prestige scores. Unemployment is not usually rated using this system.

The categorical approach provides considerable detail and specificity, but listing seven categories can be awkward. In contrast, the prestige scale is easy to use, requiring the reporting of a single number, but that number doesn't always give us a sense of a person's lifestyle. I use both the occupational categories and the prestige scores, because these advantages and disadvantages offset each other.

ORGANIZATION OF THIS BOOK

In sum, this book explores women's place in the political economy at the beginning of the twentieth century using two different standpoints. The first is an exploration, at the national level, of variations in women's experiences according to racial-ethnic background, class, and geography. Because this past is often used as the baseline for judging changes during the subsequent one hundred years, it is important that we understand it on its own terms. In addition, 1900 was at the crux of changes in the U.S. economic structure and ethnic composition, making it a key time to observe transformations in women's options. The second standpoint is based in contemporary issues. Here I explore the historical roots of seemingly new concerns, looking backward to see ways in which the past is much more relevant to the present than popular culture would lead us to believe.

I use a thematic organization to raise both specific and general issues regarding women's role in the political economy. The first three chapters examine the nature of women's employment. Chapter 2 tabulates the large volume of women's work in the informal economy that went uncounted by the census in 1900, suggesting that the roles of women in the economy then were larger than we have been lead to believe. Chapter 3 reveals which individual, household, and geographic characteristics predicted women's entry into formal employment. I show that some of the predictive traits have changed while others have remained the same, and that the influence of race, ethnicity, class, and gender could vary considerably. Chapter 4 explores which jobs women held in the formal economy, looking at the occupational segregation experienced by women of differing racial-ethnic backgrounds.

The next three chapters concentrate on broader political economic concerns frequently cast as social problems. The issues were selected to represent the three analytical levels of the individual, the household, and geographic settings. In addition, the issues connect the beginning and the end of the twentieth century. Chapter 5 focuses on domestic work, the predominant women's job in 1900, and uses it to inquire whether women might have participated in ethnic enclaves, or employment networks based on ethnicity, which now are expected to benefit men. Domestic employment was a woman's work ghetto, but in my analysis I consider the conditions under which employers went out of their way to hire women of a racial-ethnic background similar to their own. In Chapter 6 I turn to the lives of female heads of households and of single mothers (who might not head their own households). Contrary to contemporary perceptions, this group of women has been around for a long time. I show how they supported themselves in the absence of large state or federal welfare programs in 1900, and which groups of women were most vulnerable to becoming heads of a household. Then, in Chapter 7, I direct attention to the geographic or contextual effects on women's employment. I consider how residence in a rural versus an urban area or in a particular region of the country could limit or expand a woman's job options. Ironically, the area we now call the rust belt previously offered women some of the best jobs.

Finally, in the Epilogue (Chapter 8) I make the basic argument that the beginning of the twentieth century tells us a great deal about the end of it. I take a moment to reflect on the new factors influencing women's place in today's political economy as well as the less obvious older factors that still hold sway. I discuss the implications of racial-ethnic differences in shaping the existing diversity within the category of "women" and the role of local differences in shaping national patterns of women's work.

2 Home-Based Work and the Informal Economy

The Case of the "Unemployed" Housewife

IT IS POPULARLY BELIEVED that during the twentieth century there was a dramatic increase in women's paid labor force participation. Published census data appear to support this assumption by indicating that 20 percent of all U.S. women were gainfully employed in 1900 and that 63 percent participated in the labor force during 1996 (Bureau of Labor Statistics 1997). Nonetheless, scholars have concluded that this quantitative increase was not as large as it appears to be because of two data problems. First, the technical definition of employment has changed over time, becoming more inclusive of women's labor since 1940, which means that our observations are not based on consistent measures of work (Durand 1968; Jaffee 1956; Long 1958; Smuts 1960). Second, there is general agreement that women's employment was undercounted early in the century and that the 1900 rates we use as a basis of comparison are too low (Abel and Folbre 1990; Bose 1987; Ciancanelli 1983; Conk 1981; Folbre and Abel 1989; Goldin 1990). The most undercounted work was unpaid labor in family enterprises, and the "missing" workers were usually married women.

Exploring the many forms of home-based work is important to understanding women's role in the political economy and employment. First, doing so corrects the historical record. The data seem to suggest that during the entire twentieth century, men were continuously employed throughout their adult lives, while women only began this employment pattern sometime after the 1960s. An analysis of home-based work reveals that women's economic contributions to the household have also been fairly continuous.

Second, since the process of locating home-based work focuses on household income strategies, uncovering this hidden work reveals the strength of the connection between work and family life. Married women frequently engaged in economic roles that were not publicly visible, and their contributions were therefore more likely than men's or single women's to be hidden in the informal economy. For example, self-employed men who owned a farm or a small business were counted as gainfully employed, even though they did not engage in wage labor. But their wives' work in the same business was treated by the Census Bureau and by society either as part of the informal economy or as encompassed in their family role, rather than as part-time employment.

Third, uncovering the extent of women's home-based work, and of wives' apparent unemployment, reveals the role of ideology in shaping census definitions of work. Indeed, there was a double standard in reporting work, based on gender and family position. However, changes over time and cross-national comparisons prove that different methods have been and can be used to count similar forms of labor. Because the choice among these methods depends on one's objectives, the route to improved reporting of women's work is not merely a technical one of revising census methods but also involves a more equitable evaluation of women's work and a concomitant change in ideology.

Finally, perceiving home-based work as gender differentiated also entails understanding how race and ethnicity shaped the variations in women's lives. The contemporary visibility of street vendors or undocumented child-care workers, combined with our image of tenement garment shops at the turn of the century, leads us to assume that home-based work or other employment in the informal economy was and still is dominated by immigrants or working-class families. However, this impression is based on a limited number of jobs. Adding other forms of home-based work modifies our view of the gaps in women's employment rates among blacks, whites (both third-generation immigrants and later), or ethnic groups (including immigrants and their U.S.-born children).

In this chapter, I argue that the reported increase in women's employment in the twentieth century was due in large part to changes in the theoretical definition of work which, perhaps inadvertently, recognized and counted women's labor. In addition, as the century progressed there was a transition in the primary location of married women's work away from home-based employment, such as on a family farm or in a family business, taking in boarders, or doing factory outwork, to employment at sites away from home. This shift to out-of-home, formal-economy employment increased women's visibility as workers and was more in line with the prevailing idea of the types of work that should be counted. Incorporating women's previously uncounted home-based work into employment rates changes our estimates of the relative labor force participation rates of men and women, and among different groups of women, at the turn of the century. In fact, many ostensibly unemployed housewives were laboring in the informal economy. Because the 1900 "base rate" of women's work should have been higher than the 20 percent who were counted, the increase in women's participation over the course of the century is not as dramatic as is often argued. However, the small, readjusted *quantitative* change in rates that results from counting previously uncounted work is not nearly as important as the *qualitative* change in the nature of women's work, which moved out of the home-based family economy and became both waged and more market dependent.

To develop this argument, I will explain the census definition and coding changes that occurred over the course of the twentieth century and examine some of the forms of home-based work that were ignored, especially when the work was done by wives. The census changes were not merely technical; I illustrate how the definitions of employment reflected both ideas about women's proper role and the political needs of the U.S. government. With this information as background, I review methods that can be used to locate and recount women's work. Then, I proceed to calculate the amount of previously unrecorded home-based work in order to show how these figures change our impression of U.S. men's and women's relative economic contributions in 1900. In addition, I show the effect that counting home-based work has on the employment rates of black and white women and women of various national origins, as well as on aggregate regional differences in women's work. Next, I uncover the conditions that were likely to lead wives and female household heads to perform home-based work. In concluding this chapter, I summarize the importance of women's home-based work and its implications for understanding changes in women's labor throughout the twentieth century.

WHO WORKS? HOW THE CENSUS HAS COUNTED EMPLOYMENT DURING THE TWENTIETH CENTURY

In certain ways, women's productive work participation is structured by the same considerations today as in 1900, with many women employed in ways compatible with their family life or spouse's job. However, in 1900 more of this employment was located in the home—a place where it was less likely to be reported—and more men were self-employed, making use of unpaid family labor that was also largely uncounted. Part of the reason for the undercount of work is embedded in census definitions of employment, which affected the records of women's work in 1900 more so than at the end of the century.

The census definition of "gainful employment" used from 1870 through 1930 (and known as the gainful worker census series) did not encourage recording or counting women's work. The term "gainful worker" defined as "employed" those persons age ten and over who reported any occupation, whether or not they were working or seeking work at the time of the census. By 1890, a person's occupation was considered to be "[that] work upon which he chiefly depends for support, and in which he would ordinarily be engaged during the larger part of the year" (Wright 1900). Although before 1910 one did not have to work for pay in order to be counted, unpaid housework has always been explicitly excluded.

In contrast, the current definition of participation in the civilian labor force, first used in 1940, includes two components, the employed and the unemployed. People age 16 years or older are considered employed if they work for pay during the week of the survey, if they work 15 hours or more as unpaid workers in a family business, or if they have a job but are not working for such reasons as illness, bad weather, or vacation. To be considered unemployed, one has to both not be working during the survey week, usually in April or May, and to have made specific efforts in the preceding four weeks to find a job. Anyone else is not in the labor force.

There are many obvious as well as subtle differences between the 1900 definition of employment and the current one that helped relegate women's work to the uncounted informal economy at the turn of the century. The impact of the early census methods was large for married women but relatively small for single women, who were more likely to work in locations outside of the home, where their employment would be recorded.

One definitional change entailed raising the age threshold for inclusion among the employed from 10 to 16 years, a move that reduced the entire potential labor pool. The higher age criterion reflected the prevalence of mandatory school attendance laws, but it also meant that the work of young teenagers in baby sitting, newspaper delivery, or other tasks was no longer counted as employment.

Another more important fact to consider is that the recent census definitions of labor force participation focus on current employment, providing a concise economic picture of who actually holds a job at a given point in time. In contrast, the 1900 census recorded the usual or customary job, whether or not a person was actually working or even seeking work, and thus essentially described the social division of labor. This earlier definition, which focused on an individual's usual task, encouraged most wives to indicate their primary employment as housewife. Because married women did so many kinds of work—housework, factory outwork, laboring in the family business, taking in boarders—none of these jobs was considered their primary activity, even when they were temporarily working for pay or permanently working part-time. Furthermore, enumerator instructions made it clear that women's home-based remunerative tasks—caring for boarders, selling eggs, and the like—were not to be counted as work by the census unless they provided the majority of a woman's economic support (Ciancanelli 1983). Such tasks were viewed as a natural extension of women's work for their families

(Bernstein 1984), creating what Folbre (1993) has called a "social identity bias" in how work was counted. Thus, unemployed men and even those out of the labor force in 1900, such as the retired or disabled, could be recorded as having an occupation, whereas women who generated income at home, worked part-time, or labored in a family business were usually recorded as housewives. As a result, the 1900 census encouraged an undercount of women's work and an overcount of men's work. Although current methods represent a considerable improvement in this regard, they also tend to exclude seasonal or "casual" workers, who are often women or migrant farm workers (or both) working only part of the year.

A third and central component of employment led to unrecorded women's work: its home-based nature. When married women were engaged in productive work in 1900, it was most frequently performed at home rather than away from the home, where it might more easily have been recorded as gainful employment. Yet the recorded home-based work in remunerated jobs such as seamstress, milliner, laundress, and boardinghouse keeper accounted for only 14.4 percent of all employed women ages 15 to 64 at the turn of the century. Such jobs could be considered self-employment, but there was no such occupational category in the census until 1910, when it was added to indicate persons working "on their own account" rather than for a wage or salary. Even with this change it was difficult for women employed at home to be seen as holding a job if the work was part-time. In contrast, women's home-based work today is more likely to be recorded as self-employment and includes jobs requiring licensing (such as in-home child care), commission work (such as sales of home products, cosmetics, or real estate), or independent consulting (such as computer programming or home decorating). Yet even now, much employment in what economists call the underground, hidden, informal, or irregular economy goes uncounted. For example, women may engage in off-the-books domestic work or other self-employed service work; do factory outwork, in which they are considered subcontractors on tasks ranging from data entry to garment assembly; or give piano lessons, run garage sales, or maintain an illegal rental unit in the house (De Grazia 1982;

Molefsky 1982). As these examples suggest, the shift from home-based work to the formal wage economy has not been a continuous linear process for women, who still engage in undercounted formal work or uncounted informal economy work. In fact, the recent increase in small businesses may have increased the volume of women's (and men's) home-based work.

A fourth way in which the census influenced women's employment rates was through its treatment of unpaid work. The current stipulation is that unpaid workers should be counted if they labor for fifteen hours or more per week in a family business. Although unpaid work in a family enterprise also could be counted in 1900, it was not distinguished as a category of work until 1940. Indeed, throughout the census's gainful worker series from 1870 to 1930, with the exception of 1910, enumerators were instructed to record women working on family farms or in family businesses as housewives rather than as employed. Thus women who would now be enumerated as family workers were not counted at the turn of the century, while men who purportedly headed those same family enterprises were always counted.

All the more striking, women's unpaid family work went uncounted at a time when they had considerable access to it—in 1900, 37 percent of the population lived on farms. Although unpaid work in a family business is now explicitly included as labor force participation, only 3 percent of the U.S. population lived on farms by 1980. Ironically, when the census crafted a better definition of gainful employment as part of a major reorganization of its job classifications in 1910 and encouraged enumerators to "never [take for] granted, without inquiry, that a woman, or child, has no occupation," it later bemoaned the "overcount" for women's work that was produced because women who regularly did outdoor farm work on family farms for no wages were recorded as farm laborers. The Women's Bureau and government farm experts had wanted this result to show that most farms were family-run, but the net result was that for many years, demographers discounted 1910 as an aberration in the rates of women's gainful employment.

One major reason why women's unpaid labor went unrecorded in 1900 was that it was hidden by male self-employment. Because women's contributions to male-headed family enterprises were unpaid and were performed alongside housework, their efforts were less socially visible than men's. The historical movement of women's labor from home-based units to outside the home, where they generated a separate paycheck, was undoubtedly helpful in making their work more countable and visible. However, married women's entry into the paid labor force in large numbers did not eradicate home-based, informal economy work, nor did it ensure women's escape from male-dominated work units.

THE CENSUS AND THE DOUBLE STANDARD: HOW IDEOLOGY WAS REFLECTED IN AND REINFORCED BY THE CENSUS DEFINITIONS OF WORK

Underlying many of the technical differences between the censuses at the beginning and end of the twentieth century was the explicit application of a double standard in counting men's and women's work in 1900. Census authorities had an expectation of how many women ought to be counted, and they shaped questions, enumerator instructions, and even their data analysis (Conk 1981) to conform to that social expectation. Men could report their usual employment and whether or not they were currently engaged in it, have their statements accepted, while women's reports were subject to additional criteria used to exclude them from labor force totals. Married women who reported gainful employment were asked if the work was done at home or if it was done only occasionally. The presumption was that married women workers were rare. Since urban men, such as those who constructed census questions, no longer associated the home with work for themselves, it was difficult for them to associate women's home-based labor with work. Indeed, unpaid family labor when performed primarily by adult women was not considered an occupation. Self-employment in the form of taking in boarders was not included either, unless women relied solely on it to "eke out a living." Women usually had to be earning a wage to be counted as employed, which is why married women's employment rates were very low but their daughters' rates were much higher: young, single women generally worked for wages in the formal economy. In contrast, only about two-thirds of all men reporting work actually earned wages (Sobek 1997) because of the more lenient criteria used to judge them.

Why did the census use a double standard for counting women's and men's work at the turn of the century or later change its definitions of employment and its enumeration methods? The explanation is not procedural only but lies in the different ideologies and government needs reflected in the measures.

A brief examination of other late nineteenth century censuses helps to put the U.S. definition of gainful employment in context. Earlier counts, like the British census of 1851 and the censuses of England and Wales in 1861 and 1871, were based on classic liberal doctrine and were intended to present Britain as a community of workers and a strong nation (Deacon 1985). In this view, women were productive workers in the home, whether as housewives or as workers in a family vocation. Home-based work was equally as important as other occupations, and consequently female relatives of farmers and small businessmen were automatically put in their own separate occupational category. The 1871 and 1881 censuses of Victoria, Australia, used a similar approach, resulting in women's participation rates of 41 and 43 percent in those years (Deacon 1985). In contrast, New South Wales, Australia, used a more conservative classification that divided the population into breadwinners or dependents—women doing domestic work, unpaid workers in the home, children, and the infirm. This system, which yielded lower women's participation rates of only 24 to 29 percent for the census years from 1871 to 1901 (Deacon 1985), became the system all Australian statisticians agreed to use after 1890. Its intent was to provide an image of a country in which not everyone needed to work, thus appearing to be a good place for British investment. As Deacon (1985, 35) suggests, "[by using the new] method women were seen as minor economic actors, by the other as important contributors to the nation's prosperity."

The U.S. censuses of 1870 to 1930 reflected an ideology that was similar in substance to the revised Australian one. This ideology, which emerged in the second half of the nineteenth century, especially among the middle class, has been called the "cult of domesticity" or the "cult of true womanhood." The cult of domesticity tried to elevate the social status of mothering and to treat women's homemaking as a profession (Kessler-Harris 1982), even if a profession whose goal was for a woman to subordinate herself to the needs of the family (Matthaei 1982). This Victorian definition of the homemaker obscured her economic function (Anderson 1987). Although the sexes could have been envisioned as different but equal, each heading its own sphere (Matthaei 1982), the reality was that women's sphere was to become economically dependent on men's sphere (Jensen 1980; Sokoloff 1980). This patriarchal ideology served to justify and solidify a new economic structure in which male household heads had to work hard to support a family—a goal most attainable by the middle class. It also had the effect of motivating working-class men in unions at the beginning of the century to battle for the family wage—a single wage supporting one family. For their part, women employed outside the home found they had to justify themselves even though it was becoming harder to find remunerative work they could do at home. Many African-American women objected to these new role constraints, and they, along with immigrant and working-class women, found the new model unattainable because their families needed their earnings.

Support for the ideology of dual or separate spheres was built into the U.S. census definition of gainful employment, which excluded women's home-based labor unless it was the major source of household income. This criterion both reflected the pervasiveness of the ideology of domesticity and simultaneously provided the mechanism for collecting data to support the perception of dual spheres, just as the census of New South Wales had done. It assumed rather than tested the dual-spheres concept. Consequently, the contrast of those early low rates with the present ones directs our attention to the apparent major increase in women's labor force participation since World War II, or to the cohort effects of steadily increasing married women's employment over the century. However, focusing on the numbers draws attention away from several key changes. It was the overlapping shifts in the census definition, beginning in the late 1930s, and in the location of women's work that allowed that labor once more to be classified as employment.

The Depression and subsequent New Deal social welfare legislation meant that considerable political pressure was placed on the Census Bureau to provide accurate information about the U.S. labor force, especially unemployment rates (Anderson 1988; Conk 1981). Congress mandated a voluntary registration of the unemployed in 1937, and the Works Progress Administration developed a Sample Survey of Unemployment in 1939 (Anderson 1988). This research paved the way for the Census Bureau's dramatically changed definition of employment, new occupational coding scheme, and modified verification procedures in 1940. In total, the switch from measuring gainful employment to labor force participation reduced the size of the work force by 1.2 million people (Durand 1968, 13), primarily by excluding men who were not actually working at the time of the census. However, in April 1945 the Census Bureau improved its monthly survey questions, thereby adding 2.25 million workers to its estimates who had been incorrectly recorded on the earlier forms as not in the labor force (Durand 1968, 13). Although the sex composition of this group is unclear, employed wives are the most likely to have been reclassified. Certainly the abatement in the dual-spheres ideology during World War II, intended to encourage wives' employment, would have facilitated an improved count of women's work.

The modified definitions introduced in the 1940s, which increased the visibility of women's work, would remain in effect with only minor changes for the rest of the century. Although the political pressures of the Depression most directly generated the procedural modifications, the changes also occurred because of the long-term transformation in the U.S. economy from an agricultural to an industrial base, and a parallel shift in the dual-spheres gender role ideology. Such linked changes in the economy, roles, and census methods are not unusual, nor are the problems restricted to the United States. Indeed, internationally, variations in agricultural surveys and population census methods affect the count of women's work more than of men's work, generally through the differential undercount of women's home-based or agricultural labor (Benería 1982; Durand 1975; United Nations 1995). Although census definitions and enumeration methods both conform to and support gender-related ideologies, many groups interested in women and international development issues, including the United Nations-based INSTRAW (International Research and Training Institute for the Advancement of Women), have been lobbying for consistency and improved methods of counting women's home-based economic contributions. Only in 1993 did the International Conference of Labour Statisticians finally agree on a *definition* of the informal sector (United Nations 1995). When such work is actually *counted* better, as I do here, it becomes evident that the major change in women's work over time is not quantitative but rather a qualitative shift from unwaged to waged work and from dependence on family to dependence on the market.

Reevaluating Women's Work in 1900

Since pre-1940 census definitions of work are clearly different from contemporary ones (Anderson 1988; Conk 1978, 1981), accurate historical labor force comparisons require adjustments to make the measures used at the beginning and end of the century more similar. Two different approaches have been used to compensate for the gender-based double standard embedded in early censuses and the definitional discontinuities. The first approach encompasses a variety of "gender-equity" methods (Sobek 1997) that attempt to make men's and women's work more equivalent under the gainful worker definition. This is accomplished by counting as employment women's labor in a family enterprise or in other kinds of part-time paid work done at home, just as it was counted for men. The second approach attempts to make different measures of women's work more equivalent over time by projecting our current definition of labor force participation back in time, generally by excluding men's self-employment (just as women's self-employment was excluded in the earlier censuses). The choice between these two methods—counting women's self-employed home-based work or ignoring men's self-employment— depends on the purpose. While both are useful, my recalculations of turn-of-the-century women's work are based on a modified version of the gender-equity method that I developed (Bose 1987), since this way of counting work is more consistent with recent ideas about family businesses and agricultural work. A gender-equity approach to the 1900 census also moves away from the dichotomous public-private, dual-spheres conceptualization that rendered women's home-based work invisible and treated it as valueless. Instead, the gender-equity approach is rooted in an understanding of work as a continuum from formal, to informal, to home-based paid or unpaid work; this approach further recognizes that individuals (as well as households) may be carrying out more than one of these activities at any point in time. Such a broad conceptualization has become common in international studies of women's work (Benería 1992; Rothstein 1995; Ward 1990; Ward and Pyle 1995). It has also been used to rethink a wide variety of topics, including rural women's work (Bose 1987; Wright 1995) and service work (Glazer 1993) in the United States. Although I do make limited use of the second approach, projecting current definitions back in time, its narrow focus on wage equivalency in the recalculations tends to reduce both men's and women's labor force participation.

In the present day, it is common for an adult woman to seek employment outside of the home in order to keep a child in school and out of the labor force, but in 1900 the reverse was true. Families needing a second income might urge their adolescents or single adult relatives to find an outside job so that adult women could stay at home to supervise the household, engage in expenditure-reducing tasks, take on some paying work, or all three (Wright 1995). The early twentieth century economy frequently reduced married women's work options to these roles, which the dual-spheres ideology did not distinguish from housework. As part of their home-based roles, women were expected to contribute unpaid labor to a family farm or small business. Although work that was never recorded cannot be fully recaptured, we can estimate the volume of unpaid work in a family business on the basis of the occupation of the household head. If the family needed cash, an important income opportunity for women at home was to take in boarders and lodgers. This income-generating work can be estimated when women claim no occupation but boarders or lodgers are noted in the census records. However, other income-producing homework, such as taking in washing or doing sewing and other textile factory outwork, cannot be located unless the women themselves reported it. Thus these recalculations still represent a low estimate. There are no national statistics on the amount of homework or the degree to which it was undercounted, although there were local estimates for the turn of the century (Sobek 1997, 85). Such work is better counted when performed in a factory or in someone else's home.[1] However, we can find some of women's missing formal employment by examining the difference between the larger number of employees reported by manufacturers, which ICPSR summarized by county, and the smaller number of individual women who reported manufacturing jobs. To do so, I divide the employer numbers by the sampling fraction of the 1900 census data (one in 760) to make the aggregate numbers reported for counties more comparable to the sampled individual ones.

All of my calculations are based on the original data about individuals found in the manuscript census, made available through the 1900 Public Use Sample. Such data retain any enumerator errors in job titles, but not those introduced by the 1900 census job coding and verification procedures, as the job titles were recoded in the 1970s, when this data set was computerized. I focus on women in the sample who were between the ages of 15 and 64 (29,673 women), since they were not likely to be in school and were below the current retirement age of 65. Among these women, 22.5 percent, or 6,662, reported employment, with the lowest recorded rates for wives of male household heads (4.1 percent).[2] Since the greatest volume of unacknowledged home-based work was done by these apparently unemployed wives, my recount of women's work focuses on them.

FARMS AND BUSINESSES

Let us first look at women's unpaid work on family farms or in family businesses. When a male household head was engaged in agricultural endeavors, 15.7 percent of the household women reported gainful employment. If he was a merchant of goods that might involve retail sales (boots and shoes, clothing, dry goods, groceries, and the like), 21.8 percent of household women reported employment. In contrast, when the male head held any other job than farming or small business, fully 27.4 percent of household women reported work. Thus, as I have suggested elsewhere (Bose 1984), men's self-employment reduced women's recorded employment. For example, in 1900 only 4.6 percent of farm wives reported gainful employment, although most (71.3 percent) of these said they were family laborers or family farmers. Even in 1940, when the definitions became more inclusive, only 2 percent of farm wives claimed to be unpaid family workers (Sobek 1997).

Yet there is every reason to expect that women in farm and small business households were actually working unpaid in the family business. Estimates at the time (Sullivan 1926) indicate that the amount and nature of women's farm work varied with the farm's access to railroads, single versus multiple crop dependency, and type of livestock, but that most women were involved in some significant way. Indeed, Wright's (1995) study of rural wives born between 1905 and 1932 indicates that they were always engaged in some mixture of income-generating and expenditure-saving activities, even when additional farm labor was hired for harvests. Even recent estimates that try to project wage-equivalent contemporary work definitions back to the turn of the century suggest that between 20 percent (Goldin 1990) and 40 percent (Ciancanelli 1983) of farm wives met that criterion. Clearly there is no consensus on the amount of farm wives' farm work. Nonetheless, the choice is important both quantitatively, because farm wives were the largest group of women doing unrecorded home-based work, and qualitatively, because it should be consistent with our definition of countable employment. Since my calculations are based on a gender-equity perspective, I count wives' farm work in the same way men's farm work was counted in 1900.

Agricultural work encompasses a broad spectrum of jobs, but in 1900, fully 86 percent of male household heads engaged in agriculture were family farmers—the group in which we are most interested. Another 10 percent were farm laborers and 4 percent held a variety of other jobs, but the wives of men in these smaller groups could not be assumed to be working on family farms. Thus a gender-equity perspective suggests that 86 percent of the wives of men in agricultural jobs should have been considered family farmers. Certainly some farms had servants and hired hands to help with the labor, but most—91.6 percent—had neither. Even when hired hands lived on a farm, often there were no servants, reducing wives' farm work but effectively leaving them with boardinghouse tasks (in an additional 4.1 percent of cases). Thus, women's farm-related labor was probably needed on virtually any farm with no resident servants.

If we assume that, in the absence of servants, 86 percent of the wives of men engaged in agriculture should have reported themselves as unpaid family workers, an additional 16.9 percent of all women ages 15 to 64 years, or 5,026 women, would have been reported as employed through farm work. As we will see shortly, family farm work was particularly important for black women, because 52.2 percent of them lived in households engaged in agricultural work, while only 42.9 percent of third-generation or later white women, 21.7 percent of U.S.-born ethnic women, and 17.1 percent of immigrant women did so.

Relatively few employment-age women, 3.1 percent, lived in households headed by small merchants. At the turn of the century, it was not unusual for families in these circumstances to live above or behind their stores and to have household members engaged in sales work or bookkeeping for the business. Starting in 1910, self-employment became a job category, and wives were the largest group of unpaid family workers in these family businesses, followed numerically by sons (Sobek 1997). Although it is unknown exactly how many wives engaged in such work, if we assume that only half of them did so, then an additional 0.8 percent of all women, or 242 women, would have been counted as employed. Whether this assumption is a little high or a little low, these wives represent a small component of women's undercounted work and do not greatly influence the reestimate.

Boarders and Lodgers

A larger component in reestimating women's employment rates is remunerative home-based work. Taking in boarders or lodgers was a primary way for women to earn income in the informal economy: 10.4 percent of all women ages 15 to 64 reported living with boarders or lodgers, with the greatest likelihood in urban areas. Boarders were more common than lodgers in 1900, and they required extra work because they received meals as well as housing. The actual number of either group might have been even higher than the recorded number, for two reasons. First, boarders or lodgers could have been present at other times during the year but absent when the census enumerator arrived, and so not counted. Second, female relatives were often recorded as family members rather than as lodgers, whether or not they contributed income for their support (Bernstein 1984). In addition, the census often ignored women's work with resident boarders because enumerator instructions usually considered such work to be part-time and a component of the informal economy rather than countable employment. This particular undercount problem was most severe in 1900 in overall percentages, and for immigrant women in particular in 1910 (Sobek 1997).

Although taking in boarders could substitute for work in the formal economy, thus decreasing the probability of a woman's reporting a job, it actually was associated with increased employment. When boarders were living in a household, employment among wives increased from 4 to 5 percent, the work rates of daughters rose from 33 to 38 percent, those of other female relatives increased from 31 to 40 percent, and employment among women heading households went up from 52 to 59 percent. Furthermore, the reported job was not always boardinghouse keeper. Among employed women who had boarders at home, one-third (36 percent) reported a manufacturing occupation, a quarter (24 percent) held jobs in the domestic service sector, and another third were divided between agriculture (12 percent) and professional (8 percent) or white-collar (10 percent) jobs such as teaching, clerk/copyist, sales, or bookkeeping. Surprisingly, only

10 percent said they were boardinghouse keepers or landlords. Although female household heads and wives were the only women to report this occupation, 76 percent of employed female household heads and 84 percent of employed wives reported other work. For the most part, taking in boarders was an indicator of economic need and only one of several sources of household support, often performed concurrently with women's other employment rather than as an alternative to it.

Yet large numbers of women who lived with boarders and lodgers were not recorded as having any occupation. Since we have already counted women's work when the head was self-employed in agriculture or small business, here my focus is on other households. Married women were the largest group to carry out this income-producing work, but fully 95 percent of them reported no job when boarders or lodgers were present in a non-farm or non-small-business setting. Women household heads, though fewer in number, were even more likely than wives to be living with boarders or lodgers (19.3 and 11.7 percent, respectively) and to need the additional income these residents represented, while almost half of them also reported no work. Assuming that all wives and female heads of households who took in boarders or lodgers were earning money, then an additional 3.9 percent, or 1,149, of all women in the sample would have been employed. Although this contingent is not as large as those engaged in farm work, it is substantial.

OTHER SOURCES

Other forms of paid home-based work cannot be measured with any precision. Thus, even this reestimate will leave out some income sources such as factory piecework or illegal profits from gambling or prostitution. However, we can add unreported manufacturing work to the formal economy count. Comparing manufacturers' reports of women employees with the totals reported by individual women in the census Public Use Sample locates an additional 2.3 percent (690) of women ages 15 to 64 who were employed, quite possibly at home.

TABLE 1.   Employment Rates Incorporating Home-Based Work, All Women
Ages 15–64, 1900

Type of work	% Employed
Formal economy work	24.8
Census-counted employment	22.5
Uncounted factory work	2.3
Uncounted home-based work	21.6
Unpaid family farm work	16.9
Unpaid family shop work	0.8
Boarders and lodgers	3.9
Total recounted employment	46.4

SUMMARY

The major components of my reestimate of women's gainful
employment in 1900 are summarized in Table 1, which gives the
recounted rates for both formal employment and informal, home-
based work. When added, these rates yield a total of 46.4 percent
of all women ages 15 to 64 employed in 1900. Since this rate is a
little higher than the 1881 Australian count (43 percent), which
used employment definitions recognizing women's work in family enterprises, this U.S. reestimate has considerable face validity.[3]

In comparison to women, 91.2 percent of all men ages 15 to 64
reported gainful employment in 1900. Thus, women's recounted
employment rate at the turn of the century was approximately
one-half (51 percent) of men's in that period, rather than just one-
quarter of men's rate, as the published census data suggest.
Changing the 1900 definition of women's work to match that of
men's work, as I have done, means that the increase in female
employment over the course of the twentieth century, from 46.4
percent in 1900 to 58.8 percent in 1994 (U.S. Bureau of the Census 1995), is not as large as previously thought. However, it also
means we should not focus on this moderate quantitative increase
but rather on the important qualitative shifts in the location of
women's work and in its determinants.

At the turn of the century, much of married women's labor was
home-based, with considerable self-management, but it was also
very family dependent. So much home-based work was possible

because rural-urban differences in employment opportunities were large and because a great many more people lived on farms. When we apply my work reestimation methods specifically to wives in 1900, their employment rate rises from a paltry 4.1 percent to 43.2 percent. This volume of work did not become visible until later in the century, when married women worked away from home, in locations where their labor was more likely to be counted, and until part-time work was considered employment by the census. The problem was not that full-time work in the formal economy was easier to count but that census officials had chosen to focus on this work, at least for women. The qualitative shift in women's work was facilitated by a decline in family farms and by increased urbanization, which gave wives easier access to jobs and helped reduce the importance of marital status as a determinant of women's work. However, this change was not a linear process. In fact, using a gender-equity estimation procedure for all the decennial censuses beginning in 1880, Sobek (1997, 93) reestimated that married women's labor force participation actually declined until reaching a low point in the 1950s, and then began to rise again.[4] This is numerically possible because the loss of women's home-based work was not equally replaced by urban jobs for wives, and because of other constraints, including the domination of the ideology of the family wage and the economic crisis of the Great Depression.

HOME-BASED WORK AND RACIAL-ETHNIC OR GEOGRAPHIC DIFFERENCES

Women's uncounted work in the informal economy was not evenly distributed among race and ethnic groups or across geographic areas of the United States. In the early twenty-first century, we associate such off-the-books work with immigrant or working-class families, but we cannot assume that this was the pattern in 1900. In fact, investigating home-based work challenges our knowledge of racial, ethnic, and regional differences in turn-of-the-century women's employment rates. The gaps in labor force participation rates between black and white women, between immigrant mothers and their U.S.-born daughters, between urban

TABLE 2.   Reestimate of Employment Rates (%) for Women Ages 15–64, by Race or Immigrant Generation and Geography, 1900

| Group | Home-based uncounted work | | | | Formal census count | Recounted total employed |
	Unpaid farm	Unpaid merchant	Boarders, lodgers	Total cols. 1–3		
Race and immigrant generation						
White, 3rd+ gen.*	21.5	0.9	3.3	25.7	16.1	41.8
Black, 3rd+ gen.*	19.2	0.1	2.0	21.3	44.7	66.0
Immigrant	11.3	0.9	7.2	19.4	22.5	41.9
2nd gen.†	9.3	1.0	3.3	13.6	26.6	40.2
Geographic area						
Urban	1.9	1.1	6.0	9.0	28.4	37.4
Rural	32.7	0.5	1.7	34.9	16.1	51.0
North Atlantic	6.2	0.9	5.5	12.6	27.4	40.0
Other regions	21.6	0.8	3.2	25.6	20.3	45.9
Average, all women	16.9	0.8	3.9	21.6	22.5	44.1

Note: Methods of recounting work are the same as used in Table 1, except that uncounted factory work cannot be included. Formal and recounted work rates are for all women, but only wives and female heads did the uncounted work that is added. The recounted total women's employment rate (column 6) was derived by adding the total uncounted work from three sources (column 4) and the formal census-counted work (column 5).

*Third-generation or later in U.S.
†Second-generation U.S. immigrant.

and rural women, and between the Northeast and other regions might well change when all such work is counted. The effects also could be more task-specific. Including unpaid family farm work might affect only the rural-urban gap, while counting work for boarders might change only the difference between immigrants and others. Table 2 addresses these issues, estimating the three sources of women's uncounted home-based work in 1900 (columns 1 to 3) by race and immigrant generation and for geographic areas.[5] The total informal economy work (column 4) and the formal census-counted work (column 5) are then added to obtain a recounted total women's employment rate (column 6).

Incorporating uncounted home-based work in employment rates slightly reduces the gap between races and immigrant generations. The gap in counted employment between third-generation (or later) whites and African Americans is reduced from 28.6 percent to 24.2 percentage points in the reestimated total, primarily because of white women's greater farm presence. However, that gap remains large, and black women's recounted employment rate (66 percent) greatly outpaces that of all other women. Lines 3 and 4 of Table 2 show that the 4.1 percentage point difference in the recorded census employment rates between immigrant women and their native-born daughters is reduced to only 1.7 percentage points in the recounted rates, largely because of the inclusion of immigrant women's work with boarders.

In contrast, including home-based informal economy work has a huge impact on geographic differences in women's employment, completely reversing the patterns found in reported rates. Urban women, who reported gainful employment rates 12.3 percentage points higher than rural women (28.4 and 16.1 percent, respectively), would have had employment rates 13.6 percentage points lower than those of rural women in recounted employment (37.4 versus 51.0 percent). The reported employment rates of women in the North Atlantic region, which in the census data were 7.1 percentage points higher than elsewhere (27.4 versus 20.3 percent, respectively), are reestimated to be 5.9 percentage points lower than in other regions (40.0 and 45.9 percent). While incorporating work with boarders lifts urban and North Atlantic women's employment rates by about 6 percentage points, counting family farm work raises rural and non-North Atlantic women's employment rates so high that they outpace those of urban and North Atlantic women. These geographic trends occur because in 1900 the bulk of women's uncounted labor was on farms, which is no longer true.

Counting family farm work also changes relative race and immigrant employment rates. Contrary to our impressions from the 1900 census, neither immigrant nor second-generation ethnic women's recounted work rates (41.9 and 40.2 percent) are greatly different from those of third-generation (or later) white women (41.8 percent). Third-generation white women were not less likely to work than ethnic women, they were merely more likely to do so in home-based labor.

Many of our impressions of the past are incorrect because we use present-day, urban frames of reference. When people in the United States think of the informal economy, they do not think of farm work, even though worldwide, agriculture is the major form of women's uncounted economic contribution. Since farming is no longer a large component of the U.S. economy, what women's home-based work at the turn of the century conjures up for most people is taking in boarders, factory outwork, or child care, not farm work. Yet farm work was more common, especially among native-born women, who were most likely to be married to men who owned land. Indeed, 44 percent of white and 43 percent of black third-generation or later U.S. women lived on farms in 1900. Our images of women's work in 1900 are drawn from novels like Anzia Yezierska's *The Bread Givers* (1925), but they would be better based on Laura Ingalls Wilder's *Little House on the Prairie* (1953) or the novels of Willa Cather.

Many fictional works as well as research monographs have been written about urban immigrant women at the turn of the twentieth century, especially the Irish, Russians, and Italians. In truth, only Scandinavian women were as heavily concentrated on farms (40.7 percent) as were black and white third-generation women. Some groups (Germans, Eastern Europeans, English Canadians, British, and Latin Americans) had between 19 and 22 percent farm residence, but the more urban French Canadian, Irish, Russian, and Italian women were less likely (under 13 percent) to live on farms.

Table 3 provides a broader, national view of officially counted work and uncounted informal economy labor for the ten largest ethnic groups (of immigrant and second-generation women) at the turn of the century, whether they were urban or rural residents. The most noticeable change caused by adding women's uncounted work to the reported census figures is that the employment rate of Scandinavian women moves from average to third highest, behind black and French Canadian women, largely because of their previously ignored but voluminous farm work. The other groups are more urban, but only two of them, Italians and Russians, were overrepresented in small merchant businesses, compared to the U.S. average of 0.8 percent. The numerical

TABLE 3.   Reestimate of Employment Rates (%) for Women Ages 15–64, by National Origin, 1900

| Group | Home-based uncounted work | | | | Formal census count | Recounted total employed |
	Unpaid farm	Unpaid merchant	Boarders, lodgers	Total cols. 1–3		
Irish	5.3	0.6	4.5	10.4	33.2	43.6
British	9.9	1.0	4.1	15.0	20.5	35.5
Scandinavian	19.4	0.7	5.4	25.5	22.7	48.2
German	12.0	1.1	4.1	17.2	21.5	38.7
Eastern European	10.3	1.2	10.7	22.2	21.2	43.4
Russian	6.3	2.8	12.9	22.0	22.3	44.3
Italian	4.5	1.8	16.5	22.8	15.2	38.0
French Canadian	7.4	0.3	8.9	16.6	32.3	48.9
English Canadian	9.7	0.7	4.4	14.8	26.4	41.2
Latin American	14.2	0.0	2.8	17.0	17.9	34.9

Note: Rates are calculated in the same manner as in Table 2. National-origin groups include immigrants (first generation) and their second-generation, U.S.-born children. The first seven groups are European in origin and the remaining three are from the Americas.

impact of small enterprises on ethnic women's employment rates is small. On the other hand, these national data support the findings of smaller regional studies indicating that urban ethnic groups were more likely than average to take in boarders as an economic strategy. Having boarders was a particularly common form of uncounted home-based work among Italians, Russians, and Eastern Europeans, and it raised their total home-based labor rates (column 4) higher than those of most other national origin groups.

When the three forms of home-based work are combined, the total rate of uncounted work varied considerably among these groups around the national average of 21.6 percent (see Table 2, column 4). For Scandinavian and third-generation white women the uncounted work rates were higher, at about 26 percent of employment-age women, because of uncounted farm work. In contrast, among Irish women, who had very high counted work rates, the informal economy added only 10 percent more workers. This pattern suggests that formal employment and home-based work were alternative economic strategies, but the moderate

TABLE 4.   Percentage of Women Ages 15–64 Living on Farms or with Boarders,
by National Origin, 1900

Group	% Living on farms	% Living with boarders
White, 3rd+ gen.*	44.3	9.8
Black, 3rd+ gen.*	43.1	10.3
Scandinavian	40.7	14.1
German	22.2	10.0
Eastern European	21.4	15.5
English Canadian	21.2	10.3
Latin American	19.4	8.5
British	19.0	9.4
French Canadian	12.6	16.0
Irish	11.9	10.2
Russian	11.5	20.9
Italian	4.7	24.1

Note: Groups are presented in decreasing order of the percentage of women living
on farms.
    *Third-generation or later U.S. immigrant.

inverse relationship (correlation = −.31) that exists across the
racial-ethnic groups in these rates is not significant. Indeed,
British, English and French Canadian, German, and Latin American women also had relatively little uncounted informal economy
work, between 15 and 17 percent, but their rates of counted work
ranged widely, from a low of 17.9 percent among Latin Americans
to a high of 32.3 percent for French Canadians.

Similarly, rural or urban location did not entirely determine the
forms of home-based work that women carried out. Table 4 presents the various groups in order, according to their presence on
farms (column 1), and then indicates what percentage of the
women actually lived with boarders (column 2), whether or not
they reported such work. Most race and national origin groups,
regardless of their location, reported boarder residence close to the
national average of 10.4 percent. Black women were similar to
Irish women in their average rates of boarding, even though the
former were much more likely to live on farms; and the strongly
agricultural Scandinavian women and the largely urban French
Canadians also had similar rates of living with boarders (14.1 and
16.0 percent, respectively). Rural location may have determined

women's access to farm work, but access to boarders was more universal. Certainly, the two groups most likely to live with boarders—Russians and Italians—were also the most urban. However, the inverse relationship (correlation = −.5) that exists across the twelve racial-ethnic groups between farm residence and boarder residence is not quite significant.[6]

In summary, the variation described here suggests that home-based, informal economy work was neither confined to nor found uniformly among ethnic women, and that location by itself did not fully determine the forms of uncounted work done by women. Furthermore, adding home-based work to counted work increases the relative employment probabilities of some groups (Scandinavian and third-generation white women) and decreases that of others (Irish, British, and English Canadian), while leaving others unchanged.[7]

CHOOSING COUNTED OR UNCOUNTED HOME-BASED WORK

Among women, wives and female household heads were the most likely to engage in home-based remunerative labor. Under what conditions did they do so? Rural location and a husband's (or a wife's) farm ownership determined women's farm work. In contrast, taking in boarders occurred in all geographic settings, was common in many households, and is a type of work that is easily uncovered, whether or not it was counted as employment by the census. Thus, taking in boarders or lodgers is an excellent example for examining when and under what conditions wives and female household heads did home-based work.

So far, we have seen that wives' and female household heads' likelihood of taking in boarders varied according to their ethnicity and urban versus rural residence. To explore the relative importance of these and other traits, we need a technique for predicting dichotomous outcomes—in this case, living or not living with boarders. Logistic regression can be used to do the analysis, and the statistical results are presented in Appendix Table A.1. To make this table more comprehensible, I organize all the variables into groups representing five types of characteristics that could

predict home-based work. The first set of variables includes gendered, individual traits. The most important of these is marital
status—whether the woman was the household head or not, and
if so, separating employed and nonemployed heads. Age, which
suggests stage in the life cycle, is also included in this group. The
second characteristic is ethnicity, and here I compared each of the
ten largest national origin groups with black and white women.
To do so, I used just ten variables, one for each ethnic group. The
groups in the table are listed in order of their predicted likelihood
of taking in boarders. The third characteristic includes the variables representing social class, which I measured in different ways.
For wives, the male household head's major occupational group
was used to indicate resources (beyond those of agricultural work),
while home ownership and the proportion of all household members who were employed are indicated for each woman. The fourth
characteristic incorporates variables representing household composition. Children and seniors represent dependents whose presence could necessitate the additional income gleaned from having boarders or who, conversely, might take up all the available
space, leaving no room for boarding. The number of adolescents
or adults who could generate income is also included in the household composition variable set. The fifth characteristic includes
measures related to geographic location, and here I tested whether
urban residence would become important once other factors were
controlled and whether contextual measures like the average
women's manufacturing wage or the percentage of immigrant
women in a county would shape the likelihood of a woman's taking in boarders. On average, the probability of wives and female
household heads taking in boarders or lodgers was .11 (or 11 percent). The first column of the table uses asterisks to indicate which
variables had a significant impact. For each significant variable,
the second column shows the overall probability of living with
boarders, and the third column gives the change from the average
probability ($p = .11$) associated with that attribute.

The most important determinant is the sex of the household
head. A female household head was more likely than a male
household head (and his wife) to take in boarders. Furthermore,
among female household heads, women who held jobs were even

more likely to take in boarders ($p = .21$) than those without jobs ($p = .16$). Thus, it seems that for independent women, holding a job did not reduce the need for additional home-based work, and multiple sources of income were often necessary.

Ethnicity also had an influential effect. Italian women were equally as likely as employed female household heads to take in boarders ($p = .21$), while Russians ($p = .19$), Eastern Europeans ($p = .19$), French Canadians ($p = .17$), and Scandinavians ($p = .15$) were not far behind. In contrast, Germans were somewhat less likely than whites or blacks to have lived with boarders, but other groups statistically were no different. Thus, not every racial-ethnic group used boarding as an economic strategy.

Social class, or economic need, was the next most important characteristic, but the impact of these variables was less than that of either ethnicity or household headship. Those who owned their home and might easily rent rooms were relatively unlikely to do so because home ownership was indicative of having economic resources. Similarly, women living in households with a high proportion of employed adults did not need to take in boarders because they had used another method of raising income. Other households, however, did need boarders and lodgers. When a male household head was employed as an operative or laborer, wives were more likely than average to have boarders in their homes ($p = .13$). Operatives and laborers were relatively poorly paid and the work was not consistently available, necessitating another source of income. Surprisingly, when a male household head was in professional work, boarders were also common ($p = .15$). Although three-fifths of male professionals held well-paid, steady jobs, such as engineer, physician, lawyer, or government official, another two-fifths were actors, musicians, artists, teachers, or clergy, and their work was either less steady or lower paid, again making boarders an attractive income source.

The importance of geographic context was relatively similar to that of occupation. Net of all other influences, living in an urban area increased the likelihood of taking in boarders ($p = .15$). However, average women's wages in manufacturing, a measure of labor market demand, had little effect on these wives' and female household heads' decision to bring in boarders. Undoubtedly, this is because it was rare for a wife to take such a full-time job under any circumstance. The percentage of immigrant women in a county, a measure of demand for boarding, also had no impact. It seems that boarding was determined more by the supply of housing than by demand for it. Furthermore, many boarders were immigrant men rather than women.

Finally, all the variables reflecting household composition characteristics were significant, although their effect in each case was relatively small. Both increasing the number of dependents (young children or seniors) and increasing the number of potential workers (adolescents or adults) in a household reduced the probability of living with boarders. Given this apparently contradictory result, it seems that household size was the real issue. As other authors have noted (Modell and Hareven 1973), taking in boarders was a life-cycle-related phenomenon whereby the lack of a spouse or the departure of grown children from a household left space available for female household heads or couples, respectively, to take in boarders or lodgers. Age per se was not influential once other variables are considered, and economic need and available space were the important life-cycle factors.

In summary, taking in boarders was primarily determined by the sex of the household head and by ethnicity. Social class and urban residence, reflecting a household's economic needs and the local supply of potential boarders, respectively, were next in importance. Finally, household composition, or available space, came into play. Although these factors determined when boarders were taken in at the turn of the century, one cannot conclude that the same factors influenced other forms of women's home-based work, especially farm work. However, they are suggestive of factors likely to predict other urban home-based labor, such as factory outwork.

COMPARING 1900 AND 2000

What are the implications of locating women's home-based work using a gender-equity approach? On the one hand, there is evidence for an unexpected consistency: women have worked and contributed to a family's income beginning much earlier in the twentieth century than the double standards embedded in the census allowed us to see before. On the other hand, there are unanticipated changes. Once the twentieth century baseline of women's labor force participation is increased to 46 percent, the apparent rise in women's employment over the course of the century is greatly reduced, and we can turn our attention towards other more important economic and social shifts that are reflected in the reestimation.

Several interconnected changes in the nature of work occurred throughout the twentieth century. In the first half of the century the U.S. economy shifted away from agriculture, where women's work in a family enterprise was generally unacknowledged. Indeed, the number of at-home workers declined steadily until 1980, largely due to the drop in family farms. By the second half of the century, differences between rural and urban women's work options were no longer as large, and much family-based employment had disappeared. As a result, former links between work and family changed substantially. A major change was that a smaller percentage of women's work came to be done at home, with women working more for others and for wages, rather than working unwaged for a family member.

Moreover, the effects of women's marital status were muted. At the beginning of the century, wives worked in the informal economy, but adolescent and unmarried women might obtain a job in the formal economy. By the end of the century it was the wives who were employed, while adolescents stayed in school considerably longer than in 1900.

The growth of the service and retail sectors of the U.S. economy during the second half of the twentieth century created a demand for women employees and a supply of part-time jobs, which were attractive to mothers of young children. Part-time work used to be available to women only as homeworkers, whose contributions were then regarded as part of their family chores. Now, part-time work is often more like full-time, formal economy work. It is available outside of homes and inside of businesses, and thus is more visible. Thus a third shift occurred in the work-family link.

In addition, this examination of part-time, home-based work in 1900 reveals an ethnic division of labor among women in the informal economy. The common impression that first- and second- generation immigrant groups, notably Italians, Russians, Eastern Europeans, Scandinavians, and French Canadians, were active in the urban informal economy by taking in boarders proved to be well-founded. Yet, counter to other stereotypes of that period, third-generation or later black and white women, as well as Scandinavian women, were among the most involved in home-based work because of their full- or part-time family farm labor. It may be that similar stereotypes are common now, as we focus our attention on immigrant domestic or child-care workers and ignore the growth of small home-based businesses among black and nonimmigrant white women.

The qualitative changes revealed by the reestimate of women's work rates in 1900 were not only economic. Shifts in census definitions of employment and popular beliefs about women's roles also played a part. The dual-spheres ideology and the double standards embedded in the 1900 census reflected the middle-class values of the time, which did not recognize women's home-based, part-time work as countable employment. Thus the census of 1900 was not designed to count work that we might include now, and by the time definitions became more inclusive, in 1940, women's work had also shifted away from those forms of work that previously had gone uncounted.

This does not mean that the current U.S. census is nonideological. For example, women's unpaid volunteer work or child-rearing and housework are still not considered labor (or even unpaid family labor). Thus elements of the dual-spheres ideology remain in the census, separating unpaid domestic tasks from "work." Although it is probably not possible to achieve a nonideological census, we want to understand its biases and strive to develop a census that does not undervalue women's economic contributions. Contemporary feminists value women's independence and emphasize the importance of the economic power women have achieved through their jobs. Although women are less dependent today on individual men for support, they are more dependent on the labor market, and the new social expectation has become that of the supermom in a dual-income household.

TABLE 5.   Work Experience of Men and Women During 1996

Extent of employment	Men (%)	Women (%)
Full-time, ≥50 wk/yr	70.8	54.8
Full-time, <50 wk/yr	15.4	15.8
Part-time, ≥50 wk/yr	5.8	13.7
Part-time, <50 wk/yr	8.0	15.7
Total	100.0	100.0

Note: Full-time work is 35 or more hours per week and part-time work is less than 35 hours per week. Data refer to persons 16 years and older.

Source: Bureau of Labor Statistics. 1997. "Labor Force Statistics from the Current Population Survey." URL: www.bls.gov/news.release/work.t01.htm

Current definitions suggest that we are approaching gender parity in the labor market, since 63.1 percent of all women and 77 percent of men worked during 1996 (Bureau of Labor Statistics 1997). Yet we must be cautious in how these data are interpreted. More recorded women's work means more women are earning their own money, but it does not necessarily imply enough income to attain full economic independence or freedom from poverty. Much of the late-century growth in women's work can be attributed to part-time jobs, which generally pay less than full-time ones. As illustrated in Table 5, more than twice as many women (29.4 percent) as men (13.8 percent) work part-time. At the other end of the continuum, fewer women (54.8 percent) than men (70.8 percent) work full-time year-round (Bureau of Labor Statistics 1997), and, in 1996, even those who did earned an average of 73.8 percent of the median male income (Hartmann and Whittaker 1998). Many single mothers are supporting themselves and their children on this lesser income. This is a somewhat precarious independence.

Although unpaid work in a family enterprise has diminished over the century, remunerative home-based work has not disappeared, although its exact volume is difficult to measure. Estimates are usually concerned with the effect of uncounted work on measures of the gross national product (about 14 percent of the 1980 gross national product, according to Molefsky [1982]) or on tax evasion. For example, Feige (1996) calculated that unreported income in 1993, a proxy for the underground economy, equaled 20 percent of the total adjusted gross reported income. These studies pay relatively little attention to gender issues.

Feminist writings on homework (Boris 1994; Boris and Daniels 1989; Gimenez 1990) do examine women's role, but they have emphasized the changing nature of this work over time rather than its quantity. Women's home-based work is now found in diverse industries, but it is especially common in professional and personal service, while earlier forms of home-based work, namely factory outwork and farm labor, now seem to be under-represented (Silver 1989). Various authors have examined the different home-based work conditions of waged, often subcontracted, home workers and those who are self-employed. Others have looked at the economic and political factors determining which tasks get transferred from on-site workers to home workers (Glazer 1993). Clearly, home-based work continues to be important to the U.S. economy and for women, although its primary forms may have changed.

The next chapter looks at paid work in the formal economy—women's counted gainful employment. Can and should we include uncounted home-based work in analyses of women's labor force participation? The examination of home-based work in this chapter raised important substantive concerns, but our measurements could not be precise. The reestimate of women's work had to ignore uncounted factory outwork and could only estimate women's participation in other home based-work. Furthermore, there is value to the turn-of-the-century census responses, which simultaneously indicate women's propensity to claim labor force status and the kind of women's work people recognized as "important" at the time. Fortunately, an all-inclusive compromise is possible without combining recorded and unrecorded work into one employment measure. We can predict women's work as recorded by the census while including home-based work factors, such as living with boarders or in a male-headed farming household, among the predictor variables that should reduce women's recorded employment. This approach, used in the next chapter, has the advantage of showing the interactions between home-based and formal economy work.

3　Race, Ethnicity, Class, and Gender

Determining Women's Employment

THE EARLY TWENTIETH CENTURY was a time of rapid industrialization that began with the mixed commercial-, early manufacturing-, and agriculture-based economy of the 1880s and culminated in the swift technological development of industry associated with World War I. What factors impelled women's entry into gainful employment during this era of change? There is no doubt that women's opportunities were in flux, with some occupational sectors opening to them and others closing.

Throughout this forty-year period (1880 to 1920), women's major forms of employment were in the domestic and personal service industry. Gradually, native-born white women were able to leave private household work to enter newly open occupations, which left Asian, Hispanic, black, and immigrant white women increasingly concentrated in domestic work. Jobs in the garment and textile industries, which had been women's main point of entry into paid labor in the early nineteenth century, were also transformed. In many industries immigrant men had replaced native-born white women as the primary labor force before 1880, but the numbers of (mostly immigrant) women employed in garment and textile work did not crest until 1910 and 1920, respectively. In 1900, "operative" was no longer the most common women's job in the textile industry; rather, it was seamstress or dressmaker (Oppenheimer 1970).

At the opening of the twentieth century, white-collar occupations, as well as those that came to be known as pink-collar ones, had begun hiring women. Public school teaching had become an important female-dominated job before 1880, but other white-collar jobs changed more slowly. The three census categories of stenographer-typist, bookkeeping-cashier-accountant, and clerk had negligible numbers of women in 1880, but by 1900, when the bureaucratization of work began in earnest, women constituted 77, 29, and 7 percent of those respective clerical occupations (Katzman 1978; Reskin and Roos 1990). Furthermore, by 1900 women already made up 80 percent of telephone operators, and even retail sales jobs had opened to them. The year 1900 fell in the middle of a growth period in new jobs for women, at the same time that many of their traditional jobs in household domestic work and garment manufacturing still predominated. It was a period during which the foundation was set for women's roles in the twentieth century U.S. political economy.

It was also a period in which rates of immigration, especially from Europe, were consistently high. Germans and the Irish had been among the earliest and largest groups to arrive on U.S. shores. Southern and eastern Europeans followed later, representing a quarter of the immigrants in 1870 and a rising proportion thereafter. By 1909, 15 percent of the population was foreign born, but this European migration slowed dramatically with the national origins quota system of 1921. Nonetheless, the major northward migration of the black population began around World War I, initiating new demographic changes. Although the Asian immigrant population was relatively small, one of its outstanding characteristics was that it was primarily male. After the Chinese Exclusion Act of 1882, which caused a forty-year decline in the U.S. Chinese population, this imbalance was solidified. Even among Japanese immigrants, women accounted for less than 4 percent in 1900.

The influx of immigrants at the beginning of the twentieth century created significant diversity in women's gainful employment rates. Differences between black and white women are often recognized and used as a baseline for judging the declining racial gap in women's work rates over time, but other groups are ignored in this historical view. In 1900, most married women, with the exception of black wives, were unlikely to report employment because of their limited work and child-care options, as well as popular preferences for mothers to stay at home with their young children (Bose 1984). This phenomenon supported the notion that the only important differences among women were "black and white." Yet, as is often the case, this view is too simplistic.

Without a baseline for 1900 that uses a more diverse set of racial-ethnic groups, it is all too easy to assume that black women were more likely to work for wages than immigrants and that immigrant women were more likely to work for wages than native-born white women. However, the actual differences in gainful employment rates between racial-ethnic groups were much greater than that. Indeed, unique racial-ethnic patterns overlapped with the generally shared marital status effects. Racial-ethnic differences in employment rates have been found throughout the century, and first- and second-generation immigrant women often exhibit a wide range of employment rates (Logan 1997; Sassler 2000), suggesting that diversity is not merely an old pattern but also a continuing one. Uncovering this range in gainful employment rates and understanding the various factors that led to it are the objectives of this chapter.

In previous research, often by historians, employment patterns unique to a racial-ethnic group typically were found by using case studies, as described in Chapter 1. Although not always focused on gender issues, these studies examined an individual region or city, such as Detroit (Zunz 1982) or Buffalo (McLaughlin 1973), one or more immigrant (Pleck 1978) or religious groups (especially Jews; see Glenn 1990; Morowska 1996), racial groups (Ichioka 1988), working-class women (Kennedy 1979; Kessler-Harris 1982; Tentler 1979), or a particular occupation, such as collar workers (Turbin 1992). The detailed information in these studies is very useful, but the racial-ethnic groups are difficult to compare. For example, how can we contrast clerical workers in Pittsburgh (DeVault 1990) with blacks in the West (Katz 1987)? In this chapter, I begin this process by describing and comparing different racial-ethnic employment patterns using national data instead of case studies.

In subsequent sections, I develop a conceptual model of the factors that determined women's employment. Many historical case studies of women's work emphasized the primacy of the social class factor. However, contemporary social stratification theorists (Baca Zinn 1989; England 1993; Glenn 1987; Hill Collins 1990, 1993) argue for a more complex model, one that is more contextual and more interactive. Therefore, my model illustrates how the multiple levels of class, race, ethnicity, and gender played out against (and with) each other.

My conceptualizations of gender, race, class, and even geography go beyond the tempting-to-use, simple dichotomous categories of male-female, black-white, middle class-working class, or North-South. Indeed, the meanings of "gender," "race," "ethnicity," and "class" actually lie in their social implications. Accordingly, I use whole groups of social attributes (measured as variables) to indicate each of these concepts. For example, in 1900, gender took its social shape through the institutions of marriage and the family. Women's opportunities were delimited by their marital status and age, as well as by the number of other potential workers in a household. Race and ethnicity were expressed not only in cultural preferences but also in the differences between first- and second-generation immigrants, who were more distanced from their homeland. Geographic context was not limited to region or urban-rural residence but included more complex factors such as the local ethnic mix, which could create competition for jobs or open up opportunities. This new framework incorporates individual, household, and geographic measures into the concepts of class, race or ethnicity, and gender.

Next, I use this conceptual framework to analyze the determinants of women's gainful employment. I focus on the seven largest racial-ethnic groups in 1900: whites and blacks who were born in the United States of native-born parents, as well as Irish, German, Eastern European, Russian, and French Canadian women. Each of the last six groups has been shown to be significantly different from white women in the factors propelling its members into work (Bose 1984), but here I explore exactly what those diverse factors were. I excluded some frequently studied groups, such as Italians, because of their small numbers in the national sample and other groups, such as Scandinavians, because their gainful employment rates were no different from those of whites. These groups (and others) will be reintroduced in Chapter 4.

I examine the lives of two different groups of women. The first group encompasses all women within the usual employment age range of 15 to 64 who were related to the household head. Boarders and servants must be excluded because the household variables of the model do not really pertain to them, and the census does not provide enough other data about them to allow us to predict why they were employed. Boarders, who were usually on their own, were counted in the Public Use Sample as "primaries," with no household information provided. At the same time, servants or other employees were recorded with the household data of their employers rather than of their own families. Although some women are therefore excluded from this model, all women are incorporated in the next chapter on jobs and occupational segregation, and the lives of servants are extensively examined in Chapter 5. The second group to which I apply the model eliminates wives of the household head. "Non-wives," as I dub the remaining group, are important because they were the women most likely to report gainful employment.

In sum, this chapter introduces a model of the roles played by gender, class, race, and ethnicity in shaping women's entry into gainful employment. It does so using multiple measures of each concept. The model is comparative of multiple racial-ethnic groups. Yet it neither assumes that all racial-ethnic women are alike nor that they are different. In addition, it furnishes a national look at patterns that generally have been studied only regionally. The results reveal unexpected continuities in some of the determinants of women's work, as well as the more often cited disjunctures.

DIVERSE EMPLOYMENT RATES

In the census of 1900, women's gainful employment rates—which did not usually include unpaid family farm work or taking in boarders—varied considerably according to their racial-ethnic background. Table 6 vividly illustrates that as few as 13 percent of white women and as many as 40 percent of black women between the ages of 15 and 64 reported employment. In particular, it was the wives married to household heads whose dramatically low rates of employment—between 1 and 5 percent for most racial-ethnic groups—depressed these average rates. Wives constituted about 59 percent of adult women related to a household head. When these women are eliminated from consideration,

TABLE 6. Women's Gainful Employment (%) by Racial-Ethnic Group and
Relation to Household Head, Ages 15–64, 1900

Relation to household head	Racial-ethnic group							
	White	Black	Irish	German	Eastern Euro- pean	Russian	French Cana- dian	All race- ethnicity groups
All female relatives	13	40	25	16	14	18	28	18
Wives	2	22	2	2	3	1	5	4
Non-wives	27	61	48	39	42	62	61	37

Note: These employment rates are for women related to the household head. Therefore, female employees, servants, and boarders are excluded from these figures. Non-
wives are female household heads and daughters or other female relatives of a male
household head, some few of whom may have been married. Therefore, the focus of
this table is the effect of marital status on women's gainful employment.

employment rates for the remaining set of daughters, other female
relatives, and female household heads range from 27 percent for
white women to as high as 61 or 62 percent for black, French
Canadian, and Russian women. From this perspective, women of
color were not alone in having high employment rates. In fact, the
employment rate for many non-wives in 1900 was very similar to
the 60 percent rate for all women at the end of the century.

A GENDER, CLASS, AND RACIAL-ETHNIC INCLUSIVE MODEL: WHAT IT INCLUDES AND WHY

The model I developed for explaining these varying gainful employment rates is based on two main components:

1. the interplay of gender, class, race, and ethnicity, and
2. the characteristics of an individual, her household, and her
   geographic place of residence.

Table 7 illustrates how the model combines these dimensions into
two related axes and shows the measures I used for each concept.
The vertical axis, identified in the left-hand column, is based on
my earlier household-resources model for predicting women's
gainful employment. That model was designed to reconceptualize

TABLE 7. Relationship Between Variables of a Class, Race and Ethnicity, or Gender Model and the Individual, Household, and Geographic Levels of a Contextual Model

	Class	Race and ethnicity	Gender

Individual	Literacy: Reads a language
	
	Head's occupation:
	  Professional or
	    manager
	  Clerical or sales
	  Craft
	  Operative or laborer
	  Service
	  Agriculture
	  Unclassified
	  Unemployed
	
	Woman is household head
		2nd- (vs. 1st-) generation immigrant
		
		Racial-ethnic group (considered in this chapter):
		  White
		  Black
		  Irish
		  German
		  Eastern European
		  Russian
		  French Canadian
			Marital status: married, living with spouse
			
			Age

Household	Proportion of household adults employed
	
	Presence of non-nuclear-family members:
	  Extended family
	  Boarders
	  Servants
		None	Household age and sex composition:
			  No. of children
			    (ages 0–9)
			  No. of seniors
			    (age 65+)
			  No. of adolescent
			    boys (ages 10–14)
			  No. of adolescent
			    girls (ages 10–14)
			  No. of single men
			    (ages 15–64)
			  No. of single women
			    (ages 15–64)

Geography	County-level economic indicators:
	  Women's avg. wages,
	    in manufacturing
	  Average firm size
		County-level percentage of:
		  1st- and 2nd-generation immigrant women
		  Black women
		  Other women of color
		
		Region:
		  West
		  North and South Atlantic
		  North and South Central
			Urban (vs. rural) residence

home and work as linked rather than separate spheres (Bose 1984). To illustrate this linkage, I expanded the usually considered human capital variables, which focus on individual characteristics like education and age to predict work, by adding two other categories—the household and geographic context. I set the individual within her household constraints and resources. Rather than focusing on families alone, however, I put all aspects of women's lives at the center of the analysis (Dublin 1994).

The new model presented in this chapter augments my earlier one by classifying the household-resource variables into the social class, racial-ethnic, and gender categories that compose the horizontal axis. In Table 7, each of the individual, household, and geographic predictors of women's work, drawn from a household-resources model, is distributed across these new analytical groups. The result is an interweaving of these two frameworks that allows me to test theories that stress the priority of race and ethnicity, class, or gender in women's working lives. I will first describe how I conceptualize class, race and ethnicity, or gender and how they can be quantified using both typical and newly developed individual, household, or geographic indicators.

CONTEXTUAL EFFECTS

A major drawback to the early national-level research on work in 1900 was the limited geographic information recorded in the census, which included only the region and size-of-place where a person lived. Case studies had considerably more information, but in a national study, geographic information becomes essential to understanding why residence in a particular city or a region might be influential in women's lives. I was able to enlarge the number of these geographic or contextual variables by incorporating economic and demographic county-level data, available from Michigan's Inter-University Consortium for Political and Social Research. These additional materials allowed me to create new geographic indicators—ones that can be viewed as structuring the availability of work according to a person's social class, racial-ethnic group, and, to a lesser extent, gender.

I will briefly describe these contextual variables here. *Class*-related opportunities and income potential are indicated by average wages for women in manufacturing and average firm (company) size. Detailed information about *racial-ethnic* opportunity structures—or competition for jobs—is based on measures of the percentage of first- and second-generation immigrant women, the percentage of black women, or the percentage of women of other races in a county. Since blacks were concentrated in the South and immigrants were concentrated in the North Atlantic and North Central census areas, such measures reveal nuances within regions. *Gendered* components of geography were reflected in urban residence, since cities usually facilitated women's employment. Urbanness could now be measured using population density as well as city size. My expectations about how these contextual indicators would influence women's work are described in the sections that follow on class, racial-ethnic, and gendered variables.

SOCIAL CLASS

Many researchers have considered immigrant status to be synonymous with working-class status. However, I do not assume this was always true, and instead transfer immigration-related measures to the racial-ethnic category. I prefer to see social class as embedded in many other measures of economic position. Wage and salary data, the most obvious indicators, were not available until 1940. However, two key economic measures can be constructed from the census data.

The first is an individual measure: the occupation of a household's head. I included it because I thought that women's employment would be more likely when the head's status was low, since additional income might have been necessary. If the woman herself was the household head, I expected that the lack of a husband would increase the likelihood of her own employment, regardless of racial-ethnic background. Indeed, women were not usually considered household heads unless they had substantial resources (such as farm or home ownership) or brought in more than half of the household income. The second important measure seemed likely to be the proportion of family members who were employed. Presumably, the greater the proportion employed, or the higher the economic need, the more likely it was that a woman would be drawn into employment. In contrast, when a smaller proportion of household members were employed, a "family wage" or single salary was probably supporting the family.

Household composition could reflect social class in other ways, too. I included the presence of servants because they would reflect higher income and thus a lower likelihood of a woman's being employed. In contrast, previous literature suggests that the presence of boarders denoted a need for additional income, which would increase a woman's probability of recorded work (Bose 1984). The role of extended family members, on the other hand, was less clear-cut. The presence of additional people in the household was likely to reduce per capita income, imposing an additional financial burden that might lead women to seek jobs. This was facilitated if family members provided child care, like the raisin-picker's sister I described in Chapter 1. On the other hand, if these relatives were employed, they could bring additional income to a household, reducing a woman's likelihood of performing paid work.

Literacy as an individual-level variable also signals social class. Today we expect better educated women to be employed. However, in 1900, women's literacy was positively related to a household head's social status, and if the family was well off, women's employment would have been viewed as unnecessary. Of course, when literate women are employed, we would expect them to hold better jobs.

Even contextual variables have social class outcomes. I thought that the higher the average women's manufacturing wages were in a county and, to a more limited extent, the larger the firm size, the more likely it was that women, especial first- and second-generation immigrants, would have been employed. At the same time, I thought that manufacturing work would have a limited impact on black women, since they were confined by segregation to domestic work and agricultural pursuits and were often prohibited from holding such manufacturing jobs.

RACE AND ETHNICITY

Cultural attitudes toward the general acceptability of women's employment and of the particular type of work selected (such as factory jobs, domestic, or home-based work) were shaped by a person's race and ethnicity. Black women were the most likely to work, but other women's employment rates varied widely by group. Therefore, when I examined women's employment in a general way, I always included separate ("dummy") variables denoting each racial-ethnic group (Bose 1984). However, in this chapter, I examine each group separately. Hence, the most relevant variable for each racial-ethnic group (except whites and blacks) is immigrant generation. Second-generation immigrant women, who were further removed from their cultural origins, were considered likely to behave differently from their immigrant counterparts. Among groups with high rates of female employment, we might expect to see second-generation rates lower, especially if those families became economically better off. In that case, they might choose to protect young women from employment. I use second-generation status as a proxy for ethnic identity, although immigrant generation more accurately represents an interaction between the norms of gender and those of ethnicity.

Other measures of race and ethnicity are geographic and contextual in nature. Region is important because the employment opportunities of some groups, such as Italians, varied depending on the region or city in which they were living (Cohen 1992). For example, while many Italian women in the North Atlantic area were seamstresses, in the North Central census region I found a second-generation 42-year-old Italian woman merchant, and in the rural West a 15-year-old Italian immigrant working as a food canner and preserver. This happened because region actually represents a geography-based link to the industrial and agricultural economic structure. Since most employed first- and second-generation immigrant women worked in northeastern urban factories or in service jobs, I expected that residence outside of the Northeast region would lower their employment rates.

At a more local level, the racial-ethnic composition of a county could influence women's work, too. For example, I thought that greater density of first- and second-generation immigrant women ought to result in a higher probability of those same women finding employment. They would be more able to use the networks of ethnic enclaves, just as I suggest occurred in domestic work (discussed in Chapter 5).

The impact of a county's racial mixture (represented as percent black and percent women of other races) could be the same, but the added feature of segregation complicated it. For instance, if there was a racial-ethnic hiring queue in the North, where immigrants were the preferred employees, then higher percentages of black residents could actually increase first- and second-generation immigrant women's recorded work rather than enhance the opportunities of black women. Therefore, I anticipated that immigrant and second-generation women's work would be more sensitive to a county's racial mix than black women's work would be to the county's ethnic concentration (percentage of first- and second-generation immigrant women).

GENDER

Finally, my model assumes that women's work is shaped by their gender as well as by class, ethnicity, or race. Gender is embedded in an individual's age and marital status as well as in the more collective form of household sex composition. Thus gender is not merely a dummy variable defined as female or male; in fact, there are no men in this analysis. Rather, gender takes its social shape through household and individual contexts. Accordingly, marital status (expressed as being married with one's husband present) ought to reduce women's recorded employment; it should be a primary determinant for first- and second-generation immigrant women while considerably less important to black women's work. Increasing age should follow a similar pattern, with women's employment decreasing as they entered marriage and the childbearing years, marking life-cycle stage or family generation.

Household composition also had a variety of gendered components. The presence of young children could decrease overall women's employment, as it does today. However, children could also be an inducement into paid employment for women who were not married to the household head. The effect of senior citizens over age 65 should be similarly mixed—adding dependents in need of caretaking, but facilitating the employment of younger household members. In contrast, I believed that greater numbers of employable single men (age 15 and older) or adolescent boys (ages 10 to 14) would have reduced the need for women's employment, since men generally earned more than women.

I include urban residence as a gendered opportunity structure because considerable women's employment was possible in a small town or city factory. In rural areas, as described in Chapter 2, women were more limited to unrecorded family work on a farm, their contributions often hidden by men's self-employment in agriculture. In this model, I retain the dichotomous approach of urban versus rural, since the continuous variable of population density was a less sensitive predictor of women's employment.

COMPARING THE RACIAL-ETHNIC GROUPS: MEASURING THE MODEL VARIABLES

The mean values of the variables in this model are summarized in Table 8, where they are grouped theoretically according to class, race and ethnicity, or gender. The final column provides the national average on each variable for all women between the ages of 15 and 64, incorporating the fourteen racial-ethnic groups identified in this book.

All of the measures for the year 1900 differ significantly by racial-ethnic group, although each group is not necessarily distinct from all others. For example, black and Irish women had the highest rates of female-headed households, but none of the other groups differ from each other on this measure. Furthermore, no racial-ethnic group is consistently like any other across all indicators. To illustrate, black and white women were similar in that both lived in agricultural areas and in counties with low percentages of first- and second-generation immigrant women. Yet black and white women had very different average household prestige scores, and they were concentrated in different regions.

TABLE 8. Mean Values of Independent Variables for Women of the Largest Racial-Ethnic Groups (Household Heads, Spouses, Daughters, and Other Relatives), Ages 15–64, 1900

Variable	White	Black	Irish	German	Eastern European	Russian	French Canadian	All women*
					Racial-ethnic group			
Class								
Reads (%)	95	55	95	97	81	69	86	90
Head's occupation (%)†								
Manager or professional	12	2	11	13	9	14	4	11
Clerical or sales	5	1	5	5	4	10	4	5
Craft	11	3	12	18	13	21	24	12
Operative or laborer	14	22	30	23	36	26	39	19
Service	3	11	7	5	3	—	3	5
Agriculture	45	55	13	23	23	13	13	37
Unclassified	1	1	2	2	2	9	1	1
Unemployed	8	6	17	11	7	6	10	10
Total	99	101	97	100	97	99	98	100
Head's prestige score‡	23	12	24	24	18	25	17	22
Female-headed households (%)	6	13	11	8	5	4	7	8
Proportion employed in household	.31	.33	.36	.33	.32	.33	.36	.32
Extended family (%)	26	31	27	22	17	13	24	25
Boarders (%)	10	10	11	10	16	22	17	11
Servants (%)	6	1	4	5	5	5	2	5
Avg. wages, manufacturing ($)	229	207	272	248	258	290	294	239
Avg. firm size (no. of employees)	8	9	13	11	12	12	16	9

TABLE 8. *Continued*

| | | | | Racial-ethnic group | | | | |
Variable	White	Black	Irish	German	Eastern European	Russian	French Canadian	All women*
Race/Ethnicity								
Immigrant, 2nd gen. (%)§	Omitted	Omitted	66	61	26	9	41	20
Racial-ethnic mix by county								
% in county, 1st- or 2nd-gen. immigrant women	24	7	55	55	63	67	58	34
% in county, black women	11	48	3	4	3	3	1	12
% in county, other races	0.2	0.1	0.1	0.1	0.1	0.0	0.2	0.2
Region of residence (%)								
North Atlantic	25	3	61	31	39	68	72	29
South Atlantic	17	42	3	3	2	3	—	14
North Central	33	5	26	58	52	27	24	34
South Central	21	49	4	5	5	—	1	18
West	4	1	6	3	2	2	3	5
Total	100	100	100	100	100	100	100	100
Gender								
Marital status, % married, with spouse	61	56	52	63	71	71	61	61
Average age (yr)	33	31	35	34	32	30	33	33

(continued)

TABLE 8. *Continued*

				Racial-ethnic group				
Variable	White	Black	Irish	German	Eastern European	Russian	French Canadian	All women*
Gender *(continued)*								
Household composition								
Avg. no. children (ages 0–9)	1.08	1.50	0.91	1.09	1.48	1.55	1.37	1.13
Avg. no. seniors (age 65+)	0.15	0.11	0.16	0.15	0.08	0.03	0.04	0.14
Avg. no. adolescent boys (ages 10–14)	0.29	0.35	0.24	0.29	0.37	0.30	0.40	0.30
Avg. no. adolescent girls (ages 10–14)	0.28	0.39	0.23	0.29	0.30	0.27	0.33	0.29
Avg. no. single men (ages 15–64)	0.55	0.51	0.79	0.63	0.55	0.43	0.75	0.58
Avg. no. single women (ages 15–64)	0.91	0.99	0.79	0.56	0.40	0.39	0.58	0.94
Urban residence (%)	38	27	82	69	68	85	77	49
No. of cases	14,272	2,781	2,215	3,293	460	268	301	27,009

Note: Chi-square or analysis of variance tests indicate that every variable is significantly different by racial-ethnic category ($p \leq .001$).
* "All women" includes women between the ages of 15 and 64 from all racial-ethnic groups, but only those who were female household heads or directly related to the household head as wives, daughters, or other relatives. Excluded are servants, boarders, and other primaries.

†Household head's occupational distribution does not always total 100 percent owing to missing information or rounding. All information on occupations in this table includes women who may themselves be household heads. Such women's occupations are not used to measure household status when predicting women's gainful employment. Instead they are recorded as female household heads; that percentage is provided in this table.

‡The head's prestige score is included as a useful summary descriptive measure but it is not used in further analyses.

§Omitted variables: Blacks and whites are defined as native born with parents who were also U.S. born. Thus, the percentage of second-generation immigrants variable is irrelevant for them.

Table 8 provides a glimpse of such racial-ethnic similarities and differences. I discuss a few of these comparisons as I describe the measures themselves.

Social Class

At an individual level, a *person's literacy* (coded 1 = can read in some language) is a dimension of social class, indicating potential access to white-collar jobs. In general, literacy rates were quite high, except among black and Russian women.

The *employment of the household head* also reflects a family's standard of living. I recoded the heads' occupations into eight groups that are similar to those used in other sociohistorical studies of this period. The categories are professionals and managers, which are upper-tier white-collar jobs; clerical and sales tasks, which are lower-tier white-collar jobs; craft work in the skilled blue-collar fields; operatives and laborers, who were often described as semiskilled or unskilled workers; service workers; and those in agriculture. In addition, some people were employed in jobs that were so unclear that the census coders could not classify the work, while others were temporarily unemployed. (For purposes of comparison in later multivariate analyses, agriculture was the excluded category for the series of occupational dummy variables.) A quick glance at the table reveals that the heads of German and Russian households were more likely than average to be in professional or managerial positions. Eastern European, French Canadian, and Irish household heads were the most likely and white household heads the least likely to hold jobs as operatives or laborers. Meanwhile, black and white household heads were concentrated in agriculture. Women who were household heads also are included in this data. However, they are not included when predicting women's work, since it would be tautological to predict a woman's employment from the head's occupation when she herself is the head. (Therefore, this was coded as 1 = respondent is the head, for multivariate analyses, as if it were an occupation.)

It is important substantively to include *female headship*, since it was as strongly related to class position in 1900 as it is now. Female headship rates ranged from a high of 13 percent among blacks to a low of 4 percent among Russian women. This phenomenon is examined in more detail in Chapter 6.

An alternative measure of the head's status is the continuous variable of *occupational prestige,* which is coded from 0 (low) to 100 (high). Black, Eastern European, and French Canadian household heads had relatively low status, while Russians had the highest status. This measure is used in later chapters, but the occupational categories turned out to be better predictors of women's work for the purpose of this chapter.

A household approach to social class incorporates information on the economically active people there, creating a measure of the *proportion of family members who were employed* out of all the combined male and female relatives over age 10, but excluding the woman respondent herself. While the range on this variable is rather small, French Canadian and Irish women lived in households with the greatest proportion employed. Because daughters living away from home as servants or boarders had to be excluded in this analysis, one outcome is that working-class households with daughters employed elsewhere appeared to have fewer family members earning income than was actually the case. Therefore this measure, as well as the number of female adolescents, may be underestimated in this model.

Other household indicators of social class were measured as the presence or absence (coded 1 or 0, respectively) of non-nuclear-family members—*extended family, boarders, or servants*—each representing either a potential form of income or a financial asset (although relatives could also be financial burdens). Russian women were the most likely to take in boarders, while white households were the most likely to employ servants. The presence of extended family was relatively uncommon in Russian or Eastern European women's households but quite common in black women's homes.

Two final variables reflect a county's economic environment. These were the *average women's wages in manufacturing* (calculated as the total women's wages in manufacturing divided by the total number of women employed in manufacturing) and the *average firm size* (calculated as the average number of wage earners in manufacturing divided by the number of manufacturing establishments). Irish, Russian, and French Canadian women lived in the highest-wage counties, while black women lived in low-wage counties. These measures of industrialization proved useful in predicting women's work. However, agricultural indicators such as farm size were tested and proved irrelevant except to Eastern Europeans, and so were excluded from the analysis.

Race and Ethnicity

The dimension of ethnicity is measured at an individual level by *immigrant generation* and not by country of origin, since this analysis is carried out separately for each racial-ethnic group. Immigrant women are distinguished from those born in the United States with at least one foreign-born parent (coded 0 = immigrant and 1 = second generation), reflecting the distance of the latter from their cultural origins. As shown in Table 8, German and Irish women had generally been in the United States longer than other groups, since nearly two-thirds of them were second-generation immigrants. In contrast, Russians and Eastern Europeans had arrived more recently and they were usually immigrants. This measure of immigrant generation is omitted for whites and blacks, who were defined as third-generation or longer U.S. residents.

At a geographic level, the racial-ethnic composition of a woman's environment is measured in four components. The first three variables indicate the diversity of a county. *Ethnic mix* is the percentage of women in a county who are foreign-born white immigrants or native born with immigrant parents (constructed from the numbers of women in these two categories divided by the total number of women). Note that black and white women lived in counties with relatively few immigrant groups, largely due to their own high rates of rural, farm residence. The *percentage of women who are black* is the number of black women divided by the total number of women, and the *percentage of women of other races* is the number of women of color minus those who are black, divided by all women. Here we see that immigrant women lived in counties with relatively few black women, although white women lived in counties that averaged 11 percent black women. Not surprisingly, most black women lived in counties whose populations were about half black. This is due to their regional concentration in the South Atlantic and South Central census regions, where 90 percent of the black population lived in 1900.

Region of residence also reflected racial-ethnic distributions, but this variable is considered at a national rather than a local level. Region is coded as a series of dummy variables based on the original 1900 census definitions, which were the West, North Central, South Central, South Atlantic, and North Atlantic. When necessary statistically, the North Atlantic region is the excluded category and the one with the highest percentage of French Canadian, Irish, and Russian women.

Gender

Marital status (measured as 1 = married and living with one's spouse and 0 = all others) is an individual-level component of socially defined gender. Eastern European and Russian women were the most likely to be married, while Irish and black women were the least likely—freeing them up for employment in an era when it was difficult for married women to obtain paid work. *Age* in years, another individual variable, also indicates life-cycle stage for women.

Household composition was measured using the total number of persons in each of six categories. Table 8 provides the average values for these categories, which are children (ages 0 to 9); senior citizens (age 65 and over); male and female adolescents (ages 10 to 14), counted separately; single men (ages 15 to 64); and single women (ages 15 to 64). These variables combine gender, marital status, and age indicators and were created using the linkage of an individual with her household. Thus, they represent the gendered aspects of household composition, as described earlier.

Note that black, Eastern European, and Russian women lived with the largest numbers of young children and Irish women with the fewest. Concomitantly, Irish women's households were among those with the greatest number of single women, while Eastern European and Russian households had the fewest.

Interestingly, black and white households tended to have more single women (present in 60 and 55 percent of their families, respectively) than single men (34 and 37 percent, respectively). In general, single men were likely to set out on their own, but single women tended to reside at home. However, in Irish and German households the numbers of single men and single women were similar. This was due to single women seeking employment away from home, often becoming live-in servants or employed boarders and living in another person's home. In contrast, the even lower numbers of single women in Russian and Eastern European households were due to women's relatively high marriage rates.

Finally, *urban residence* (in towns or cities of 1,000 or more persons) is the primary contextual measure that structures gender-based opportunities, with urban areas most likely to provide employment opportunities to women.

GENDER, CLASS, AND RACIAL-ETHNIC SOCIAL STRUCTURES PREDICT WOMEN'S EMPLOYMENT

Now we are ready to unravel which class-, race- or ethnicity-, and gender-related variables were important in determining gainful employment among women from each of the seven racial-ethnic groups. Because there are so many variables to consider, multivariate analysis is necessary. Furthermore, since the outcome that is being predicted, gainful employment, is dichotomous (a woman is or is not employed), its proper interpretation is the *probability* that an individual woman was gainfully employed. Ordinary least squares regression can be used when the average probability of an outcome is between .25 and .75, but, as we have seen, the average gainful employment for five of the seven racial-ethnic groups in the sample fell below 25 percent (or a .25 probability). Only African-American and French Canadian women exceeded this rate. Therefore, logistic regression techniques are used in this analysis. The regression results are given in Appendix Table A.2.

I will begin by describing the results for the social class variable group. Among these indicators, the occupation of the male household head was the most uniformly significant predictor of women's work. His job influenced the probability of women's employment among all but Eastern European and French Canadian women. As expected, working-class households were the most likely to have women employed. Service, operative or laborer, and craft work were the head's occupations that most consistently increased women's gainful employment, especially among black, white, and German households. Of course, when a male household head was unemployed, a woman was also more likely to work. At the opposite end of the class spectrum, living in a household headed by a male professional or manager decreased the probability of women's employment, but only for Irish and Russian women. Thus, the meaning of a male household head's job was not entirely the same for all groups. Yet, since other class measures did not affect as many groups of women, male household head's occupation was the most useful measure of social class overall.

In 1900 as now, female household headship implied household economic need. Parallel to many contemporary households, when a black, white, or German woman was the household head, she was more likely to report employment. The situation of female household heads is covered in more detail in Chapter 6.

In contrast to the predictable effects of household headship, the effects of literacy were opposite to those we might expect now. At least among white women, those who could *not* read were most likely to work, probably because they were taken out of school to help support the household. Today, women with little education are less likely to work, while those with higher education are more likely to be employed. Indeed, formal education is now crucial for most jobs, but that was not true in 1900.

Household composition predicted employment in the manner I predicted. In households with greater proportions of employed adults, the probability of gainful employment increased for black, white, and German women: when economic need demanded it, a woman would be pulled into the labor force. However, the presence of extended family influenced only Irish women, whose employment probability was increased. The more people there were to support, the more likely it was that Irish women would work. This was facilitated by the fact that many immigrant Irish women were single. For example, one single second-generation

Irish woman, who was 28 years old and a teacher, lived with two other relatives, a man and a woman, who were both single—perhaps siblings or cousins. Since the household head's occupational status score was only 14 points, this young teacher probably had the best income-generating job in the household.

As expected, the presence of servants decreased the probability of white and Russian women's employment, reflecting upper-class household income sufficiency. Meanwhile, the role of boarders was mixed. They increased white and Eastern European women's employment, indicating lower-class need for more income. Among Russians, however, boarders served as an alternative income source that reduced a woman's recorded employment.

Contextual measures of social class, such as the county-based data on average women's manufacturing wages or average firm size, had no impact on black women because they were rarely employed in manufacturing industries owing to discrimination. On the other hand, firm size did increase French Canadian women's employment, and higher manufacturing wages did the same for white and German women.

The measures of race and ethnicity had only one individual-level indicator—second-generation immigrant status. This indicator had relatively little impact, significantly reducing gainful employment only for Russians. The implication is that there were fewer significant cultural differences in women's employment between immigrants and their U.S.-born children than is often suggested by historical case studies. Instead, social class differences among the generations, which are statistically controlled in this analysis, caused apparent cultural differences in women's work.

Geographic contextual effects were also muted. German women were unlikely to work in the West. Meanwhile, white women were less likely to report work in the North and South Central states, as were Russian women in the North Central area. In these latter cases, women's employment was depressed because it was rarely available or reported in Midwest farm regions. In contrast, French Canadian women were more likely to work in the North Central states, probably because of the availability of the urban manufacturing jobs, in which they were often concentrated. Other groups, including black, Irish, and Eastern European women, were unaffected by region. This may be most surprising among black women, since it is easy (though incorrect) to assume that they were more likely to be employed in the South than in the North. Differing regional opportunities seem to have had no impact on them, probably because of the pervasive occupational race segregation.

The various county-based indicators of race and ethnic mix overshadowed these regional effects. The percentage of black people in a county was one of the most significant and positive predictors of black women's work. Similarly, greater percentages of any first- or second-generation immigrant group increased German and Irish women's work. These findings reveal a positive effect of broadly construed ethnic or racial enclaves, since high concentrations of blacks increased black women's employment and high concentrations of immigrant women increased the employment of at least some of these groups.

Other findings suggest there was some competition between racial-ethnic groups, or at least a racial-ethnic hiring queue for work. For example, higher concentrations of either black or first- and second-generation immigrant women tended to increase the employment of white women.

Finally, I turn to the group of variables representing the social structuring of gender. Gender, as reflected in marital status—that is to say, being a wife—was the most important predictor and suppressor of recorded work for all seven racial-ethnic groups. Age followed a similar life-cycle pattern, with gainful employment decreasing among Irish, German, and Russian women as they got older. However, age per se had no impact on black, white, Eastern European, or French Canadian women—for them, marital status was the primary life-cycle concern.

Household composition affected the employment of women from every racial-ethnic group, but different specific composition characteristics influenced each one. The most uniform outcome was that the availability of single adult men in the household decreased the need for paid work among black, white, German, and Irish women. In these cases there was a gender-based labor trade-off in the household. In contrast, the presence of either adolescents (usually girls) or single women's labor increased the probability of reported work among every group except blacks. When there was no gender trade-off, women often worked.

The role of dependents varied. The presence of senior citizens increased black, white, and German women's employment, suggesting that the elderly provided back-up child care and were dependents themselves, rather than an alternative source of income. In contrast, the presence of children under nine had mixed effects. Children increased the likelihood of employment among black women but decreased the probability of work among Irish and Eastern European women. Black women were responding to an increased need for household income, as one would expect today. Although two groups seem to have stayed home with their children, the others were unaffected by children's presence. This finding is somewhat surprising. Our stereotypes of the early twentieth century would have led us to assume that having children automatically pushed all women out of the labor force, but instead it was marriage that tended to do so. As Goldin (1990) has suggested, marriage bars in jobs played a significant role in reducing women's employment.

Urban residence is the only gendered geographic feature included in this model. It increased the employment of black and white women, who as groups were most likely to live in rural areas. Yet it had no effect on the other racial-ethnic groups. Most of them lived in urban areas anyway, where the local demographic racial-ethnic mix or types of job opportunities available were more important.

What do these various findings suggest about the relative contributions of class, racial-ethnic background, and gender to determining women's employment? Although the logistic regression analyses give a good idea of how each predictive variable changed women's probability of employment, ordinary least squares regression can suggest answers to this question. (These results, described below, are not shown.)

Collectively, the race and ethnicity variables explained surprisingly little variation in employment status among separate groups of women: between 0 and 4 percent, being highest for

African-American and Irish women. Hence arguments that Irish women were treated similarly to blacks in this period receive some substantiation.

On the whole, the class variables explained fully 20 percent of the variation in employment status for black women and averaged between 5 and 12 percent of the variation among other racial-ethnic groups. While class arguments have previously been made for immigrant groups, it appears that they were even more valid for black women. In contrast, the gender variables explained only an additional 8 percent for black and 11 percent for white women, but fully 18 to 25 percent among first- and second-generation immigrant groups.

The actual balance of class and gender factors varied considerably for each racial-ethnic group. Class factors clearly were the major determinant of employment for black women. Class and gender factors were on an even footing for white women, while for immigrant groups, gender factors were much more important than class, and the predominant gender factor was marital status.

REDUCING THE HOUSEWIFE FACTOR: EMPLOYMENT AMONG WOMEN WHO WERE NOT WIVES OF THE HOUSEHOLD HEAD

Unique patterns of gainful employment among racial-ethnic groups become more visible when we focus on women who were not wives of male household heads but instead were daughters (or some other relative) of any household head or were themselves female household heads. Although I call these women non-wives, some few of them actually were married. For example, in one immigrant Russian household of eight, a young married woman of 17 lived with her husband, her parents, three young children, and an adolescent boy. This young woman was not employed, and she had been in the United States for just four years.

Most first- and second-generation immigrant wives had low gainful employment rates that were little different from those of white wives (see Table 7). The numerical predominance of wives in each racial-ethnic group is what made marital status such a major predictor of women's employment. When wives of household heads are excluded, different women's work patterns emerge. To illustrate this I performed a second set of logistic regression analyses for the remaining non-wives (also between the ages of 15 and 64) in order to judge the effects of class, gender, and racial-ethnic group variables on their gainful employment. This analysis focused on white, black, Irish, and German women because of the insufficient numbers of non-wives in the other sample groups. The statistical results are provided in Appendix Table A.3.

In several ways, black and white non-wives were similar. For both, the two class measures—proportion of household members employed, and the woman herself being the household head—were the most consequential predictors of gainful employment. For German women too, the most important factor was being a female household head, although proportion of household members employed also was significant, to a lesser extent. In contrast, few measures of social class predicted Irish women's employment.

Race and ethnicity influenced the opportunities of all four groups. Among Irish women but not Germans, being a second-generation immigrant increased employment. Researchers today would expect to find the Irish pattern, assuming that being raised with U.S norms would increase women's employment. However, that was not always true in 1900. High percentages of first- or second-generation immigrants in a county increased employment for white, Irish, and German women, while higher proportions of black or other nonwhite women increased black women's employment. Once again, this finding suggests a positive effect of ethnic or racial enclaves. After these other factors were considered, region per se had little impact, except that white women had lower probabilities of being employed when they lived in the North and South Central regions. I explore this central region effect further in Chapter 7.

Gender-related variables were significant, but the only consistent pattern was that non-wives' gainful employment decreased when single men were present in the household. These women were the next household labor source to be mobilized after single adult men were enlisted. Other household composition effects were not uniform. Although relatively few non-wives were married, marriage decreased the likelihood of employment for black, white, and Irish women. As for age, younger non-wives were the most likely to work, but only among the Germans and Irish. The presence of any dependent, either young children or senior citizens, increased black and white non-wives' employment rates, but among Irish women the presence of young children decreased employment.

Once again, I summarize the relative contributions of gender, class, and racial-ethnic variables to predicting non-wives' gainful employment by using ordinary least squares regression. (In this case, the use of this statistical technique is entirely appropriate because of non-wives' high work rates. The actual regressions are not shown.) For black women, the explanatory value of social class measures was extraordinarily high—they explained 21 percent of the variation in employment. Social class indicators were also paramount for Irish, German, and white women but they had a lesser impact, explaining 7, 8, and 9 percent of the variation in these groups' employment, respectively.

Eliminating wives married to household heads from the earlier analysis reduced the major role of gender for white, Irish, and German women. The gender effects were now concentrated in the household composition measure, the presence of single men, rather than in a woman's marital status. The small contribution of gender variables for Irish and white women (3 percent explained variation) was the same as among black women (although it was 6 percent among Germans). Nonetheless, gender factors were less important for black women than race and ethnicity measures (5 percent of explained variation). In contrast, the effects of race and ethnicity variables were miniscule for the other three groups of women (0.4 to 2 percent of variation).

DISCUSSION AND CONCLUSIONS

Women's gainful employment at the beginning of the twentieth century was not determined solely by the class position of their household. Rather, gender, class, race, and ethnicity need to be considered simultaneously. Gender-related characteristics, especially marital status and household composition, were the primary factors influencing women's employment among the five largest national origin groups and were equally as important as class factors for white women. Class characteristics were the primary impetus to employment among black women, with gender factors a distance second. Racial-ethnic factors were not of highest importance for any group.

Nonetheless, when wives of household heads (who make up the vast majority of our sample) are excluded, class influences became primary among white, Irish, and German non-wives and remain primary for black non-wives. Racial-ethnic effects moved into second place for blacks, while gender took that role for the others. Because the relative balance of class, gender, and racial-ethnic factors shifted according to both position in the household (wife of household head or not) and the particular racial-ethnic group, it is clear that earlier dichotomous models posing social class versus gender as the determinants of women's employment were too simplistic.

In addition, no single variable except marital status was significant for all groups of women, and only the presence of single men was consistently important among the white, black, Irish, and German non-wives. This was the only way in which gender, or perhaps patriarchal influence, had a uniform effect.

Therefore, the similarities in the broader employment patterns among some racial-ethnic groups coexisted with considerable racial-ethnic uniqueness. In fact, Table 8 shows that most of the variables in this model had significantly different values across racial-ethnic groups. Unexpectedly, such unique cultural effects were not associated with being an immigrant. Rather, first- and second-generation immigrants tended to share labor-force patterns, with only a few exceptions among Irish non-wives and all Russian women. Indeed, the Russian pattern does confirm case study descriptions by Susan Glenn (1990).

Can my general model be used to study the entire twentieth century? My answer is a definite yes. The basic structuring effects of class, gender, and racial-ethnic features continue to be important, even though the significance of certain variables has changed over time. Furthermore, the new geographic contextual variables improved upon employment predictions that included only region of the country. In fact, the measures of employment opportunity and county racial-ethnic mix absorbed much of the variation that would have gone to region or population density in the past. This helps to specify the nature of the economic opportunity structures that varied for each racial-ethnic group.

Among the social class measures, the importance of the household head's job has weakened over time. With the decline of the single breadwinner and the growth of two-income families, no matter what a husband's job, a wife is likely to work. Indeed, family characteristics are no longer significant predictors, at least of wages, among working mothers (Research-in-Brief n.d.). In contrast, the role of literacy in 1900, which was negligible, has been supplanted by the prominence of education, as well as other human capital factors. The growth of white-collar jobs and the decline of blue-collar ones facilitated this change. One factor that has remained fairly stable is being a female household head—a status that continues to push women into the labor force. A second factor, local labor market conditions, continues to influence women's work today, as I describe in Chapter 7. Of course, the key indicator today might not be manufacturing wages but rather the attributes of the service economy or public sector employment (Jones and Rosenfeld 1989). Research by the Institute for Women's Policy Research (Research-in-Brief n.d.) indicates that women's employment in high-technology industries and in male-dominated or mixed-sex occupations is essential to raising women's wages.

As for race and ethnicity, there is still considerable variation in labor market behavior, depending on national origin. Whether or not the local racial-ethnic mix matters is a topic in need of research. Certainly we know that residential segregation is associated with increased poverty, which suggests that racial-ethnic queuing in the labor market can be associated with residential mix.

Finally, among the gender factors, the relative consequence of the variables also has changed. Marital status, especially being married, now has little deterrent effect on women's employment.

However, very young children can still reduce women's overall employment rates or decrease an individual woman's employment hours from full-time to part-time. These effects are certainly much less than in the past but are more visible because marriage is no longer the crucial factor. Other family composition features have become less important, especially because fewer households include servants, boarders and lodgers, or extended family. What the balance might be today among class, gender, race, and ethnicity factors has yet to be determined.

4   Occupational Concentration

The Links Between Occupational
Sex and Race Segregation

THE MANY FORMS of women's uncounted, and often unpaid, work in the informal economy were explored in Chapter 2,
while Chapter 3 examined factors that shaped women's entry
into paid work in the formal economy. This chapter describes
the occupations women held in 1900 and, more important, con-
siders the implications of the work they did. The range and variation in occupations among women from different racial-ethnic
groups reflect the nature and breadth of their economic opportunities, while the jobs most women held in common reveal the
restrictions of their occupational segregation.

Overall, women's work options were much more limited than
men's. In 1900, 91 percent of all employed women were found in
only 12 percent of the census's detailed occupations. This high
level of occupational sex segregation has been used as a baseline
against which to evaluate the slightly lower rates seen now
(Goldin 1990; Gross 1968). Yet the attributes of early twentieth
century occupational segregation, especially as they affected the
lives of different age or racial-ethnic groups of women, are rarely
examined.

The origin of sex segregation in the U.S. workplace is usually
dated back to the period of emerging industrialization. Sex segregation owed its creation in part to gendered social expectations
for women and men, such as the idea of the family wage, which
dictated that although a single woman might be employed, a wife
ought to be supported by her husband. Men were considered the
typical employees and were expected to work full-time. Paid
employment for women that could be part-time and compatible
with children's school hours rarely existed except as factory outwork, taking in laundry, or housing boarders. In fact, some jobs,

86

like teaching and clerical work, had explicit "marriage bars" preventing married women's employment in those occupations (Goldin 1990). State-level legal barriers constrained women's work options too, for example through protective legislation that limited their hours of employment, night work, and participation in specific occupations such as selling liquor. Sex segregation reinforced gendered power relations by limiting women's access to good jobs and increasing their dependency on men. Although occupational sex segregation has declined somewhat over the century, it is still the major impediment to improving wages for women. In addition, it reduces women's workplace authority, job prestige, and chances for promotion (Reskin 1984; Reskin and Hartmann 1986; Reskin and Padavic 1994; Treiman and Hartmann 1981; Xu and Leffler 1992).

Any study of occupational segregation is inherently comparative. Men must be brought into the picture to illustrate how work around 1900 was divided into female- and male-dominated jobs and which, if any, of the latter were also open to women. Furthermore, because women come from diverse backgrounds and do not share all the same opportunities, black women, white women, and first- or second-generation immigrant women of various national origins will experience different degrees of sex segregation. A comparison of these racial-ethnic groups exposes the relative degree of gender equity within each, but the results must be interpreted cautiously. In 1900 as now, low levels of occupational segregation (which is usually a good thing) could occur for some groups without their having access to good jobs (which is always a drawback). Racial-ethnic groups with the lowest family incomes and highest rates of poverty often experience the most gender equity because both women and men are segregated into a small number of occupations and typically have limited opportunities for higher education (Almquist 1987). In such cases, sex segregation is influenced by race and ethnic segregation in occupations.

One purpose of this chapter is to untangle the ways in which segregation by sex and segregation by racial-ethnicity were intertwined in the labor market. My approach represents a departure from most prior research, which merely contrasted the two forms of segregation. For example, it is widely recognized that rates of occupational segregation by sex have been higher than those by race (defined as black–white) since at least 1940 (Reskin and Padavic 1994). Some researchers have argued more broadly that "throughout the twentieth century sex has been more important than race in allocating workers to occupations" (Reskin and Padavic 1994, 62), or at least that "occupational sex segregation has been more resistant to change than race segregation" (Reskin and Roos 1990). However, in the absence of data on race and ethnic segregation for 1900, it is equally plausible to argue that race segregation was more limiting than gender restrictions.

Even as clerical, retail, and professional jobs were opening up to white middle-class women, African-American women remained largely limited to farm and domestic work. Declines in racial segregation, at least among men in the 1940s and 1950s, happened only because of the northern migration of the black population out of the South and away from agricultural work, rather than through improving opportunities in each region, which did not occur until the 1960s (Fossett, Galle, and Burr 1989). Similarly, Wilkie (1985) found that declines in racial segregation between black and white women in the period between 1910 and 1970 were consistently due to changes in the occupational structure or occupational mix. In contrast, overall racial segregation within occupations increased up until 1950, with subsequent dramatic declines, especially in the 1960s, when women could move out of traditionally "black" occupations and into "female" ones (Wilkie 1985).

Given these complications, I argue that the "which is greater" approach is misleading and too simplistic. Race and sex segregation are neither alternatives nor merely additive, but instead intersect in more complicated interactions. They are experienced simultaneously in people's lives, and one conditions the other. The race system operates differently for men and women, and the sex system operates differently for blacks and whites (Kilbourne, England, and Beron 1994).

Looking at sex segregation separately for different racial-ethnic groups, as I do, and at race segregation separately for different sexes (men and women), as other researchers have often done, is the first step in identifying how the two types of segregation were and are intertwined. The next step is to calculate several segregation indexes that contrast groups across race and sex simultaneously. A few researchers have begun to study this issue for the late twentieth century. Carlson (1992) compared the occupational segregation of black men, black women, white men, and white women from each other for the period 1950 to 1989, and Reskin and Cassirer (1996) computed occupational segregation indexes for all (1,326) possible pairs of 52 racial-ethnic-sex groups (26 racial-ethnicities, 2 sexes) for 1990, but no one has considered the joint effects of race and sex segregation for earlier periods. My analysis uncovers the patterns of economic similarity and difference among racial-ethnic-sex groups in 1900 and provides a baseline against which to compare data from these more recent studies. In addition, I show that the relationship of race segregation to sex segregation was not consistent even at a single point in time (1900) but varied across industries and differed for white-versus blue-collar work, for urban versus rural areas, and for the North versus the South. Finally, I examine the implications of growth in white-collar work and decline in rural residence for occupational segregation and economic opportunities after 1900.

JOBS, DETAILED OCCUPATIONS, MAJOR OCCUPATIONAL GROUPS, AND INDUSTRIES

At the outset, we should distinguish between a job, an occupation, and an industry. A job is the work one is paid to do, and an employer usually defines that job. The census combines similar work bearing various firm-specific job titles into a number of "detailed occupations," of which there were 298 in 1900. For example, a young Irish woman working for the Cluett Brothers Collar factory in Troy, New York, might have her job title, "collar starcher," recorded on a census enumerator's form (Turbin 1992). For the purposes of its tabulations, the Census Bureau would later classify her job in the detailed occupational category of "shirt, collar, or cuff maker."

National employment trends are frequently and succinctly described by organizing these detailed occupations into major

TABLE 9.   Women's Employment in Major Occupational Groups, Age 15 or Older, 1900

Occupational group	% of working women in category	% of category that is women (vs. men)	Avg. prestige score of women in category
Professional and technical	9	36	69
Managers, officials, proprietors	1	4	54
Clerical	4	22	51
Sales	3	17	47
Craft	2	4	32
Service	42	74	11
Operative	20	31	19
Laborer	3	4	6
Agricultural work	16	9	13
Total	100 (n = 6,844)	—	—
Average	—	19	22

occupational groupings. I use nine such groups based on the 1970 census classification system. These groups are more intuitive than the 1900 system, which lumped together an enormous number of jobs under the single heading of "manufacturing and mechanical," and they are less confusing than the post-1980 census classification systems, which mix industries and occupations. The 1970 categories distinguish four white-collar occupational groups (professional and technical work; managers, officials, and proprietors; clerical; and sales workers) and three blue-collar groups (craft workers, laborers, and operatives), plus service and agricultural occupations. Table 9 shows the distribution of women's employment in these nine major occupational groups in 1900.

Most employed women were found in the services (42 percent), but they also frequently entered operative jobs, agriculture, or the professions. The other five groups combined—craft, laborer, managerial, clerical, and sales occupations—employed only 13 percent of all working women. Even though the clerical and sales fields were rapidly opening up to women in 1900, relatively few of them were employed in these areas. However, the increase in corporate paperwork quickly fueled both the expansion of clerical occupations and women's entry into them.

Although the nature of the detailed occupations in clerical work is fairly obvious, other groups are not as well understood. Service work, for example, in 1900 encompassed many female- or male-dominated detailed occupations such as servant, midwife, janitor, bartender, bootblack, and firefighter, among others. Operatives ran machinery and sometimes worked on assembly lines. Operative occupations were also diverse and included packer, canner, box maker, paper mill operative, milliner, seamstress, knitting mill operative, and many more. In contrast to service and operative work, craft occupations could involve many years of training; as a result, significant numbers of women were found in only a few of the crafts. These included jewelry making, bookbinding, and tailoring.

The nine occupational groups formed a hierarchy of social status. On a scale of 0 to 100 prestige points, laborers rated 6, service workers 11, agricultural workers 13, and operatives reached 19. These four categories of low-status occupations encompassed 81 percent of all gainfully employed women. Only 19 percent of the female labor force entered the five higher-status occupations. Women in craft occupations averaged 32 prestige points, while those in sales, clerical work, or managerial occupations averaged between 47 and 51 points, and women in the professions or technical work reached a high of 69 points. Clearly, white-collar jobs involved much higher status than most women's work, which averaged 22 points (see Table 9).

Using the 298 detailed occupations of the 1900 census to describe work or measure segregation is even more revealing than using the nine broader categories, since gender-based specialization in work is obscured as categories are combined. Yet even the detailed occupations cannot capture all of the segregation that occurs within particular firms or business establishments (Bielby and Baron 1984, 1986, 1987). Nonetheless, population census data are organized around and collected from individuals and their families, not from specific workplaces, so it is impossible to judge job segregation at the firm level. As a result, even my fairly high estimates of sex or race segregation are actually conservative ones, because the census did not examine what happened at specific workplaces.

In contrast to *occupation*, which describes the type of work that is done, *industry* describes the type of service or product produced. The 1900 census's enumerator instructions to record "the kind of work done or character of service rendered" did not make a distinction between occupation and industry. In fact, a common error was to report industry only (Graham 1980). As a result, the 1900 detailed occupations were organized into five major groups that approximated industries, with specific industries delineated only under manufacturing. Women's predominant industrial groups were domestic and personal service, which employed 39 percent of all working women, and manufacturing or mechanical pursuits, which employed another 29 percent. The remaining three industries—agricultural pursuits, professional service, and trade and transportation—each employed only 15, 9, and 8 percent of the female labor force, respectively.

Changes over time in the nation's industrial composition have affected the availability of employment for women, because the production processes that are specific to an industry determine what occupations are needed (Hodson and Sullivan 1990). Some occupations, such as typist or manager, are found in many industries, while others, such as farmer, are found in only one industry (agriculture) and therefore are more vulnerable to change. Indeed, at the beginning of the twentieth century, the agriculture industry was contracting as a source of employment even as the manufacturing industry and retail sales work were expanding. The growth of sex- or race-typed jobs was partly defined by such large shifts in industrial predominance, because each industry's occupations were segregated differently.

However, sex or race typing also developed out of workers' struggles over particular occupations (Baron 1991; Goldin 1990; Milkman 1987). When new occupations such as typewriter (typist) were created, contention over their sex composition would ensue (Davies 1974). Moreover, when existing occupations changed the nature of their work technology or organizational structure, usually in an effort to reduce production costs, their sex or race segregation could shift as well (Kessler-Harris 1982;

Reskin and Roos 1990). For example, in early cotton mills women operated "spinning jennies," but by 1850 technology had switched to "spinning mules," operated by fewer men. In the 1890s, when men demanded higher pay, they were replaced again by young women operating new "ring spinning" equipment at lower wages (Kessler-Harris 1982, 144). Even in periods of little industrial change, variation in industries' location across geographic regions or between rural and urban places influenced women's and men's work opportunities.

OCCUPATIONAL DISTRIBUTIONS OF BLACK, WHITE, AND ETHNIC WOMEN IN 1900

This brief summary of the occupations and industries in which women were employed, although typical of those sketches usually reported in history texts, hides the variation in work patterns found among the more detailed occupations or differences according to race and ethnicity. Therefore, Appendix Table A.4 provides a broader picture of women's occupational distributions, simultaneously showing the occupational concentrations and commonalities of the fourteen largest racial-ethnic groups in 1900. As in previous chapters, black and white women are defined as having resided in the United States for three generations or longer (being native born of native-born parents), while the other twelve groups combine immigrants and their second-generation, U.S.-born children. As mentioned earlier, these definitions are practical, because the 1900 census gives place of birth for an individual and his or her parents, but they are also useful, since national traits, if any, are often found in the second generation as well as among immigrants.

Appendix Table A.4 describes the 56 detailed census occupations in which any racial-ethnic group had at least 1 percent of its employed women. These are the most typical jobs, not the highly unusual ones. For each group, the table shows the percentage of employed women per detailed occupation, rounded to the nearest whole number, with a plus sign indicating when some few women, but less than 1 percent, worked in such occupations. The detailed occupations are organized into the nine broader census occupational categories. On these lines, the table shows the total percentage of each racial-ethnic group employed in all the occupations of that category, whether or not the job is listed in the table. Any difference between the total percentage for the category and the sum of those employed in the jobs listed within the category is usually small, since the missing occupations usually did not employ women. The nine-category totals indicate the full occupational distribution for each racial-ethnic group.

Reading down each column of Appendix Table A.4 reveals both the occupational range and boundaries for working women of each group. The total number of detailed titles with at least one employed woman shows the *diversity* of options for each group, while the number of titles with at least 1 percent of a group's employed women indicates where they were typically *concentrated*. White women had the widest variety of options: at least one employed white woman was recorded in each of 115 detailed titles. The next largest groups, the Irish and Germans, also showed considerable diversity, with women employed in 78 to 80 different occupations. However, most groups were concentrated in just 16 to 23 occupational titles. Even Italian women, who are often discussed as having limited work options, actually had the same degree of occupational concentration, once employed, as most other groups. Indeed, they were found working as dressmakers, sewing machine operators, packers, metal workers, and produce merchants, among other job titles. The exceptions were French Canadian women, who were the least concentrated, being recorded in 30 typical occupations, and women of color (black, Native American, Latin American, and Asian women), who were the most concentrated. The few women recorded in this census sample for the latter three (non-black) groups of women of color makes their true occupational range uncertain, but the concentration of nearly all black women in just nine job titles highlights the strength of racial segregation in women's work.

The occupational patterns also exhibit social class differences. White and British-origin women held jobs like teacher and nurse that gave them significantly higher prestige, or social status, than other groups. In contrast, black women's jobs were significantly lower in prestige than most, although all women of color and several other groups fell below the national average of 22 on the prestige scale (see last line of Appendix Table A.4).

Higher social class was also reflected in access to white-collar work. Nationwide, 17 percent of employed women worked in the professional, managerial, clerical, or sales jobs that constituted the white-collar occupations. Yet between 20 and 25 percent of native white, British, Irish, English Canadian, and German women worked in these jobs. They were overrepresented here and, by implication, were less trapped into the lower-paid service or operative jobs that were typically held by women in 1900. Education was necessary for white-collar jobs, and women from all five of these groups had high literacy rates, with 95 percent or more able to read a language. These high rates were facilitated by the fact that the British-, Irish-, and German-origin groups were composed more of second-generation immigrants, whose families had greater resources to invest in women's education than did first-generation immigrants. In contrast, Russian, Italian, Asian, black, and Latin American women rarely held white-collar employment, undoubtedly because of their low rates of literacy, which ranged from 27 to 69 percent. Additionally, 90 percent or more of Russians, Italians, and Asians were first-generation immigrants, with few resources, and blacks and Latin Americans had been discriminated against in the South and Southwest, respectively, for several generations. In discussing a parallel difference in 1910, Sassler and White (1997) observe that the daughters of earlier immigrant groups not only were disproportionately likely to work in high-status occupations, but that their white-collar jobs gave them higher socioeconomic status than the sons in the same immigrant groups. In contrast, daughters of the more recent immigrant groups had lower-status occupations than other young women and had lower status than sons of the same ethnicity. Sassler and White argue that women from earlier immigrant groups were likely to come from families with less need for their employment, giving them more choice in when and where they might work and leading them to avoid manufacturing or domestic work, but giving them access to white-collar jobs. The group patterns that Sassler and White identify are roughly the same as I found for 1900.

Scandinavian, Eastern European, and French Canadian women present an intermediate case in terms of access to white-collar work. They had fairly high rates of literacy (97, 81, and 86 percent, respectively) but low rates of white-collar employment. This apparent contradiction highlights how immigration status can override education as an influence on employment opportunity. Most members of these three nationality groups (60 to 76 percent) were immigrants rather than second-generation residents in the United States. Although immigrants had slightly lower literacy rates than their second-generation children (91 versus 99 percent), the more important factor was that their literacy was not always in English, which would be necessary for clerical and sales positions. This remained a problem at the end of the twentieth century, when educated immigrants to the United States often still had trouble finding jobs commensurate with their education. However, in 1900 as in the present, second-generation immigrants were equally as likely as third-generation white women (24 versus 25 percent) to hold white-collar jobs, while immigrants and black women rarely did (8 and 2 percent, respectively). The importance of geography is an additional factor that is highlighted by the experience of Scandinavians, Eastern Europeans, and French Canadians, since they were more likely than other national-origin groups to live in rural areas where there was little access to white-collar jobs.

These three factors—literacy, second-generation status, and urban location—each increased the access of all women to white-collar work. However, the interaction of these factors was not apparent in the case of Irish, British, and German women because they held all three advantages. Two additional factors—being young and being single—also increased the probability of white-collar work; however, those are age- and gender-related characteristics, not class-related ones like the first three.

Although a few groups of women held a disproportionately large share of white-collar jobs, the predominant employment for most, including white, Irish, British, English Canadian, Scandinavian, German, Eastern European, and Latin American women, was in service work. Fully 42 percent of all employed women worked in service occupations, and some, especially Scandinavians, specialized in them (68 percent). Because of the importance of this work to women, it is the subject of the next chapter.

Operative work was the second most frequent type of labor, employing 20 percent of all working women. It paid better than domestic service and did not require being on call twenty-four hours a day. Russian, Italian, and French Canadian women were actually able to specialize in this work, holding over 50 percent of their employment as operatives in textile, garment, or food-processing work. While women from these three groups also entered service work, it was at comparatively low rates (14 to 26 percent). Thus, within blue-collar work, there was considerable occupational specialization according to national origin.

The routes to employment were different for many women of color. Asian, Native American, and black women were extremely overrepresented in agricultural work, with between 39 and 47 percent of their employment on farms, in contrast to only 15 percent of white women and 1 to 6 percent of other groups. Nonetheless, the majority of employed black women (51 percent) did service work, split between servant, hand laundry, and other similar occupations. In part because of this occupational segregation, married black women had pioneered in moving hand-done laundry work from a task performed by live-in servants to a paid service job done out of their own homes. Neither they nor Asian women were hired for factory operative jobs with any frequency. Nonetheless, other forms of blue-collar work were important and, after agricultural tasks, the few employed Native American and Asian women in this census sample were most likely (27 to 29 percent) to be laborers. Because most Native American women (97 percent) lived in rural areas, they were employed in "laborer" occupations that were considered traditional in their communities. Several married or widowed women in their late thirties or early forties who lived in large households were fisherman, while a younger single woman reported hunting and trapping. Several Japanese women in their mid-twenties who were married and without children said they were general laborers. None of the Chinese women reported jobs.

OCCUPATIONAL COMMONALITIES AMONG WOMEN

Considering all these differences, what jobs, if any, were typical for most women? The answer to this question is found by reading across the lines of Appendix Table A.4.

Servant was the only detailed occupation recorded for women of virtually every racial-ethnic group. It also was the single largest women's job and it can be described as an occupational niche for women (see Chapter 5). The next most commonplace occupations—(live-in) housekeeper-steward and hand laundry—were very closely allied to servant tasks. The predominance of all three jobs highlights the importance of service work for women in 1900. Indeed, even at the end of the twentieth century, janitor and maid/cleaner were still among the top ten jobs held by black women and the top three jobs held by Mexican and Central American women (Reskin 1999; Reskin and Padavic 1994). Although some women still have domestic work as an occupational concentration, the organization of the work has changed considerably, and domestic service is no longer the archetypal women's job.

Working in clothing production also was fairly common for women in 1900, but the precise way of doing so varied. Seamstresses and dressmakers were found among all racial-ethnic groups except Asians and Native Americans. When we combine these two roles with milliners and tailoresses, all jobs in which women worked on a single garment, then between 8 and 22 percent of each group was employed in sewing occupations. Textile machine tender, or operative, was also a widespread role, but women from different racial-ethnic groups worked in different operative occupations. Combining six textile operative job titles together, including work in cotton, silk, knit, wool, worsted, or other textile mills, I find between 1 and 9 percent of German (1 percent), Russian (2 percent), third-generation white (2 percent), Irish (5 percent), Eastern European (6 percent), British (7 percent), and Italian (9 percent) women were operatives. Among the other groups, fully 37 percent of French Canadian women were textile operatives. In contrast, women of color (black, Asian, Native American, and Latin American) were entirely excluded, and Scandinavians rarely found such work.

Another women's occupational niche was "farmer," a role found among all except three groups—Italians, French Canadians, and Russians. Because of the undercount of women's work in agriculture, the recorded numbers are low, varying between 2 and 14 percent of employed women in the other ten groups. Women recorded as farmers were frequently female household heads or widows who owned farms.

None of the white-collar occupations were common to all racial-ethnic groups. However, teachers (between 1 and 10 percent) or clerk-copyists and bookkeeper-accountants (usually 2 percent in each job title) were found in many groups, except among Eastern Europeans, Italians, Latin Americans, Asians, or Native Americans. Today it is exactly these clerical occupations, as well as sales work, that have gained numerical prominence. Secretary was among the top three jobs for Cuban and Japanese women, while cashier was among the top three jobs for Chinese, Philippine, Asian-Indian, and Korean women in 1990. Secretary and cashier were both among the top three jobs for European, Native American, African-American, Mexican, and Puerto Rican women (Reskin 1999).

WOMEN'S WORK, MEN'S WORK: AN INTRODUCTION TO SEGREGATION

When women are typically employed in a limited number of jobs, as I have just described, the result is occupational segregation. Indeed, 91 percent of all working women were employed in only 37 of the detailed occupational titles. To get a better picture of what this meant in the lives of working women from diverse racial-ethnic groups, Table 10 shows the specific few occupations that each employed at least 5 percent of a group's working women and the percentage of female workers employed in all those jobs.

At one extreme, Scandinavian, black, Native American, Latin American, and Asian women were almost entirely consigned (71 to 100 percent) to their most frequent jobs. What made this occupational segregation so limiting was that both blacks and Asians were restricted to various forms of farm or servant jobs at the

TABLE 10.   Census Detailed Occupations Employing ≥5 Percent of Working Women, by Race and Ethnicity, Age 15 or Older, 1900

All women		White, 3rd+ gen.		Black, 3rd+ gen.	
Servant	23%	Servant	16%	Servant	28%
Laundry	6%	Farmer	10%	Laundry	18%
Farmer	6%	Teacher	10%	Farm labor, family	17%
Teacher	6%	Housekeeper	8%	Farm labor	15%
Dressmaker	6%	Dressmaker	7%	Laborer, general	6%
Housekeeper	5%			Farmer	5%
Farm labor, family	5%				
Total	57%	Total	51%	Total	89%
No. of jobs ≥5%	7	No. of jobs ≥5%	5	No. of jobs ≥5%	6

Irish		British		Scandinavian	
Servant	30%	Servant	17%	Servant	51%
Dressmaker	6%	Teacher	9%	Laundry	6%
Teacher	6%	Housekeeper	8%	Dressmaker	6%
Housekeeper	5%	Dressmaker	6%		
		Nurse, not trained	6%		
Total	47%	Total	46%	Total	73%
No. of jobs ≥5%	4	No. of jobs ≥5%	5	No. of jobs ≥5%	3

German		Eastern European		Russian	
Servant	28%	Servant	29%	Servant	16%
Dressmaker	8%	Tailoress	8%	Seamstress	11%
		Housekeeper	7%	Uncodable	9%
		Laundry	5%	Textiles, not spec.	8%
		Seamstress	5%	Dressmaker	6%
		Saleswoman	5%	Tobacco operative	6%
				Shirt, collar	5%
Total	36%	Total	59%	Total	61%
No. of jobs ≥5%	2	No. of jobs ≥5%	6	No. of jobs ≥5%	7

lowest economic level. Scandinavian women also were heavily concentrated in the occupation of servant: their 51 percent employment in domestic work was even higher than among black or Irish women. At the other extreme, German women had relatively little concentration, with only the two occupations of servant and dressmaker employing many women and accounting for only 36 percent of their female labor force.

TABLE 10.   *Continued*

Italian		French Canadian		English Canadian	
Dressmaker	11%	Cotton mill		Servant	21%
Uncodable	11%	operative	23%	Nurse, not trained	13%
Laborer, general	6%	Servant	10%	Dressmaker	8%
Metal worker	6%	Clerk, copyist	8%	Housekeeper	5%
Sewing operative	6%	Textile work,			
Housekeeper	6%	not spec.	6%		
Unspecified	6%	Dressmaker	5%		
		Boarding house-			
		keeper	5%		
Total	52%	Total	57%	Total	47%
No. of jobs ⩾5%	7	No. of jobs ⩾5%	6	No. of jobs ⩾5%	4

Latin American		Asian		Native American	
Servant	38%	Farm labor	29%	Farm labor	27%
Laundry	14%	Laborer, general	29%	Hunter	13%
Seamstress	14%	Farmer	14%	Fisherman	13%
Housekeeper	10%	Servant	14%	Farmer	13%
Farmer	5%	Peddler	14%	Laundry	13%
Teacher	5%			Landlord	13%
Laborer	5%				
Landlord	5%				
Uncodable	5%				
Total	101%*	Total	100%*	Total	92%*
No. of jobs ⩾5%	9	No. of jobs ⩾5%	5	No. of jobs ⩾5%	6

Note: Some of the occupational titles have been shortened due to space limitations. Laundry is hand laundry work (census occupation 121) as opposed to laundry work in steam laundries (occupation 122); nurses are training unspecified (census occupation 127), as opposed to trained nurses (occupation 126); and housekeepers are domestic residents (census occupation 947), as opposed to nonresident housekeepers and stewards (occupation 156).

*The percentage employed in the jobs listed totals between 90 and 100 percent because there are relatively few Native American, Latin American, and Asian origin women in the census sample. With larger numbers, there would undoubtedly be more diversity in occupations. The Latin American total of 101 percent is due to rounding error.

The other groups fell somewhere between these extremes and reveal some distinctive occupational specialties. French Canadian women were disproportionately employed as operatives, especially in cotton mills (23 percent), but also in other textile mills (an additional 14 percent), while Eastern European, Russian, and Italian women frequently did hand sewing as seamstresses, dressmakers, and tailors (between 14 and 20 percent; see Appendix Table A.4).

To fully understand what women's compression into a limited number of jobs in 1900 tells us about occupational segregation, men need to be brought into the picture, since women's work concentrations were relative to those of men. Table 11 shows the top twenty occupations held by male and female workers, with the numbers to the left of each occupation indicating its rank, beginning with "1" as the most common women's job. Women's top twenty jobs encompassed 82.5 percent of the female work force, while men's top twenty jobs totaled only 66.9 percent of the male work force. The occupations are grouped according to the balance of women and men in them, indicating whether or not each was female- or male-dominated. Taking into account the number of women in each title, women's top twenty occupations had a weighted average of 65.9 percent women in them, while men's top twenty occupations had a weighted average of only 8.4 percent women. It not surprising that women labored in many female-dominated occupations: servant, hand laundry work, dressmaker, seamstress, milliner, or teacher. Yet fully half of women's top twenty occupations were male-dominated or gender-neutral, while only one of men's typical occupations (servant) was female-dominated, and that was ranked 19.

There are at least two dynamics at play here, and they explain this apparent contradiction. First, when women worked in a male-dominated detailed occupational category, such as sales, they were not necessarily in the same job as men or selling the same items for the same company. Their workplaces could easily have been separate. Second, simply because women were likely to enter an occupation did not make it female-dominated work. For example, because women were approximately 20 percent of the labor force, they could be considered overrepresented, but not the dominant group, in professional work, where they were 36 percent of the employees, and in the operative occupations, where they were 30 percent of the employees. In the latter occupational group, women actually reached 50 percent of the workers only among cotton mill operatives. Within most other

TABLE 11.   Sex Segregation of the Top Twenty Typical Occupations, for Men and Women, Gainfully Employed Workers Age 15 or Older, 1900

Occupations held by women and % female workers in each		Occupations held by men and % female workers in each	
Female-dominated		**Female-dominated**	
[1] Servant	87%	[19] Servant	87%
[2] Laundry work (hand)	89%		
[4] Teacher	75%	**Male-dominated**	
[5] Dressmaker	99%	[1] Farmer or planter	6%
[6] Housekeeper (domestic		[2] Laborers (general)	4%
residence)	100%	[3] Farm labor	11%
[9] Nurses (training not		[4] Farm labor (family)	16%
specified)	95%	[5] Carpenter or joiner	0%
[10] Seamstress	97%	[6] Clerk or copyist	16%
[14] Housekeeper	91%	[7] Drayman, teamster	0%
[16] Milliner	97%	[8] Sales(men)	25%
[19] Stenographer	70%	[9] Uncodable employment	21%
		[10] Coal miner	0%
Gender neutral		[11] Merchant (not specified)	2%
[15] Cotton mill operative	51%	[12] Steam railroad laborer	1%
		[13] Machinist	0%
Male-dominated		[14] Painter, glazer, varnisher	0%
[3] Farmer or planter	6%	[15] Farmers (family)	7%
[7] Farm labor (family)	16%	[16] Blacksmith	0%
[8] Farm labor	11%	[17] Bookkeeper/accountant	25%
[11] Sales(women)	25%	[18] Engineer/fireman	
[12] Laborers (general)	4%	(not train)	0%
[13] Clerk or copyist	16%	[20] Iron and steel worker	2%
[17] Uncodable employment	21%		
[18] Tailor	34%		
[20] Bookkeeper/accountant	25%		

occupational groups—agriculture, laborer, craft, or managerial work—women were greatly underrepresented as recorded workers. However, in the newer jobs such as sales, clerk or copyist, and bookkeeper or accountant, women were represented at nearly the equivalent of their rates in the entire labor force. This sounds equitable, but such newly expanding and still relatively small occupations were merely in transition to becoming female-dominated, as the occupation of stenographer already had. Transformations of this kind are actually fairly common and are described later in this chapter.

The degree to which one sex dominated a job was not the same for each racial-ethnic group in 1900. A table describing this would be unwieldy, but a few examples drawn from the nine occupational groups can illustrate the point. Most women held jobs within major occupational groups having a weighted average of 40 to 49 percent women in them. Yet Latin American and Scandinavian women were in occupational groups that were more female-dominated, averaging 54 to 58 percent women, and Russian, Italian, and Asian women were employed in more nontraditional categories averaging less than 35 percent women.

If we look now within the occupational groups, women were 74 percent of the workers in service occupations. Yet this figure varied from a high of about 85 percent among Scandinavians and French and English Canadians to a low of 2 percent among Asians. If it seems odd that Asian women did so little service work (and Asian men did so much), keep in mind that the Chinese Exclusion Act created a tremendous sex imbalance in the U.S. Asian population. As a result, most of the few Asian women were married and not available for live-in servant work, while many members of the surplus single Asian male population were employed as servants, especially on the West Coast.

As another example, among recorded agricultural workers, women averaged only 9 percent, but this figure ranged from 26 percent among blacks to 2 percent among Scandinavians. Women were 36 percent of all professional and technical workers, but this rate ran from as high as 59 percent among Irish workers down to zero among Italian and Asian workers.

These varying percentages represent different degrees of control over, or concentration in, particular occupations by women of diverse racial-ethnic groups. However, the larger numbers need to be interpreted cautiously. First, women could predominate over men in a job category, as did Irish women, who were 59 percent of Irish professional workers, but the small numbers of workers in that category could limit this success. Only 9 percent of all employed Irish women were professionals, in contrast to 15 percent of white women. Second, simply because the percentage of women in an occupation was higher for one racial-ethnic group than for others does not necessarily imply they were overrepresented in that work. To judge overrepresentation we need to compare employment in that one occupation to the average female employment rate. For example, black women were 26 percent of black agricultural workers, a higher proportion than for any other group. On average, however, 33 percent of black women were in the labor force, so that one could say black women were actually underrepresented in agriculture.

Indexes of occupational segregation were designed precisely to control for, or to take into account, these percentages of a group (such as women or men) in the labor force as a whole. The measures provide a succinct way to summarize the information on occupational distributions for women of different racial-ethnic groups.

MEASURING OCCUPATIONAL SEGREGATION

The most frequently used segregation measure, particularly for historical data, is the Index of Dissimilarity (Duncan and Duncan 1955), which is based on the difference between men's and women's percentage distribution across a set of occupations. The measure, D, ranges from 0 to 100 and represents the percentage of women (or men) who would have to change jobs to produce a non-sex-segregated labor force in which the sex distribution would be the same for each occupation. The results are easy to interpret. For example, since women were about 19 percent of the 1900 labor force age 15 or over, there would have been no sex segregation ($D = 0$) if women were also 19 percent of each job or occupational group. On the other hand, if the sex segregation index turned out to be 60, then 60 percent of all women (or men) would have had to change jobs in order to achieve 19 percent women in each job. This measure is advantageous because it can be used with any number of job categories. In addition, since it takes into account the percentage of women in a group's labor force, it can sensibly compare the levels of sex segregation among different race or national-origin groups in a way that the newer size-standardized index (D_s) is unable to do (Charles and Grusky 1995). Finally, D can be adapted to measure race segregation at work, comparing the number of blacks (or whites) who would have to change jobs to achieve labor force equity.

I calculated the measure for workers age 15 or older, rather than limiting the analysis to the working ages of 15 to 64, both to make these calculations comparable to those of other researchers and to incorporate all of the adult workers in each occupation. This broader age range reduces the average female gainful employment rate to 19 percent from 22.5 percent, since women age 65 and older were less likely to be employed than men of that age.

As I mentioned earlier, jobs can be categorized into a variety of groupings: detailed census categories, or major occupational and industry groups. Many of the published historical comparisons of gender segregation, or dissimilarity, are based on the nine major occupational groupings. However, when there are sufficient numbers of people, I calculate the segregation index for the larger number (298) of detailed census occupational titles in 1900, because most sex-based specialization at work occurs within finer occupational categories (see, for example, Bielby and Baron 1984, 1987; Jacobsen 1994; Sokoloff 1992). Thus, as the number of categories increase, so also does the degree of revealed segregation.

Grouping jobs at various levels of aggregation is facilitated by the 1900 census's Public Use Sample, since it records each occupation using both the 1900 and 1950 census categories. For segregation indexes based on 298 detailed jobs or the five major industries I use the 1900 occupational codes. However, I created the nine major occupational groupings using the 1950 coding system, since it was less industrially based than the 1900 system. One should not alternate between the 1900 and 1950 coding systems for longitudinal analyses, but for studying the single year, 1900, these two systems produce very similar results (Jacobs 1989).

Other researchers have used dissimilarity measures for different historical periods. They generally agree that the index of *sex segregation*, based on detailed census job categories, held steady at between 65 and 69 from 1900 through 1960 (Gross 1968), and even as late as 1970 (Jacobs 1989). The index increased slightly (worsened) in the 1920s and the 1950s, but it decreased some (improved) in the 1940s (England 1981). Only during the 1970s did the index show a significant decline (England and McCreary

1987), exhibiting faster change for nonwhites than for whites (Beller 1984). In the 1980s, the segregation index continued to drop at a slower rate (Reskin and Roos 1990). Even if we look only at nonagricultural jobs, which are more segregated than farm work, there was a seven-point drop in sex segregation from 1910 to 1970 and again from 1970 to 1986 (Jacobs 1989).

In 1940 indexes of occupational *race* segregation among both women and men were rather high, at 65 and 44, respectively, and actually increased (worsened) among men through 1960. However, these rates declined thereafter, and by 1980 the greater racial segregation among women had declined (improved) to match that of men, reaching 26 to men's 30 by 1990 (King 1992; Reskin and Cassirer 1996). During this same fifty-year time span, indexes of occupational sex segregation (among both blacks and whites) remained almost twice as high as the index of occupational race segregation among men (Reskin and Padavic 1994). Indeed, Jacobsen (1994) concluded that the slowed decline in occupational sex segregation, combined with the high rates of firm-level segregation, made it unlikely that overall sex segregation rates would fall as low as race segregation ones by the year 2000. Of course, even in the 1990s, every racial-ethnic group of women varied in how segregated it was from each of the other groups. The range went from a low segregation index of D = 4 between British and Scottish women to a high value of D = 49 between Central American and Eastern European women, indicating that racial-ethnic segregation among employed women can be almost as high as occupational sex segregation (Reskin 1999).

Unfortunately, there is no published information on the early twentieth century relationship between occupational race and sex segregation comparable to the newly developing literature about the end of the century. Neither sex segregation among a variety of racial-ethnic groups nor the interaction of race and sex segregation has been studied. Therefore, my analysis sets a twentieth century baseline for occupational sex segregation across both industrial and occupational groups, while exploring the complex ways in which race and sex segregation interact.

OCCUPATIONAL SEX SEGREGATION
WITHIN RACIAL-ETHNIC GROUPS

Sex segregation indexes provide a succinct way to summarize the information found in Tables 9 and 10 and in Appendix Table A.4 about women's occupational distributions, as well as to show the variation in sex segregation among racial-ethnic groups. These indexes are shown in Table 12 for men and women of the fourteen largest groups in 1900.

As is typical in other research, when the number of job categories increases, in this case from five industries to nine major occupations to 298 detailed occupations (reading across the rows of Table 12), the index of sex segregation also increases. The fact that the segregation index is so much lower across industries than across occupations is partially a numerical phenomenon. Research based on the manufacturing sector during all or part of the period 1950 to 1980 (Wallace and Chang 1990; Wharton 1986) suggests that there would be more measured industrial segregation in 1900 if the census had subdivided the manufacturing sector into its diverse component industries. This would create more categories and reveal that female employees ranged from less than 1 percent in construction or steel manufacturing up to fully 66 percent in the textile industry.

Nonetheless, there were substantive differences between sex segregation in the five industries and the nine major occupational categories. The first difference is that industries tended to be less segregated than comparable occupational categories. For example, 38 percent of service *industry* workers were female, but service *occupations* were 74 percent female. The primary source of this difference was that each industry contained a greater diversity of occupations than did other categorizations. For example, the trade and transportation industry labor force averaged 10 percent women, but it included managerial occupations that had very few female employees (4 percent) and clerical or sales work, which were composed of 22 and 17 percent female workers, respectively. It was not unusual for men and women to be in the same industry; it was more unusual for them to be in the same occupation.

TABLE 12. Indexes of Sex Segregation for Various Racial-Ethnic Groups for Gainfully Employed Workers Age 15 or Older, in 1900

Racial-ethnic group* (no. of employed women/men)	Sex segregation index		
	Five major industries	Nine major occupations	298 Detailed occupations†
Total labor force (F = 6,950; M = 29,864)	32	54	67
White, 3rd+ gen. (F = 2,564; M = 14,844)	39	58	70
Black, 3rd+ gen. (F = 1,479; M = 3,031)	33	44	59
Irish (F = 842; M = 2,124)	25	57	78
British (F = 241; M = 1,281)	32	55	—
Scandinavian (F = 193; M = 947)	54	74	—
German (F = 686; M = 3,356)	31	58	77
Eastern European (F = 107; M = 622)	20	50	—
Russian (F = 64; M = 354)	25	58	—
Italian (F = 35; M = 379)	44	61	—
French Canadian (F = 103; M = 289)	14	61	—
English Canadian (F = 205; M = 693)	29	63	—
Latin American (F = 16; M = 112)	35	64	—
Asian (F = 6; M = 210)	42	48	—
Native American (F = 15; M = 56)	9	19	—

*Black and white women are native-born persons of native-born parents. Other groups include immigrants and second-generation U.S.-born persons. Groups are arranged geographically by region of national origin.

†The index was not calculated when the number of employed women was less than 298. In all these cases, except for Asians and Native Americans, the χ^2 values for the table of sex by occupation are significant at $p \leq .001$, indicating different job distributions by sex.

Recent literature argues that there is an industry-level effect on occupational segregation and that industrial organization can create or reduce gender inequality (Bridges 1982; Wallace and Chang 1990). An overview of such studies concludes that women tend to work in lower-paying industries and that this causes some of the sex difference in pay (England, Christopher, and Reid 1999), although there is no agreement on how to best group these industries to show the negative wage effects.

A second difference between industries and occupations is found in the racial-ethnic patterns of sex segregation. *Industrial sex segregation* indexes were *higher* for white (39), black (33), Latin American (35), and Asian (42) workers than among nine of the other groups, whose indexes varied from 14 to 35. Although this division may appear to be related to race, it actually was tied to rural residence and gender dichotomies in agricultural work. Most of the groups with high industrial segregation, Latin Americans, blacks, and whites, had resided in the United States for a long time and were the most likely to own or tenant land. The men in these three racial-ethnic groups shared an employment concentration in the agricultural sector, while the women rarely recorded farm work. Asian women actually did work frequently in agriculture, but Asian men were segregated into service work. In contrast to these agriculturally based patterns, French and English Canadian, British, Irish, German, Russian, and Eastern European men and women experienced less industrial segregation because both sexes were heavily concentrated in manufacturing jobs. Their urban residence decreased their industrial segregation, but it did not change their occupational sex segregation within these industries. All in all, at the turn of the century, industrial segregation was largely a proxy for rural-urban differences.

There was more *consistency* in the level of *occupational sex segregation* among various ethnic groups and whites: ten groups fell in the range of 55 to 64 (Table 12, column 2). Only Scandinavians had an unusually high occupational segregation index (74), owing to their almost dichotomized labor force roles: two-thirds of the employed women were restricted to service occupations, especially servant work, while 41 percent of the men were in agriculture. In contrast, women and men of color, especially

blacks and Asians, were among the *least* occupationally sex segregated (at 44 and 48). This was not an advantage. Instead, it
reflected race barriers restricting *both* men and women to poorly
paid agricultural, laborer, or domestic service jobs (Almquist
1987; Goldin 1990). This picture changes very little when we
look at occupational sex segregation indexes based on the finer
298 detailed census occupations (Table 12, column 3).

SEX SEGREGATION AND BLACK/WHITE RACIAL SEGREGATION AT WORK: CONTRASTS AND INTERCONNECTIONS

Because levels of sex segregation varied according to race or
national-origin group, the next logical step is to determine
whether race segregation varied by sex. Can race or sex segregation be labeled the more serious problem in 1900, and how did
either relate to the quality of jobs available?

Because race is essentially a social construct, we must consider
how to define it for this purpose. As described in Chapter 1, the
1900 U.S. census defined five races—white, black ("Negro or of
Negro descent"), Chinese, Japanese, and Indian (Native American). Yet the dearth of people from the latter three groups in the
data sample means that most were considered to be black or
white, even though "black" included a wide range of mixed-race
people. Indeed, throughout much of the twentieth century, race
has been socially defined dichotomously as black and white.
Therefore, on both technical and conceptual grounds, I use the
dichotomous approach in measuring race segregation.

This decision represents a departure from the broader approach of fourteen racial-ethnic groups used in earlier tables.
Previously people were categorized as third-generation or later
black or white, Native American, or as members of eleven
national-origin groups each composed of immigrants and their
second-generation children who, except for Asians and some
Latin Americans, were mostly white. Indeed, it was sensible to
combine first- and second-generation immigrants since they
were barely segregated occupationally from each other (D = 11
for nine occupations).

However, now, as a first step, I collapse the fourteen groups into three by combining the eleven national-origin groups into a single category while retaining the two third-generation or later black and white groups. The small number of Asians and Latin Americans were included in the first category, since they were immigrant groups whose experience was somewhat different from that of African Americans, even though they were (and are) also treated as racial minorities within the United States. The few Native Americans in the data sample were eliminated for this particular analysis.

This new categorization—first- and second-generation immigrants (or ethnic groups), blacks, and whites—results in three comparative racial-ethnic segregation indexes, each shown in a row of Table 13. The first index, between (first- and second-generation) immigrant workers and white ones, shows the least segregation (row 1), while the highest levels of segregation occur in the third index, between ethnic and black workers (row 3). Levels of black-white segregation fell somewhere in between (row 2). This pattern reflects two different dynamics—one based on geography and a second one based on race. Geographically and industrially, blacks and whites shared a concentration in agriculture that made their work more similar to each other's than the work of blacks was to that of (first- and second-generation) immigrants. On the other hand, (first- and second-generation) immigrants' and whites' shared "whiteness" (that is, race) meant their work was more similar to each other's than the work of blacks was to that of whites, primarily because of the racial barriers in many urban industrial and white-collar occupations. Although not shown, immigrant generation also mattered somewhat: first-generation immigrants were less segregated from blacks than were their second-generation children (40 versus 48, respectively) due to employment barriers such as language or education. Nonetheless, the absolute levels of racial-ethnic segregation in occupations (shown in Table 13) were generally lower than the ones for sex segregation (shown in Table 12).

Still, to judge the relationship of race and sex segregation in 1900, we need to look at their interplay. This is difficult to illustrate with three racial-ethnic groups having two sexes each, since

TABLE 13.   Three Indexes of Racial-Ethnic Segregation for Gainfully Employed
Workers Age 15 or Older, in 1900

Index (W = 17,410; B = 4,512; E = 13,384)*	Five major industries	Nine major occupations	298 Detailed occupations
White (3rd+ gen.) from 1st- and 2nd-gen. immigrant workers	25	26	30
White (3rd+ gen.) from black (3rd+ gen.) workers	30	32	41
Black (3rd+ gen.) from 1st- and 2nd-gen. immigrant workers	43	43	49

Note: The racial-ethnic categories are the same as in prior tables except that the eleven groups of first- and second-generation immigrants are collapsed into a single category. Both blacks and whites are third-generation or later residents of the United States. Native Americans are excluded from this analysis. Compare this breakdown with that used in Table 14.

*Numbers of people for each race and ethnic group are presented for the 298 detailed occupations. They would vary slightly for the five major industries or for the nine occupational categories.

comparing these six categories with each other requires 15 separate segregation indexes. Using even larger number of categories, 52, Reskin and Cassirer (1996) were forced to show average segregation indexes for each group, losing some of the flavor of the differences they found. Therefore, in order to clarify the interactions of race and sex in creating occupational segregation, I redefined race using the more typical dichotomous approach of black and white. These are no longer the same categories as used above. The effect on the category "black" is minor, but the category "white" is greatly expanded, since the majority of first- and second-generation immigrants are now combined with them. The few Asians and Native Americans in the sample are excluded from this analysis since they are considered neither black nor white.

The dichotomous racial approach produces four race-sex categories with six segregation or dissimilarity indexes comparing them, as shown in Table 14. Once again, the aggregate-level occupational indexes of race segregation (row 1) were far lower than the indexes for sex segregation (row 4), although the industries were fairly similar (D = 36 vs. D = 32) in both. Disaggregating,

TABLE 14.   Race Segregation by Sex and Sex Segregation by Race (Black/White) for
Gainfully Employed Workers Age 15 or Older, in 1900

	Five major industries	Nine major occupations	298 Detailed occupations
Race segregation by sex (no. of employed blacks/whites)*			
Black workers from white workers	36	37	41
(B = 4,548; W = 31,896)			
Black women from white women	52	46	58
(B = 1,492; W = 5,400)			
Black men from white men	30	33	38
(B = 3,054; W = 26,488)			
Sex segregation by race (no. of employed women/men)*			
Women workers from men workers	32	54	67
(F = 6,935; M = 29,864)			
Black women from black men	33	44	59
White women from white men	35	59	73
Interaction of race and sex segregation			
Black women from white men	45	50	72
White women from black men	49	72	82

Note: Compare this table with Table 13. The categories used here reflect the more
typical U.S. racial dichotomy. The definitions of "back" and "white" have been modified to include people from any immigrant generation (first, second, third, or later)
of any group. The effect on the black category is minor, since only 36 persons, usually of Latin American and Caribbean origin, have been added. However, the effect
on the white category is large, since the majority of first- and second-generation immigrants have been combined with longer-term white residents. Only the few Asians
and Native Americans in the sample are excluded from either racial category. This
dichotomous racial approach results in four race/sex categories with six segregation
indexes comparing them (see the six rows in bold). The trichotomous approach used
in Table 13 would have resulted in six possible racial-ethnic/sex categories, requiring 15 segregation indexes to compare all the categories to each other.
   *Numbers of people for each race and sex are presented for the 298 detailed occu-
pations. They would vary slightly for the five major industries or for the nine occupational categories.

or breaking down, these indexes shows that (both occupational
and industrial) race segregation was stronger among women than
among men (rows 2 and 3), and occupational sex segregation was
lower among blacks than among whites (rows 5 and 6). Consequently, race and sex segregation in 1900 were already interconnected in patterns researchers have found from 1940 up until the

1980s. This interconnection makes it difficult to say one was "more serious" than the other.

Making general statements about race or sex segregation indexes is also difficult because of their wide range in values. Whether by occupation or by industry, the *least* segregation was found between black and white men. This does not mean, however, that they worked side-by-side or achieved similar incomes. Blacks were not evenly spread throughout the United States in 1900: most (90 percent) lived in the South, usually in rural areas, and were geographically segregated from whites, 75 percent of whom lived in northern states, primarily in urban places (Massey and Hajnal 1995). Furthermore, while southern men of both races were most likely to work in agriculture, 60 percent of whites but only 24 percent of blacks owned and worked their farms (Schweninger 1990). These inequalities in land ownership meant that blacks were often occupationally segregated as farm laborers, hired by white farm owners, and consequently earned less as well.

The *greatest* occupational segregation, measured using the 298 detailed categories (Table 14, row 8, column 3), was between white women and black men whose race and sex were both different from each other, simultaneously compounding two types of occupational segregation. This economic segregation primarily occurred because white women were employed in manufacturing or as live-in servants, jobs from which black men were usually excluded. Yet even such high rates of occupational segregation could vary with geography. In the rural and urban North, as well as in the urban South, between 81 and 86 percent of white women would have had to change occupations in order to have the same distribution as black men, but in the rural South that figure was "only" 47 percent. This was facilitated by the concentration of the black population in the South, especially the rural South, and by the greater predominance of agricultural employment in the South than in the North. As I will show below, agriculture was generally less segregated than other fields.

The size order of the indexes also tells us about hierarchy and social distance. A useful example is found by comparing several different indexes for white women in the detailed occupations

(Table 14, column 3). Although 58 percent of them would have needed to change occupations to be desegregated from black women, a 73 percent change would be required to desegregate from white men, and fully 82 percent would have had to shift work to desegregate from black men. White women were most similar to, or least segregated from, black women, yet this racial disparity in work opportunities was much wider among women than among men (black and white men's segregation index was 38). Black women, for their part, experienced occupational race segregation from white women (D = 58) and sex segregation from black men (D = 59) about equally; for them, one was not stronger than the other. However, for both groups, the interaction of race and sex segregation (Table 14, rows 7 and 8) produced the highest levels of occupational disparity.

These relationships also had implications for social activism. For example, white female labor organizers, working for unions, equal pay, or protective legislation, who wanted to work cross-racially in that period would have had difficulty (Hewitt 1991). They had more in common with black women than with any other group but had considerably less cross-race mutual work experience than did men; and black women shared as many work experiences with black men as they did with white women, giving them less incentive to work cross-racially. Furthermore, what black and white women had in common was agriculture and service work—occupations that were less likely to unionize. Indeed, the relatively high rates of occupational segregation between them reduced the likelihood of their interacting at all.

Segregation levels across the five major industries (see Table 14, column 1) were more consistent than across occupations, having aggregate race and sex indexes that were low and fairly equal. Yet occupational segregation did vary *within* the industries.

Table 15 reveals an interesting pattern in the interrelationship between occupational and industrial segregation. Industries employing greater percentages of women (service, the professions, and manufacturing) had the highest levels of occupational sex segregation, while those employing more blacks (service and agriculture) had the lowest levels of occupational race segregation. In 1900 women were entering fields where role violations apparently

TABLE 15.   Race, Sex, and Race by Sex Segregation Indexes for Detailed
Occupations Within Major Industries, 1900

	Service	Profes-sional	Manu-facturing	Agri-culture	Trade/Transport
Race segregation by sex					
Black from white workers	25	45	40	24	66
Black from white women	32	16*	43*	55	69*
Black from white men	16	60*	40	16	64
Sex segregation by race					
Women from men workers	84	66	74	24	60
Black women from black men	75	60*	90*	39	73*
White women from white men	89	66	74	9	60
Interaction of race and sex segregation					
Black women from white men	82	75*	91*	50	77*
White women from black men	81	58*	83	23	92
Total numbers					
Black women	828	22	55	581	6
Black men	694	35	315	1,744	266
White women	1,841	574	1,946	468	586
White men	3,607	1,050	7,289	9,616	4,926
No. of occupations	29	30	157	16	67
% Women in industry	38	35	21	8	10
% Blacks in industry	22	3	4	19	5

*The number of people in at least one of the two race-sex groups involved in this correlation is similar to or less than the number of detailed occupations. Although the pattern of the correlations is sensible within the industry column, a single correlation's exact value may be unstable.

required sex segregation to eliminate male-female competition, while blacks were in fields that did not threaten existing segregated race-power relations. As a consequence, aggregate sex segregation was considerably higher than race segregation in the three industries with the greatest female representation, but in the industries with few reported women (agriculture and trade or transportation) aggregate levels of race segregation were equal to or slightly higher than levels of sex segregation. Thus it is *not* true that sex segregation in the past was *consistently higher* or more restrictive than race segregation: nontraditional women's industries had relatively little sex segregation. Furthermore, most commentators (Jacobs 1989) agree that the farm work which predated "modern" nonagricultural industries was actually less sex segregated than the newer jobs (even though agriculture had far fewer occupations than other industries and its level of segregation might have been slightly higher than it appears here).

Patterns linking race to sex segregation within industries were not consistent either. On the whole, women experienced considerably more *race segregation* than did men, especially in service and agricultural work. Yet in industries from which blacks were largely excluded, such as the professions, men experienced more race segregation than did women, while in manufacturing and the trades race segregation was about the same for both sexes. On the whole, whites experienced more *sex segregation* than blacks, but blacks actually experienced more sex segregation than whites in certain industries: manufacturing, agriculture, and trade and transportation. Indeed, occupational segregation within industries varied greatly—from 9 percent among white men and women in agriculture to 90 percent among black men and women in manufacturing. This means that our perceptions of the intransigence of sex segregation relative to race segregation need to be modified. It also means that structural conditions within industries shaped the relative amount of sex and race segregation that occurred, rather than ideologies of sexism or racism taking some consistent form.

Twentieth Century Changes in Segregation: Shifts in Occupational Structure and Urban Growth

The degree of sex and race segregation in any given occupation can change over time, even while the segregation of the entire labor force remains fairly stable. Occupations are more likely to shift from male to female domination than the reverse. These changes can occur at different rates across the country. For example, clerical work became feminized between 1880 and 1920 (Davies 1974, 1982), with the largest early changeover in Chicago and the slowest changes occurring in some of the southern cities, like Baltimore

(Wyly 1996). As described in Chapter 3, public school teaching became feminized in the late nineteenth century. By 1900, the detailed categories of stenographer, typist, and telephone operator had also switched from male to female domination. Other occupations, like bookkeeping, waiting tables (Cobble 1991), and bank teller, were in various stages of initiating a change in their sex segregation in the early twentieth century, but by mid-century they had resegregated from male to female domination. Although manufacturing operative work had already shifted from a native-born female to a foreign-born male work force in 1900 (Reskin and Roos 1990), the clothing industry, including operative and machine-based jobs like seamstress, was still the second largest nonagricultural employer for women (Katzman 1978).

Changes in segregation are caused by shifts in labor supply as well as by occupational restructuring. According to Reskin and Roos (1990), the fundamental reason why a job resegregates from male to female domination is a shortage of male workers. Such a shortage occasionally occurs when an occupation is rapidly expanding, using up the supply of suitable men. However, in most cases men are leaving a job that has become less attractive because the work process has been deskilled, often as a result of changed technology, or the job rewards have become less worthwhile. As a result, women's integration into apparently prestigious male-dominated jobs can be a hollow victory. Contemporary examples of this transition include residential real estate sales and pharmacy work, which are no longer structured as self-employment in local, small or family businesses and instead have become part-time jobs in national or regional corporations (Reskin and Roos 1990).

In 1900, not only were particular occupations changing their segregation, but other shifts were also occurring in the distribution of the whole occupational structure, as some jobs, such as those in agriculture, were on the decline and others, especially in white-collar or sales fields, were on the rise.

How did these changes affect the interplay of race and sex segregation over time? One way to answer this question is to compare the occupants of newer, expanding white-collar occupations (retail, sales, clerical, professional) with those in more traditional

TABLE 16.   Race and Sex Segregation Indexes in New and Old Occupations, 1900

| | Occupations* | |
	Older	Newer
Race segregation	35	56
(% blacks in jobs)	(14.9%)	(1.7%)
Sex segregation	70	57
(% women in jobs)	(18.8%)	(19.4%)
No. of occupations†	237	103

*Older occupations are in manufacturing, agriculture, and domestic service, as well as craft and laborer, and thus are primarily blue collar. Newer occupations are in retail, sales, clerical, and the professions, and thus are primarily white collar.

†The total number of older and newer occupations is greater than 298 because this division is based on the 1950 census, which recoded and divided jobs into more detailed occupations than did the 1900 codes.

blue-collar ones (manufacturing, agriculture, and domestic work for women, plus craft or laborer work for men) in 1900 in order to suggest future trends. The new jobs required more education than did the traditional ones: 99 percent of white-collar versus 83 percent of blue-collar women were literate. Therefore, I expected white-collar occupations would be more race segregated but less sex segregated (Goldin 1990) than blue-collar ones, since requiring greater education would restrict the access of blacks but give white women more employment opportunities. Indeed, the results in Table 16 show this was true.

Newer white-collar work had an occupational sex segregation index of 57, while traditional blue-collar and service work remained at a higher index of 70, even though the overall percentage of women within each sector was similar. At the same time, the index of race segregation in white-collar jobs was 56, even though less than 2 percent of the workers were black, while the index was only 35 in older jobs where African Americans were concentrated, especially in agriculture and domestic service. Looked at another way, the older blue-collar jobs were twice as sex segregated as they were race segregated, while the newer white-collar jobs were about equally race and sex segregated in 1900. Of course, the latter statement is somewhat misleading, because few blacks could even enter white-collar jobs at this time.

Growth over the century in these newer jobs facilitated the occupational restructuring that reduced men and women's occupational differences and thus decreased sex segregation. At the same time, the new jobs replaced the older black-white similarity in agricultural work and domestic service with white-collar occupations that excluded many blacks, both through educational requirements and outright race discrimination, thus increasing race segregation in the short run. Indeed, in 1900, newer jobs had few black workers, in contrast to 15 percent in older jobs. Some of this race difference in job distributions was mitigated by the migration of blacks to the North after World War I, since black predominance in the South at the turn of the century tended to occupationally segregate them into agriculture and service work. As they moved out of agriculture, partially due to a reduced demand for labor, and out of domestic work with increased education (a labor supply factor), women's racial segregation declined (Wilkie 1985). This geographic shift had an occupational effect on blacks that was similar to the one on women when part-time work shifted out of the home, decreasing women's previous isolation in the informal economy (see Chapter 2). Indeed, between 1910 and 1970, the proportion of black women working in predominantly black occupations dropped from 88 to 19 percent, especially during the 1940s and 1960s (Wilkie 1985).

Potential changes in occupational composition also can be reflected in the jobs held by young workers, those between the ages of 15 and 24, who had just entered the labor force. They had access to a wide range of jobs because of the changing occupational structure and they were likely to be better educated than older workers: 91 percent of young versus 81 percent of older women workers were literate. Therefore, the index of sex segregation should have been, and was, lower for younger nonagricultural workers than for older ones (71 vs. 77). On average, 19 percent of all young women workers and 15 percent of older ones held white-collar jobs, but the disparity was even greater for nonagricultural workers, among whom 15 percent of young and 9 percent of older women workers did white-collar work.

TABLE 17.   Race and Sex Segregation Indexes by Region and
Urban/Rural Distinction

	North Atlantic/ North Central		South Atlantic/ South Central	
	Urban	Rural	Urban	Rural
Race segregation	64	52	64	31
(% blacks in jobs)	(2.7%)	(1.1%)	(36.1%)	(36.2%)
Sex segregation	72	76	82	44
(% women in jobs)	(23.9%)	(11.8%)	(26.6%)	(17.9%)
No. of occupations	288	208	212	167

In contrast to occupational sex segregation, occupational race segregation was identical for both older and younger nonagricultural workers ($D = 55$). Because educational and racial barriers to entry into white-collar occupations were strong, resulting in few black workers in new jobs (1.7 percent), there was no lessening of occupational race segregation for black youth. They could expect the same limited job options as older men and women. Perhaps this is one of the reasons that led them to migrate North.

The relationship of occupational race and sex segregation to geography is indeed complicated, as shown in Table 17, which contrasts the northern and southern regions of the United States and their respective urban and rural areas. There was no difference in occupational race segregation between the urban areas of the North and South ($D = 64$). That is to say, urban racial barriers in the range of jobs open to northern blacks were similar to those in the South. This seems particularly surprising because blacks represented less than 3 percent of the northern urban labor force, while they were fully 36 percent of the southern one. In addition, northern blacks were residentially integrated, typically living in city wards that were 90 percent nonblack (Massey and Hajnal 1995). However, this did not lead to integrated workplaces. Racial-ethnic segregation in hiring was the norm in urban firms and factories of both regions.

In contrast, levels of sex segregation in urban areas were influenced by region. There was less sex segregation in the urban North ($D = 72$) than in the South ($D = 82$), despite their similar percentages of employed women. Living in the urban North placed immigrant women where they could enter manufacturing jobs and gave longer-resident white women the opportunity to enter these or the new white-collar jobs, diversifying women's options. Although many black women were employed in the urban South, racial bars prevented them from entering most factory or white-collar employment. Black women's options were severely limited in order to keep the "appearance of propriety necessary to attract white women at low wages" (Kessler-Harris 1982, 140).

Patterns were different in rural areas—indexes of both race and sex segregation there were usually lower than in urban areas—because agriculture had less segregation than other industries. Furthermore, the rural South had less race and sex segregation than the rural North. Black women's high rates of agricultural employment and primary residence in the South were both responsible for this regional distinction.

Thus, all other things being equal, the transition to an urban economy would mean a short-run increase in occupational race segregation because urban white-collar and sales jobs excluded blacks. The post-World War I migration of blacks northward did not change this trajectory, and indeed, between 1900 and 1940, occupational race segregation did worsen (Sobek 1999). This was also true for residential segregation, which began the century with low levels of neighborhood segregation, but by 1970 had reached peak levels, even though state-level and regional geographic segregation had declined (Massey and Hajnal 1995).

All other things being equal, the urban transition would have slightly decreased sex segregation in the North while greatly increasing it in the South. Actual regional changes are unknown, but sex segregation among nonwhites (who generally lived in the South) did increase through 1940 (Sobek 1999). Yet, overall, there was relatively little shift in occupational sex segregation through the 1960s, because urbanization was not the only factor to influence women's employment. As the economy expanded and the demand for white-collar labor grew, single women and, later, married women were drawn into the labor force in greater numbers, but always in female-dominated jobs

(Blackwelder 1997). Therefore, sex segregation only fluctuated in a narrow range along with the economy through the 1960s, but declined thereafter. Although regional variations in segregation have not been studied for the end of the century, we do know that there is still geographic variation: The fifty largest metropolitan areas in 1990 ranged by as much as ten points in sex segregation, between 45 and 55 (Cotter et al. 1997).

CONCLUSIONS

The dynamics of the connection between sex segregation and racial-ethnic segregation at work were complex. First, the relationship between them was not consistent. Second, both forms of segregation reflected underlying social class dynamics. Finally, racial-ethnic and sex segregation were shaped and changed by shifts in the occupational and industrial structure.

Prior analyses suggested that it was possible to make generalizations such as "sex segregation is stronger than race segregation." However, this simplistic approach did not hold up within every industry. Furthermore, racial-ethnic effects on sex segregation took the form of a continuum. Women of color experienced little sex segregation from their men (D fell between 19 and 48), but race segregation meant that both men and women had low-status jobs. At the other extreme, some groups, notably Scandinavian, Italian, Latin American, and French and English Canadian women, experienced more severe sex segregation from the men in these groups (D fell between 61 and 74). Yet the women's jobs were only slightly less circumscribed and also of low prestige (with scores usually between 14 and 17 points). Their gender and recent immigration status often limited these women's options to a greater extent than men's. Other racial-ethnic groups—the Irish, British, Germans, and Russians—experienced occupational sex segregation at levels similar to those of (third-generation or later) white households, with D falling between 55 and 58. Most of these groups had been in the United States for a longer period of time and had achieved relatively higher-status jobs, with prestige between 22 and 29 points, especially in the second generation.

Obviously, occupational segregation was not merely the separation of groups working at different jobs in the same firm or at equivalent jobs in different firms. It also incorporated features of social class, since it structured access to "good jobs." Racial-ethnic background and gender were already bases of economic outcomes in 1900, as they have been described to be today (Reskin and Cassirer 1996). The clearest example draws on the situation of women of color, especially blacks, Native Americans, and Asians, who experienced relatively low occupational segregation from their men; that is to say there was more within-group gender equity. This sounds positive, but both men and women were segregated into a limited range of occupations at the bottom of the economic ladder, often in agriculture or domestic service. Indeed, black, Native American, and Asian women had jobs whose average prestige score was between 8 and 12 points, and the vast majority of them worked in only five or six occupations.

Another way to see class effects is to look at the patterns of economic and social distance exemplified through occupational segregation indexes. For example, black women, who had similar levels of segregation separating them from white women and from black men, were presented with an interesting choice of allies. In contrast, white women held jobs that were most similar to those of black women, but most separated from black men; meanwhile, white men were most similar occupationally to black men. As Reskin (1999) has suggested for the end of the century, segregation preserves inequalities by maintaining social distances and creating income differences. Segregation reduced the likelihood that groups would compete or interact with each other.

Finally, the changing nature of the national economy in the early twentieth century also structured racial-ethnic and sex segregation. In 1900 the percentage of women employed within an industry was directly related to that industry's degree of occupational sex segregation, but the percentage of blacks employed in an industry was inversely related to its occupational race segregation. When women entered an industry in large numbers, occupational segregation was used to limit their job choices. For blacks, however, industrial segregation itself limited them to low-paying jobs. Their concentration in agriculture and domestic service work did not threaten any economic power structure since such jobs provided few avenues for social mobility. Furthermore, the black population's residential concentration in the agricultural South helped substitute for occupational segregation, as neighborhood- or ward-level segregation would do later in the century (Massey and Hajnal 1995). Indeed, the U.S. Supreme Court's decision in *Plessy v. Ferguson* (1896), announcing the "separate but equal" doctrine, had recently legally sanctioned segregation in many forms.

The expansion of new white-collar occupations formed another economic barrier, increasing racial segregation while decreasing sex segregation as compared to the older blue-collar occupations. There were also barriers within blue-collar jobs. The declining agricultural sector had low rates of both race and sex segregation, while the still-growing industrial jobs had somewhat higher levels of race segregation and much higher levels of sex segregation. It would take considerable time for the shift to white-collar occupations to have any net effect on reducing sex segregation, while race segregation would continue even after black migration to the North.

Age differences in segregation among nonagricultural workers furnish additional support for this analysis. There was no difference in occupational *race* segregation according to age, suggesting the shared concerns and consistent racism experienced by black Americans. In contrast, there was an age difference in occupational *sex* segregation that enabled young, primarily white or second-generation immigrant women to step into slightly different jobs than older women, which suggests divisions among women by life cycle and education, as well as expanding opportunities for women.

Over the course of the twentieth century, and notably after World War II, racial segregation, especially among women, declined to a greater extent than sex segregation. Nonetheless, recent research suggests that the wide range of *sex* segregation among ethnic groups in 1900 (Almquist 1987; Reskin 1999) and in the groups' relative economic standing (Logan 1997) continued throughout the twentieth century. Shifts in industrial composition over the twentieth century—the decline of agriculture, the initial rise and post-1970 decline in manufacturing, and the growth of the service and retail sectors—meant the rise or demise of occupations open to different demographic groups of people. The growth of urban jobs as well as urban migration could have increased occupational race segregation, but after World War II opened up manufacturing to blacks, occupational segregation began to decline. This change received further impetus from the civil rights movement of the 1960s and from affirmative action legislation.

One trend that has not changed is the consignment of working-class immigrant women to domestic service and janitorial jobs—a pattern that continues despite the restructuring of that work from live-in servants to self-employed day workers to employees in the cleaning service industry. Because of the continued prominence of domestic work as a woman's occupational niche, it is the focus of the next chapter.

5 Ethnic Enclaves and Ethnic Queues
Women and Domestic Work

IN 1900, a full third of all employed women in the United States were doing domestic work. Immigrant women, especially from Ireland, Germany, or Scandinavia, dominated domestic work in northeastern and midwestern cities, and black women predominated in the South, but large numbers of third-generation native-born white women were still employed as servants in rural areas. This chapter focuses on the lives of women who were employed as live-in servants.

The census data for 1900 tell us little about the birth families of such women, and so many of the reasons why they entered domestic employment cannot be fully determined. On the other hand, considerable information is available about the families that employed them and with whom they lived. This information allows us to uncover the implicit criteria used to hire domestic workers, as well as where women chose to work.

Over the course of the twentieth century, women's employment in domestic service has been dominated by varying racial-ethnic groups in different regions of the country, but this type of work has not disappeared (Katzman 1978; Sutherland 1981). Research has documented the historical roles of Japanese women (and men) in domestic service in the West (Glenn 1980, 1986), of blacks in the South and in Washington, D.C. (Clark-Lewis 1994; Katzman 1978; Palmer 1989), and of Chicanas in the suburbs (Romero 1988). The recent upsurge in domestic work has drawn on contemporary immigration from Latin America and the Caribbean, especially to the West Coast (Chang 1996; Hondagneu-Sotelo 1994; Turbin 1995) and from the Philippines to Canada (Bakan and Stasiulis 1995).

The groups of women dominating this work have also varied over time. Between 1890 and 1920, foreign-born white women gained access to other jobs and were replaced in the North by black women, whose concentration in domestic work actually increased (Katzman 1978; Palmer 1989). Domestic work became the predominant job for African-American women through 1940, when World War II opened other occupations to them. Domestic work is still one of the top ten jobs for black and Hispanic women, many of whom are immigrants, especially from Latin America and the Caribbean (Reskin and Padavic 1994). Indeed, at the end of the twentieth century, the ethnic mix in domestic work paralleled that in 1900. Nonetheless, the regional distribution of immigrant groups has changed and the reorganization of domestic work has resulted in growing numbers of self-employed day workers, live-in nannies, and employees of cleaning service firms (Macdonald 1996; Napierski-Prancl 1998).

Taking into account the importance of domestic employment for women over the course of the century, it is no wonder that many authors have described this work experience. Most have carried out case studies of single groups of immigrants or have focused on women of color in order to elucidate employer-employee dynamics, especially in cross-racial settings, and to highlight the methods of domination used by white employers and the forms of resistance developed by black and Latina domestics (Cohen 1991; Palmer 1989; Rollins 1985; Romero 1988). They discuss contemporary issues as well as the historical transformation of domestic work between 1900 and 1920 from a master-servant relationship to an employer-employee one when work shifted from live-in to "job work" or live-out work settings (Clark-Lewis 1994). This research emphasis creates the impression that domestic employment always involves employers and servants of different racial-ethnic groups. Furthermore, there is an implicit assumption that servants or other domestic workers are hired in a hierarchical order of preference, or ethnic labor queue, and that in-group hiring is rare because an employee of lesser status is preferred.

That assumption, however, is not always justified. Using census data for 1900, I compared the match between an employee's racial-ethnic group and that of her employer's household head. The significant percentage of same-group matches that I found implied the possibility not merely of a reduction in cross-group antagonism, but also a potential for female servants to have obtained the economic and social advantages, shared across social classes, that are available through ethnic enclaves. Nevertheless, there were also many across-group pairs that confirm some degree of social hierarchy and various types of racial-ethnic hiring queues for domestic work.

Since servant work is rarely considered outside the context of an employer's social control, it is helpful to examine the applicability of the two major frameworks used to study the positive economic aid immigrants sometimes provide to each other. The ethnic enclave approach focuses on the ethnic resources available in an ethnic subeconomy and requires the presence of ethnic employers or entrepreneurs to hire other members of their own group, while the ethnic niche concept centers on employees and the potential positive outcomes of occupational segregation. Although both enclaves and niches are frequently discussed as avenues for men's economic advantage, they could help women as well.

Ethnic enclaves, as conceptualized by Portes for Cubans (see Portes and Jensen 1987; Portes and Manning 1986; Wilson and Portes 1980), Bonacich for Koreans (Bonacich and Light 1988; Bonacich, Light, and Wong 1977), or Min Zhou (Zhou 1992; Zhou and Logan 1989) and Sanders and Nee (1987) for the Chinese, were initially described as geographically based settings in which immigrants were employed in enterprises whose owners were of the same nationality, resulting in cross-class within-group support. In distinguishing an ethnic enclave from an ethnic neighborhood, the geographic basis of the former becomes less important. Instead, the primary focus is on a distinct ethnic labor market, which is a partially autonomous economic system in which kinship networks and other cultural values are important resources (Zhou 1992). The enclave economy both supports ethnic entrepreneurs and provides a better economic return to immigrant workers than they could find in the "open" market. Although enclave employment is usually associated with Latino and Asian immigrant groups, it applies equally well to white European immigrants (Logan 1997) as well as to native-born African Americans.

A focus on live-in servants provides a lens on the extent and nature of women's cross-class sponsorship from households of the same ethnicity, such as might be found in an ethnic enclave. Few studies have considered women's role in contemporary enclave economies, but some researchers feel enclaves are exploitative of women, while others see only a continuation of past cultural social patterns (Zhou 1992; Zhou and Logan 1989). I believe that types of enclave employment varied according to a woman's marital status because, especially in 1900, wives and mothers chose jobs that did not conflict with family obligations, whereas single women were more apt to choose employment outside the home. Single women may therefore have received more advantages from enclave work.

In an enclave economy, households could hire a servant more easily using racial-ethnic networks. When the race or ethnicity of a servant matched that of her employing household there also was the potential for some social mobility, even for those who were segregated into domestic work. For such women, who were usually single, the primary advantages of this enclave employment consisted of securing a job where there was none before and creating a space where interethnic or interracial hierarchies were eliminated. Even though domestic work afforded little access to different jobs, ethnic networks could facilitate some mobility within the occupation (Hondagneu-Sotelo 1994). There was also the possibility of finding jobs for siblings, which would facilitate geographic chain migration (Clark-Lewis 1994), as well as the potential of receiving small loans, greater protection from harassment, and other benefits based on social networks that might include marital mobility. This traditionally female occupation was not one in which to expect any better economic returns in an enclave setting for a worker's higher education (measured as literacy), citizenship (second-generation status), or English ability than under cross-race or cross-ethnic hiring, as enclave theory predicts for men's jobs. Yet for some groups, the occupation did provide intergenerational mobility, so that daughters of servants could escape this work. In contrast, domestic work was an occupational ghetto for African-American women, while the Japanese experience was an intermediate case (Glenn 1986).

Domestic work was not the only enclave-like employment available to women. Similar processes of in-group recruiting undoubtedly occurred when families sought boarders or ethnic business owners hired married women to do factory outwork in their homes. Yet such enclave employment is not easily identified through the census. In the first example, boarders are considered separate households, so the census Public Use Sample does not link them to the family with whom they resided. In the second example, information on the ethnicity of employers was never collected. In both cases it is difficult to distinguish enclaves from the larger labor market.

Ethnic niches, as described by Suzanne Model (1993) for Irish, Russian, Italian, black, and Puerto Rican men in New York City, are occupational concentrations in which overrepresentation in certain types of employment sometimes offsets weak vocational skills or labor market discrimination by simplifying work searches, eliminating ethnic barriers, or providing access to upward mobility through training and access to job ladders. Model argues that occupational niches can allow workers to develop mutual, intra-class assistance methods that facilitate economic mobility, although not all niches do this equally well. She defines a niche as an occupation that employs at least 50 percent more than a group's share of the total work force. Women's early twentieth century concentration in domestic work certainly fits this criterion, since women made up 19 percent of the work force but 87 percent of domestic servants age 15 or older. In this chapter, I examine the concentration of women from different racial-ethnic groups in servant work.

Although the existence of an ethnic enclave often creates an ethnic niche, the reverse is not necessarily true: an ethnic occupational niche does not require the existence of an ethnic enclave. Furthermore, both a niche and the ethnic matching found in enclaves can occur when employers favor some national-origin groups over others, creating an ethnically ordered labor queue (Reskin and Roos 1990). The frequency of either racial-ethnic matches or cross-group hires is not just a matter of employers' motivation to hire women different from or sharing their own racial-ethnic background. The opportunities for an employer-employee racial-ethnic match are shaped by the labor supply and the level of employer demand.

In 1900, the general level of demand remained high for domestic workers because the utility infrastructure that was to make housework lighter—electrification, sewage systems, and hot and cold running water—was not widely available at a national level. In contrast, the demand among some ethnic or black households to hire live-in servants of their own, or any other, racial-ethnic group was both varied and limited by their economic position. Finally, hiring preferences and the available labor pool shaped demand. The interaction of these two features makes it difficult, especially in the South, to determine whether African-American intraracial hiring was due to enclave-type co-sponsorship or to an employer's inability to hire anyone else, since racial discrimination, their own relatively low status, and a southern population that was largely devoid of groups other than third-generation blacks and whites limited their hiring options.

The composition and overall availability of the female labor supply were in flux, and 1900 was on the cusp of turn-of-the-century changes in domestic work. Servant work was declining relative to women's other employment options. It employed 61 percent of all female workers in 1870, 33 percent in 1900, and only 18 percent by 1920 (Hill 1929, 36). Although the decline was not linear, native-born white women were gradually able to exit private household work as better-paying manufacturing jobs opened up to them. By 1910, their rate of employment as servants had dropped to 18 percent, and by 1920 it was only 7 percent (Katzman 1978, 292). However, the flow of immigrants into the United States, which reached a peak in 1909, increased the availability of other groups to labor in this female-dominated work. In 1890, 48 percent of foreign-born white women were employed as servants; by 1900, 38 percent were in such jobs; and, with the decline in immigration, by 1920 only 19 percent were servants (Katzman 1978, 292). In contrast, for women of color, major decreases in this occupation did not come until 1930 for Chinese women and until after World War II for Japanese and African-American women (Amott and Matthaei 1991, 324).

Thus, 1900 marks a time of transformation in both the supply of and demand for women's paid domestic labor. Because of such changes, this exploration of the racial-ethnic matches between women employed as live-in servants and the households that hired them must incorporate supply factors, such as a county's average women's manufacturing wage—as a proxy for better job opportunities—and the racial-ethnic mixture of a county's female labor force, as well as demand factors, such as a household's sex composition or the social status it had attained before hiring a servant.

LIVE-IN AND DAY SERVANTS IN 1900

Who were the servants living with their employers and away from their own families? As Table 18 illustrates, in 1900 most live-in servants were female (86 percent) and, as befits the stereotype, both women and men in this occupation were young, averaging 27 and 28 years old, respectively, and never married (85 percent).

Black women were the most likely to break these stereotypes, in part because they had few other job options. They were the pioneers in retaining domestic employment once they married, although as wives, they tended to switch from live-in to day work. Therefore black women were 52 percent of day workers but only 18 percent of live-in servants. As a result, only 4 percent of the black women who were live-in workers were married (with their spouse present), while 27 percent either were widowed or had an absent spouse, making their situation more similar to that of young, single white women than one might expect. In 1900, the supply of single women for this occupation was still large enough that hiring a married woman for live-in domestic work was not a necessity for employers. Almost all of the white (95 percent) and 65 percent of the black domestic workers were literate and, in spite of the large numbers of immigrants engaged in this occupation, virtually everyone reported speaking English, perhaps learning it on the job.

A greater percentage of male than female domestics were racial minorities (42 versus 19 percent). Because of immigration restrictions on Asian women, the employment of Japanese and Chinese male servants, especially in the West, is not surprising. In contrast,

TABLE 18. Demographic Characteristics of Live-in Servants by Sex, 1900

Characteristic	Women	Men
Age		
% Ages 10–29 yr	69	62
Avg. age (yr)		
Total	27	28
White	26	28
Black	30	25
Marital status: % Never married		
Total	85	85
White	90	85
Black	68	83
Literacy: % Read a language		
Total	89	86
White	95	95
Black	65	65
Speaks English (%)	97	92
Race/immigration (%)		
White	81	58
Immigrant	36	26
2nd-gen. immigrant	18	13
Native-born of native-born parents	28	19
Black	18	30
Japanese	—	6
Chinese	—	5
Other	1	1
Total (%)	100	100
No. of servants (total = 1,100)	945 (86%)	155 (14%)

	Women			Men		
	Total	White	Black	Total	White	Black
Regional distribution (%)						
North Atlantic	47	52	24	33	43	23
South Atlantic	11	5	34	16	7	36
North Central	31	36	9	17	27	6
South Central	9	4	31	19	14	34
West	3	4	2	16	9	0
Total (%)	101	101	100	101	100	99

the large percentage of black male servants was due to more complex labor market dynamics in the North. Black men and women
servants had similar regional distributions, but white men and
women did not. A smaller percentage of white men than white
women were servants in the North Central and North Atlantic
regions, suggesting that white men but not white women had other
employment options there, and that black men took up the short-
fall among male servants. Thus, African Americans were only
8 percent of the female servants but 18 percent of the male servants
in the North. These regional patterns imply that domestic workers' tasks were generally sex segregated but also had a permeable
boundary, so that racial minority men might substitute for
women's labor in the West, but African-American men, not
women, substituted for native-born white men's labor in the North.

Although some men were hired as servants, my focus is on the
women, for two reasons. At a theoretical level, it is their ethnic
niches and ethnic enclaves which are rarely studied, and at a
methodological level, they were the predominant domestic
employees and often did different tasks than the men engaged in
this work. In addition, because over half (54 percent) of the female
servants were first- and second-generation immigrants (in contrast to 39 percent of the men), they had a considerably greater
possibility of working for co-ethnic employers.

In 1900, 21 percent of all women over age 14 were gainfully
employed, and 31 percent of these worked in the domestic occupations of servant, housekeeper, or doing hand laundry. Only 41
percent of female domestic workers were live-in servants in private households; the remainder were day workers residing with
their own families or in group quarters such as hospitals or boarding schools. Domestic work was well on its way to becoming a
day job—a situation from which we cannot judge employee-
employer racial-ethnic matches. Although live-in servants were
younger (27 versus 32 years old) and more likely to be single (85
percent never married versus 49 percent), literate, and urban than
other domestic workers, in this regard they were representative
of most gainfully employed women at the turn of the century.

The degree of women's segregation into domestic work varied
by specific racial-ethnic group. Table 19 indicates that, compared

TABLE 19. Racial-Ethnic Women's Employment Overall, in Domestic Occupations, and as Live-in Servants, in 1900

Ethnicity	No. of women employed	Women's gainful employment rate (%)	% of female workforce	No. in domestic occupations	% in domestic occupations	% of female domestic workforce	No. as live-in	% of domestics that lived in	% of female live-in workforce
U.S. white	2,592	15	37	539	21	24	248	46	27
British	294	19	4	67	23	3	24	36	3
Irish	910	32	13	326	36	15	183	56	20
Scandinavian	204	21	3	124	61	6	64	52	7
Other European	79	17	1	29	37	1	16	55	2
German	813	20	12	278	34	13	139	50	15
Eastern European	115	21	2	37	32	2	22	60	2
Italian	39	16	1	2	5	—	1	50	—
Asian	7	24	—	1	14	—	—	—	—
Russian	68	22	1	10	15	—	6	60	1
French Canadian	109	30	2	15	14	1	6	40	1
English Canadian	221	25	3	59	27	3	33	56	4
Latin American	20	17	—	10	50	—	5	50	1
U.S. black	1,545	44	22	705	46	32	157	22	17
Total/Avg.	7,016	21	101	2,202	31	100	904	41	100

Note: Data are for women age 14 years and older only. This cutoff excludes some younger women, recorded under "relationship to head" as live-in servants, who are included in other analyses.

Domestic occupations as drawn from the 1900 census codes include servants and other domestic service (occupation 131 or 148), housekeepers and stewards (occupation 156), and hand-laundry work (occupation 121).

Native Americans are excluded from this analysis. None were live-in servants, but two of fifteen employed women did hand laundry.

to their proportions in the female labor force, Irish and Scandinavian women were approximately 50 percent overrepresented as live-in servants (column 9 in contrast to column 3), while African-American women were 50 percent overrepresented in domestic occupations (column 6 compared to column 3), each constituting an ethnic occupational niche as defined by Model (1993). In addition, German women were overrepresented as live-in servants by 25 percent. Why did these groups specialize in domestic work? Many more Irish than other women immigrated to the United States alone and thus often sought the family environment of domestic service. Meanwhile, Scandinavian women in Minnesota or Wisconsin and German women elsewhere in the Midwest or on the plains had few of the alternative urban job options. Although underrepresented as a racial-ethnic group, native-born white women of native-born parentage were the single largest group of live-in servants, simply because they were the largest demographic group nationally. Thus, all five of these groups had a reasonable chance of being employed in households headed by someone of a similar race or national origin.

RACIAL-ETHNIC MATCHES:
THE SERVANTS' PERSPECTIVE

Most male and female domestics had no live-in co-workers. As Table 20 shows us, among the households that hired female servants, 83 percent employed only one woman, and as a result, 71 percent of female live-in servants worked alone. My analysis begins from the servants' rather than the household's perspective, comparing each servant to her employer rather than each employer to their servants. Although some employers are represented more than once, with this approach each servant-employer pair represents a hiring decision.

Were servants different in their race or ethnicity from the households in which they worked? One view is that servants were different from their employers and were selected according to a hierarchical racial-ethnic queue, but I expected that simultaneously there were in-group choices, constituting a form of cross-class relationship typified in contemporary ethnic enclaves,

TABLE 20.   Number and Percentage of Employed Servants in Households
Employing Live-in Servants, Totals and Female Servants Only, All Ages, in 1900

Total no. of servants per household	Female and male servants				Female servants			
	Households:		Servants:		Households:		Servants:	
	%	(no.)	%	(no.)	%	(no.)	%	(no.)
1	84	(744)	68	(744)	83	(671)	71	(671)
2	12	(103)	19	(206)	12	(98)	18	(166)
3	3	(28)	8	(84)	3	(26)	7	(67)
4	1	(6)	2	(24)	1	(6)	2	(19)
≥5	1	(6)	4	(44)	1	(5)	2	(22)
Total	101	(887)	101	(1,102)*	100	(806)	100	(945)

*Total includes two servants whose sex is unknown.

that had potential advantages for women. Indeed, on average, 35 percent of all women live-in servants matched their employers' national origin or both were native-born black or native-born white. The relationship between the specific racial-ethnic background of each servant and that of her household's head, as displayed in Table 21, is statistically significant. In other words, race and ethnicity played an important role in the hiring decisions of groups among whom domestic work constituted an ethnic niche, as well as for the other groups.

Matches occurred more frequently for some groups of live-in servants than for others. Table 21 clarifies this variation by indicating, in bold numbers, the figures for servants hired by an employer with matching background, as well as for those servants hired by third-generation native-born whites. It should not be surprising that the highest rate of hiring matches (75 percent of cases) is found for white servants, because this group also constituted the vast majority of employers. However, three distinct patterns are found for the other racial-ethnic groups.

German and Eastern European servant women were most likely to be employed by a member of their own ethnic group, with match rates of 38 and 48 percent, respectively, which resemble the ethnic enclave effect found among some contemporary Asian and Latin American immigrant groups. Although their absolute numbers were rather small, the same can be said for

TABLE 21. Comparison of Female Servants' Racial-Ethnic Group with Racial-Ethnic Group of the Employing Household Heads (Individual Level)

Servant's racial-ethnic group	Household head's racial-ethnic group													
	W	B	Ir	G	S	Br	EE	R	It	OE	EC	FC	LA	Total
White (native born)	203 (75%)	0	13 (5%)	21 (8%)	1 (1%)	19 (7%)	1 (1%)	1 (1%)	0	3 (1%)	6 (2%)	2 (1%)	0	270 (29%)
Black (native born)	119 (70%)	18 (11%)	4 (2%)	13 (8%)	0	7 (4%)	1 (1%)	0	0	2 (1%)	5 (3%)	0	0	169 (18%)
Irish	111 (60%)	0	28 (15%)	18 (10%)	1 (1%)	16 (9%)	3 (2%)	0	2 (1%)	3 (2%)	3 (2%)	1 (1%)	0	186 (20%)
German	53 (38%)	0	8 (6%)	54 (38%)	1 (1%)	16 (11%)	1 (1%)	0	0	3 (2%)	5 (4%)	0	0	141 (15%)
Scandinavian	43 (67%)	0	3 (5%)	2 (3%)	3 (5%)	6 (9%)	1 (2%)	1 (2%)	0	1 (2%)	4 (6%)	0	0	64 (7%)
British	15 (63%)	0	1 (4%)	3 (13%)	0	3 (13%)	0	0	0	0	2 (8%)	0	0	24 (3%)
Eastern European	4 (17%)	0	1 (4%)	3 (13%)	0	0	11 (48%)	2 (9%)	0	0	2 (9%)	0	0	23 (2%)
Russian*	0							2 (33%)	0					6 (1%)
Italian*	1 (50%)								0					2 (0%)
Other European	9 (56%)	0	0	1 (6%)		3 (19%)	1 (6%)	0	0	1 (6%)	1 (6%)	0	0	16 (2%)

TABLE 21. *Continued*

| | Household head's racial-ethnic group | | | | | | | | | | | | | |
Servant's racial-ethnic group	W	B	Ir	G	S	Br	EE	R	It	OE	EC	FC	LA	Total
English Canadian	25 (**76%**)	0	0	2 (6%)	0	1 (3%)	0	0	0	0	5 (**15%**)	0	0	33 (3%)
French Canadian*	3 (**50%**)											1 (**17%**)		6 (1%)
Latin American*	1 (**20%**)												2 (**40%**)	5 (1%)
Avg. head prestige†	44	18	43	45	22	50	42	43	41	46	43	10	49	945 (102%)

Note: Data in the table are grouped into horizontal panels delineated by alternating bands of gray and white background. The first panel includes third-generation or later white and black women, the second panel includes first- and second-generation immigrant groups from Europe, and the third panel includes first- and second-generation immigrants from Canada and Latin America. The fourth panel shows the average prestige score of the household head. Numbers in **bold** are percentages hired by native-born whites of native-born parents or by same-group employers.

*These groups have relatively few cases; therefore, percentages are given only for white and in-group hires.

†Head's prestige is not significantly different between or among any of the groups.

Key: W, white; B, black; Ir, Irish; G, German; S, Scandinavian; Br, British; EE, Eastern European; R, Russian; It, Italian; OE, other European; EC, English Canadian; FC, French Canadian; LA, Latin American.

Russian and Latin American women, who had 33 and 40 percent match rates, respectively. Russian immigrants in this period were likely to be Jewish, and in-group hiring may have been particularly important around religious concerns such as keeping a kosher home.

Another distinct set of women were most likely to be employed by third-generation, native-born white households, but their second most common employers were members of their own racial-ethnic background. These include British, Irish, English Canadian, and black women, who had employer matches occurring between 11 and 15 percent of the time. Although based on smaller numbers, the same is true of French Canadians (17 percent). This particular grouping of nationalities is united by past or current ties to the British Empire, including a knowledge of English.

A third set of nationalities had few hiring matches. Scandinavians were the largest group affected, but the same dearth occurred among smaller groups of servants such as Italians and a mixed group of other Europeans, for whom matches occurred in zero to 6 percent of cases. In sum, there was considerable variation among these thirteen racial-ethnic groups in the degree of within-group hiring or ethnic enclave employment, and thus in potential mobility advantages for women live-in servants. Furthermore, the three described patterns of employment matches do not seem directly related to the size of the group or to the existence of an ethnic niche such as maintained by Irish, German, Scandinavian, and black women.

A wide variety of factors might explain the race or ethnic match of individual women servants with their employers, including characteristics of each person or of the place where both resided. For example, a match might have been more likely when the servant or the household head was an immigrant or second-generation U.S. resident or did not speak English, but it might have been less likely in higher-status households. Alternatively, matches might have been more frequent in northeastern urban areas with larger percentages of immigrant women, where wages were high enough to draw native-born white women into manufacturing and leave black women or those of other national origins concentrated in domestic work.

Appendix Table A.5 shows the results of a logistic regression analysis testing the utility of such explanations by using the presence or absence of a racial-ethnic match between a servant and her employer as the outcome to be explained. Surprisingly, when women servants were first- or second-generation immigrants, the likelihood of a match was considerably lower, at .06 or .05, than the average probability of .36. This sharp difference reflects the fact that the highest overall match rate was among third-generation white servants and their employers.

A racial-ethnic match between servant and employer was also more probable if the household head's prestige was relatively low. The lower-prestige matches occurred for white and black live-in servants, whose employers' average prestige was 31 and 18 points, respectively, on a scale of 0 to 100, probably due to the concentration of these servants and employers in rural, agricultural areas. The matched employers of the predominantly urban ethnic women had an average prestige score of 42, which was significantly higher than the employers of matched white (31 points) or black (18 points) servants. Even when there was no match, the status of household heads who employed ethnic live-in servants was higher (54 points) than that of household heads who hired white or African-American live-in servants (43 and 40 points, respectively). Nonetheless, the effect of household prestige on the probability of a match was rather small: a ten-point increase in prestige would lower the probability of a match by only .03 to .33. In contrast, an increase of $100 in women's average annual manufacturing wages would reduce the probability of a racial-ethnic match to $p = .24$. This confirms that as wages rose, third-generation white women entered manufacturing jobs, leaving domestic service to other racial-ethnic women who were less likely to match their employer's background. Still, servant characteristics explained more of the variance in creating a match (29 percent) than either household characteristics (7 percent) or geographic context (0.4 percent), as indicated by an equivalent ordinary least squares regression (not shown).

Comparable patterns emerge from the employers' perspective: 38 percent of the households hiring a servant had at least one racial-ethnic match. Coded only for race, as black versus white, fully 83 percent of the households contained a match. In the former case, households with matches had an average prestige of 32 and those without matches averaged 47. Interestingly, such matches were much more likely when the household head was male rather than female (42 versus 26 percent of the time, respectively).

What created the diversity in rates of servant-employer racial-ethnic matches? Thus far, it seems that higher-status households employed first- and second-generation immigrants rather than white or black women and that white-to-white matches were more common in rural areas, where household heads had lower status. The high prestige of those employing first- or second-generation immigrant women was fairly consistent, no matter what their own race or national origin (see Table 21, last line). This suggests that the number of families attaining the status needed to hire a live-in servant might vary by racial-ethnic group. For example, Scandinavian servants rarely found a co-ethnic employer, in spite of women's ethnic niche, but this was because few Scandinavians could afford to hire them rather than a lack of inclination to do so. Consequently the next step is to examine the households that employed servants.

CROSS-CLASS RELATIONSHIPS: HOUSEHOLDS EMPLOYING SERVANTS

Families that hired live-in servants in 1900 did not represent the norm: only 5 percent of households did so, although many more hired day workers, especially laundresses. Heads of households employing live-in domestic workers had an average prestige score of 40, while those without servants averaged a significantly lower score of only 20. Most servants worked for families whose head held a professional or managerial job (40 percent). These were the highest-status jobs, in which only 10 percent of all household heads labored and which almost certainly provided middle- to upper-class income. A further indicator of their social status was that 64 percent of the servants' employers owned their own homes, in comparison to the national average of 35 percent. Another substantial group (18 percent) of live-in servants were hired by household heads who were employed in agriculture. This figure is large, but it underrepresents the 37 percent of all household heads engaged in farm work at the time. Only a few matches were based on native language. Virtually all of the household heads (99.3 percent) spoke English, but when they did not, they hired women who did not speak English either.

The role of national origin was more complex. First- and second-generation immigrant servants were employed most often by professionals (40 to 50 percent of each ethnic group), while black or white servants were equally likely to be hired by professional (31 percent) or agricultural (28 percent) household heads. These facts suggest two overlapping possibilities: ethnic servants were preferred in middle-class households or ethnic populations were rarely found in rural areas. Since both could be true, these possibilities suggest a more general question. To what extent was the presence or absence of live-in servants based on employer demand (as exemplified by a household's social class and compositional characteristics) or on the available labor supply of black and ethnic women (which itself would be shaped by regional location, population density, or a county's other employment opportunities)?

Multivariate analysis, which compares the ability of these factors to predict the presence of servants, provides some answers, with the results shown in Appendix Table A.6. One set of explanatory variables reflects the social class of the household head in homes that employed servants. These heads of household were significantly more likely to be at least third generation in the United States and white rather than from any other racial-ethnic origin group. When male, such household heads were primarily white-collar workers engaged in the professions or in management, as clerical and sales workers, or in other less easily classifiable jobs. These upper-class, white-collar men were the growing group of employers for live-in servants. In contrast, the industrial working class, engaged in craft, operative, or laborer jobs, was unlikely to employ servants. Agricultural households

TABLE 22. Comparison of Household Head's Racial-Ethnic Group with Racial-Ethnic Group of Women Live-In Servants They Employ (Household Level)

Servant's racial-ethnic group	Household head's racial-ethnic group													
	W*	B†	Ir*	G*	S†	Br*	EE†	R†	It†	OE†	EC*	FC†	LA†	Total
White (native born)	185 (38%)	0	10 (19%)	17 (16%)	1	15 (25%)	1	1	0	3	6 (19%)	2		
Black (native born)	101 (21%)	18 (100%)	4	11		4	1			2	4		2	
Irish	58		23 (43%)	14	1	12	1		2	3	3	1		
German	41		6	44 (42%)	1	14 (24%)	1			2	5 (16%)			
Scandinavian	36		2	2	3 (50%)	5	1	1		1	3			
British	14		1	3		2 (3%)					1			
Eastern European	4		1	3			9 (60%)	2			2			
Russian			2	2				2 (33%)						
Italian									0					
Other European	7			1		2				1 (8%)	1			

TABLE 22. *Continued*

	Household head's racial-ethnic group													
Servant's racial-ethnic group	W*	B†	Ir*	G*	S†	Br*	EE†	R†	It†	OE†	EC*	FC†	LA†	Total
English Canadian	16			1		1					5 (16%)			
French Canadian	3		1	1								1 (25%)		
Latin American	1									1			0	
Multiple servants														
50–90% match	6		2	5										
25–49% match	2													
No match	17		2	1		3	1				1			
Overall match with 25–100% of servants	193 (39%)	18 (100%)	25 (46%)	49 (47%)	3 (50%)	3 (5%)	9 (60%)	2 (33%)	0	1 (8%)	5 (16%)	1 (25%)	0	309 (38%)
Households														
No.	491	18	54	105	6	59	15	6	2	13	31	4	2	806
% of total	(61%)	(2%)	(7%)	(13%)	(1%)	(7%)	(2%)	(1%)		(2%)	(4%)			(100%)

Note: Data in the table are grouped into horizontal panels delineated by alternating bands of gray and white background. The first three panels show the number and percentage of matches with the racial-ethnic background of the household head when there was one live-in servant. The fourth panel indicates the number of matches when there were multiple servants in the household; in this case, at least 25 percent of the servants needed to match the head in order for there to be considered a match at the household level. The fifth panel combines the single- and multiple-servant figures and gives an overall match rate.

*In these five groups, many households (n ≥ 20) hired female live-in servants. Percentages (in **bold**) are given for same-group hires and for most (or next most) common group to be hired.

†In these eight groups, relatively few households (n < 20) hired female live-in servants. Percentages (in **bold**) are provided only when all live-in servants are drawn from the same group as the head.

Key: W, white; B, black; Ir, Irish; G, German; S, Scandinavian; Br, British; EE, Eastern European; R, Russian; It, Italian; OE, other European; EC, English Canadian; FC, French Canadian; LA, Latin American.

are the excluded group in this analysis and thus serve as the basis of comparison for the others. They were declining in number over time and represented the older model of families who employed live-in servants: agricultural heads of households were more likely than manual workers but less likely than white-collar workers to have servants. Not surprisingly, the households that employed servants had a significantly lower proportion of household members employed, as they were more likely to draw on a single, high income, or a family wage, than other families. All of these factors—the household head's racial-ethnic group, sex, and occupation—combine to indicate the importance of class in determining when live-in domestic help was hired. In fact, these variables had the largest impact on the hiring decision, as indicated by the unit change in probability for them.

In contrast, the household's composition had little impact on the decision to employ live-in servants and, where it did, the effects were opposite to those expected in typical supply-and-demand models. Young children needed a good deal of care and created a demand for more female labor, yet the households that employed servants actually had fewer children—only 45 percent of those households had youngsters, compared to 55 percent of families without resident domestic servants. At the same time, controlling on all factors, the number of single women or female adolescents available to help out with the housework was not different in households with and households without servants. There were more extended family members present in homes that employed servants—27 percent had them, versus 19 percent of other households—and they might have pitched in to do some housework. However, it appears that they were dependents, increasing the demand for domestic help rather than reducing it. By and large, households that employed servants had no more, and perhaps fewer, demands for help with household labor than other families.

Nonetheless, geographic, or contextual, effects influenced the presence of servants. Household heads in the West and North Central regions were significantly less likely to employ live-in servants than household heads in the North Atlantic region and the South. Even after taking into account their differing population densities, the general labor shortage in the West and the lesser class variation in the North Central region meant that few households actually employed live-in servants there, relying on day servants or none at all. An increased labor supply of immigrant or black women in a county, represented by their respective percentages, also increased the prospect of employing live-in servants. Their presence was important because they were the women most likely to enter gainful employment. However, specifically in the South, these effects were reversed for black women, and their increased presence was associated with fewer live-in servants. This supports what Katzman (1978) and others have found: black women pioneered being employed while married, doing so by shifting from live-in to domestic day work, and this process began in the South. As a result of this trend, immigrant women's advantage as live-in servants was that they represented a supply of unattached labor, without children of their own and willing to live away from their birth families.

In sum, the decision to hire a live-in servant in 1900 was not driven by the household's demand or need for women's labor, but rather by social class and regional labor conditions. One consequence was that relatively few first- or second-generation immigrant or black household heads achieved the status necessary to hire any servants, let alone one of their own national origin. Among the households that did employ women as live-in servants, the vast majority were headed by third-generation whites (61 percent), while Germans (13 percent), British or Irish (7 percent each), and English Canadians (4 percent) were also represented in substantial numbers, as indicated in Table 22. Households of other national origins rarely could afford to employ servants, making it difficult for Scandinavian, Russian, Latin American, or African-American women workers to obtain this type of ethnic enclave work with its potential for cross-class aid.

Nonetheless, when families could afford to employ live-in servants, some of them did hire workers similar to themselves. The first three panels of Table 22 show the number and percentage of matches with the racial-ethnic background of a household head when there was one live-in servant. Panel 1 shows the outcome for black and white servants, panel 2 provides the results for women of European origin, and panel 3 does so for Canadians and Latin Americans. The fourth panel denotes the matches for households with multiple servants, using a criterion of the head matching at least 25 percent of the servants. Overall, 38 percent of the household heads employed some servants who matched their own racial-ethnic background.

White and British-origin households were the only ones that employed more women servants than were available from their own groups. Consequently, they needed to do some out-group hiring and, at a maximum, could employ only 55 and 41 percent of their servants, respectively, from their own backgrounds. The remaining racial-ethnic groups had too few employing households to possibly hire all of the women servants of their backgrounds and thus, theoretically, they could always hire someone similar to themselves. However, those who could afford live-in servants did not always hire intra-ethnically or intraracially.

Significant possibilities for enclave-like, in-group hiring were created by black households, which always employed black workers (100 percent). Eastern European (60 percent), Scandinavian (50 percent), German (47 percent), and Irish-headed households (46 percent) also usually employed members of their own national-origin groups. For these four groups, excluding Eastern European women, servant work was an ethnic niche as well. Moderate intra-ethnic hiring occurred among Russian (33 percent) and French Canadian (25 percent) households. Third-generation whites also appeared to have moderate rates (39 percent) but, since their maximum rate would be 55 percent, they actually belong in the high-rate group. In contrast, very low intra-ethnic hiring rates were found among English Canadian (16 percent) and British (5 percent) households, and a mixed group of other Europeans (8 percent). If there were racial-ethnic hiring queues or a hierarchy of preferences in the employment of live-in servants, such norms were not shared by everyone.

Consequently, the view from the household or employer level as creators of ethnic enclave employment possibilities was different from that of the individual servant in finding ethnic niches. For a large group of women, matches were usually possible. Third-generation white, German, and Eastern European households were likely to hire intra-ethnically, and servants from those groups were usually employed by someone of their own background. A second group—black, Scandinavian, and Irish households—also frequently hired servants of their own racial-ethnic background, creating some of the advantages of an ethnic enclave and the possibility of some social mobility. Yet many servants from these groups were unmatched with their employers simply because there were too few high-status households among these groups. Finally, other groups, especially English Canadian and British employers, as well as a mixed group of other Europeans, had the ability to create matches but chose not to do so. Instead they preferred to hire third-generation white or German servants, an indication that these groups had developed a degree of ethnic hierarchy or queuing in their hiring practices and rarely considered employing members of their own group.

ETHNIC HIERARCHIES OR QUEUING: FACTORS DETERMINING SERVANTS' RACE OR ETHNICITY

Although the first choice of most employers was to hire a live-in servant from their own racial-ethnic group, British and English Canadian employers were not the only ones to make use of hiring queues. Because there were insufficient white live-in servants to meet the demands of white employers and because some racial-ethnic groups, such as the Scandinavians, Irish, and African Americans, had not achieved the class status to hire all the live-in servants of their own background, considerable cross-group hiring had to occur. The first column of Table 22 shows the hiring preferences among white employers. Although they usually hired white servants, their next most frequent choice was a black live-in servant, followed by an Irish, German, or Scandinavian woman. To what extent does this hiring queue merely reflect the regional distribution of the various groups in 1900, with southern whites hiring black servants, northeastern whites hiring German and Irish servants, and Midwesterners hiring Scandinavian women?

One way to determine when some racial-ethnic groups were more preferable than others is to examine which households employed black women, first- and second-generation immigrants, or white women as live-in servants. I used two different multivariate analyses (logistic regressions) to explore this issue. One compared the choice of hiring black versus first- or second-generation immigrant women (shown in Appendix Table A.7) and a second compared hiring black versus white servants (shown in Appendix Table A.8), the latter of which selects heavily from rural settings. In each instance I compared the effects of the demand for female labor, represented by the household head's social status and racial-ethnic background, and the household's composition, with the effects of supply factors, especially geographic location, on the hiring outcomes.

Equivalent ordinary least squares regressions (not shown) indicate that the geographic factors explained twice as much variation (30 percent) in the selection of a black servant over a first- or second-generation immigrant "ethnic" employee as did the household's social status and labor supply (15 percent). The comparable figures were 21 percent (geographic factors) and 11 percent (household factors) in the black versus white servant comparison.

Next, I focused on the specific geographic variables that significantly predicted who was hired. Appendix Table A.7 shows that first- and second-generation immigrant women were likely to be employed as live-in servants in counties with high percentages of immigrants and especially by household heads who were themselves from various national-origin groups, usually from immigrant groups that had arrived in the mid-nineteenth century. Black women were extremely likely to be hired as servants in the South Atlantic or South Central regions, where the probability increased from an average of .25 up to .75 and .74, respectively, and this chance increased further in southern counties with high percentages of blacks. These two effects of geographic context reflect a modified homophily (similarity) or ethnic enclave principle. Irish, German, and other ethnic employers were significantly more likely than third-generation, native-born whites to hire ethnic domestic workers. However, such choices were also influenced by labor supply, making nationality-to-nationality matches more possible in the Northeast but rare in the South. In fact, southern residence predicted cross-race, rather than similar national-origin group, hiring.

One additional geographic feature was also important—average women's manufacturing wages in a county. Higher wages, by providing alternative opportunities, decreased white and ethnic women's employment as live-in servants. As a direct result, they increased the probability that an African-American woman would be hired as a servant, since most manufacturing jobs were not open to them. This effect was not due to ethnic enclaves or the demographic distribution of people but instead reflected a combination of data on a county's economic context and social information about racism in hiring patterns.

In the choice between employing a third-generation black woman or a third-generation white woman as a live-in servant, shown in Appendix Table A.8, the influence of some of these geographic effects was attenuated. This was a choice that usually occurred in rural areas, where immigrant women often were scarce, so the restricted range of some of the geographic variables reduced their explanatory power.

Other predictors mattered much less than geography. Most household labor supply measures had no significant impact, except that having more single adult women in a family predicted an African-American servant rather than a servant from one of the other two groups. The role of household status was more complicated. High-status households preferred to hire live-in servants from any racial-ethnic group except blacks, but would hire black women in preference to third-generation white women as servants.

These findings reflect a racial-ethnic hierarchy or hiring queue in employment practices, but one that varied by region. Ethnic women were the preferred servants, especially outside of the South. This trend encouraged intra-ethnic matches and meant that intra-ethnic similarity had importance where it could be most easily acted on, in the North and Midwest. In contrast, the hierarchical order of preference simultaneously created cross-race hiring patterns in the South. Taken together, many different geographic or contextual variables shaped the possibilities both for ethnic enclaves and for ethnic queues in hiring.

CONCLUSION

To varying degrees, employers in each racial-ethnic group hired servants sharing their own background. These matches created within-group cross-class relationships for employed women, potentially similar to ethnic enclaves in their advantages. On average, 35 percent of all female live-in servants worked in a household where the head shared a heritage similar to their own. Although this percentage was definitely lower than some end-of-the-century enclave employment rates, which have reached 70 percent for New York City's Chinese population (Zhou 1992), it certainly was sizable. From the perspective of specific groups, 75 percent of white women worked in households headed by another white person, 22 percent of first- and second-generation immigrants were employed by co-ethnics, and 11 percent of the African-American live-in servants were hired by other African Americans. Although the matching rates varied widely according to specific ethnicity, Eastern Europeans, Scandinavians, Germans, and the Irish primarily hired servants of their own national origin or background. Thus, a substantial amount of enclave-like hiring occurred, both from a servant's perspective and from that of employers, 38 percent of whom hired someone from the same racial-ethnic background as themselves.

Despite a general trend toward hiring someone of the same background, ethnic queuing was important to the hiring process. From the employer's perspective, the primary variation was by race: 38 percent of third-generation white household heads and all African-American employers hired racially similar women. Coding all groups as either black or white, and ignoring ethnicity, in 83 percent of households employer and servant were racially matched. In some advertisements for servants, especially for child-care work, race was even specified, although northern white employers might seek white workers (Wrigley 1998) and southern white employers might prefer black workers for this task (Palmer 1989). In general, the preferred order of hiring, at least among people of higher social status, was initially to seek first- or second-generation immigrants over native-born black women, and to select native-born black women before native-born white women. This overall picture masks within-region differences. Southern (white) employers had a cross-racial preference: native-born black women were hired before native-born white women. In the North, the most likely employees were first- or second-generation immigrants, which created a considerable amount of enclave employment, and the second choice was a third- generation native-born white women. In addition to these regional differences, racial-ethnic groups varied in their willingness to employ women of their own background. Some, such as blacks, Irish, German, Scandinavians, and Eastern Europeans, were very likely to do so, perhaps because servant work was also one of their ethnic niches, while others, including English-Canadian and British households, avoided hiring women of their own groups even when they could.

The influence of an individual's race or ethnicity on the match between women employed as live-in servants and the households that hired them was constrained not only by personal preference but also by supply and demand. The supply of racial-ethnic women's labor, in addition to other geographic contextual features, was key to determining specifically who was hired. First, the geographic distribution of immigrant groups limited within-ethnic-group hiring to the North Atlantic and Midwest regions, while the distribution of African Americans created considerable cross-race hiring in the South. Thus, the regional distribution of various groups had an independent effect on the presence and ethnicity of a servant. Second, the alternative job opportunities that were found in counties with high women's manufacturing wages reduced the supply of first- and second-generation immigrant women who might become live-in servants but increased the demand for African-American women's labor. Finally, the degree of urbanization, which was usually a key geographic feature, proved to be unimportant in creating matches at the beginning of the twentieth century.

In contrast to labor supply, labor demand, taking the form of social class, played a key role in determining who employed live-in servants. Occupationally, professionals and white-collar workers were the most able to afford and actually hire servants, while operatives and craft workers were least likely to do so. Agricultural families were the second most typical employers, but they were proportionately underrepresented in this role, having declined over time in their ability to hire servants. Nonetheless, they were the source of a high degree of same-group hires for third-generation, native-born white women. Social class was closely tied to race and ethnicity, so that many groups simply had too few affluent families to hire all the servants of their own background, significantly limiting the creation of ethnic enclaves for women in these occupational niches.

At the beginning of the twenty-first century, once again we have considerable potential for increased within-group hiring and ethnic enclave effects, because there has been a renewed labor supply of immigrant women, who are often channeled into domestic work. In addition, there is increased demand for household labor associated with the greater numbers of middle-class, dual-earner families, including blacks and Latinos. Milkman (1997) has shown that paid household work is currently expanding in metropolitan areas with large immigrant populations and considerable income inequality, indicating a sizable professional class of potential employers.

Yet, the restructuring of domestic work into a service industry has equivalent, if not greater, potential to strengthen racial and ethnic hiring queues. By the 1920s, day workers had become much more common than live-in servants, causing the Census Bureau to distinguish between workers who lived in and workers who lived out. Day workers were self-employed and had the responsibility of finding their own jobs, which could be done through ethnic networks of other workers (Hondagneu-Sotelo 1994; Romero 1988). However, since 1972 the live-in/live-out distinction has been replaced by the new census category of "cleaners and servants." This reflects the fact that a new genre of cleaning service firm has developed that sends teams of workers to clean a series of homes in the course of a single day, often using an agency-provided car and equipment. This structure changes the nature of the employer-employee relationship. As Napierski-

Prancl (1998) describes, the employer is now a firm, instead of a homeowner, the homeowner has become a client of the service industry and domestic workers are no longer self-employed but usually are temporary or part-time employees with a contractual relationship. Because poor women are often recruited for these jobs, sometimes directly through social service agencies, a cross-class employment setting continues, but without any element of personal relationship with the client. Thus, the potential for advantageous enclave-like employment is largely lost, unless the service is run by co-ethnics.

Nonetheless, the volume of live-in domestic work is growing with the expanding aid of small, private domestic placement agencies. Bakan and Stasiulis (1995) show that, at least in Canada, these agencies act as gatekeepers, following racialized practices and using racialized criteria in recruiting and placing Third World migrant (noncitizen) women as domestic workers in the homes of First World employers. Furthermore, the growing demand for childcare workers is creating a different kind of work in private homes. Some women become nannies, especially immigrant or undocumented workers from Mexico, Central America, China, and the Philippines, creating cross-racial settings (Chang 1996), while others, who are often young European women trying to spend some time in the United States, become au pairs, creating cross-ethnic settings.

Domestic work remains both a female and an ethnic niche. Social class factors still determine the demand for domestic work, while the increase in immigration still influences the female labor supply for this task. Employment structures such as private domestic recruiting agencies and cleaning service firms tend to solidify cross-group employment. However, the continued significance of day work holds the potential for some level of enclave hiring, and the growing number of cleaning service firms have reduced the oppression and tensions related to the intimacy of this type of in-home employment.

6 Female-Headed Households and the "Hidden" Headship of Single Mothers

Strategies for an Era Without Government Support

DIFFERENT TERMINOLOGY is used now than at the end of the nineteenth century for describing women who head households or are single mothers. The earlier discourse spoke of deserving widows, deserted wives, and "fallen" mothers of illegitimate children; now we debate policy proposals affecting single-parent families, teenage mothers, and welfare mothers. The vocabulary we use has shifted for multiple reasons, including the dynamics of the social welfare profession, the social visibility of various racial-ethnic groups, and actual changes in family and household composition.

According to Gordon (1994), Brush (1997), Kunzel (1994), Mink (1995), and others, urban reformers in the North who were developing the field of social welfare shifted their professional discourse several times between 1900 and the 1950s, in part to increase the perceived worthiness of various groups of women who could become their clients. Similarly, feminists of the 1920s, as well as those since the 1960s, have attempted to reduce the moral judgments inherent in the popular nomenclature.

Another element underlying the shifting terminology was the regional racial-ethnic composition of the United States. In 1900 many political debates centered on immigrants, who generally resided in urban areas of the North Atlantic and North Central regions. African-American women, who tended to live in the South and in rural areas at the beginning of the twentieth century, went unnoticed by reformers. Racial differences did not attract much attention until around World War II, when the northern urban migration of African Americans motivated social commentary about the perceived high rates of unwed mothers among them. Analyses of the causes of single motherhood, which previously focused on class, began to add race: white working-class women were considered delinquents, white middle-class women were labeled neurotic, and black women were thought to exhibit a cultural pathology (Kunzel 1994; Odem 1995; Solinger 1992). This primarily professional discourse was transformed into a public controversy on race and so-called "matriarchal families" at the beginning of the 1960s.

Shifts in terminology over the century also were driven by demographic changes in households and families. The number of female-headed households had increased gradually throughout the twentieth century (Gordon 1994). They were not a new phenomenon in the 1960s, as many believe. However, the population of single mothers, which had been fairly constant since 1890, did begin to grow during the 1960s (Gordon and McLanahan 1991). The loosening of divorce laws and the subsequent rise in divorce rates, as well as the welfare rule of "no man in the house," were among the major factors increasing rates of single motherhood in that period.

In addition, since mid-century, single mothers have been more able to become female household heads. Early in the century, they had difficulty living on their own, in part because there was little child care and few part-time jobs. So, single mothers and their children often lived as "subfamilies" in a household headed by a relative. Some left their children in orphanages or in the care of relatives while they took full-time jobs, often as live-in servants. Since the 1960s, single mothers have had greater economic independence and have been better able to maintain their own households, in part because of the strong demand for women's employment (although in low-paying clerical, sales, or service industry jobs) and in part due to the welfare improvements of the War on Poverty. Thus, the terms "single mother" and "female-headed household" became conflated in the public mind during the 1960s. This confusion was further sustained since other female household heads, especially widows, were no longer under public scrutiny. With longer life expectancy, widows were less likely to be mothers with dependent children. They were considered part of a larger senior citizen constituency that was often covered by Social Security, disability funds, a pension, and, most importantly, the provisions of the Retirement Equity Act (1984), and therefore widows were no longer viewed as a social problem.

In contrast, single motherhood in the United States has been considered a socioeconomic problem of one sort or another from at least as early as 1890 through the present. Initially and for several decades, it was popularly discussed as a women's issue, leading to the creation of mothers' aid pensions by states and locales between 1910 and 1920. During the feminist decline of the 1930s through the 1950s, this changed. Single motherhood became less publicly visible and was redefined as a problem of morality and responsibility. Thus, when it reemerged as a concern in the 1960s, single motherhood appeared new (Gordon 1994), especially since it had been reconstructed as an issue related to race and then to the feminization of poverty (Palmer 1983; Pearce 1978). In the 1990s, both social policy and popular debate over single mothers were redirected once more. This time the goal was to require single parents to participate in the labor force and to restrict the duration of welfare benefits. Interestingly, once these time-limited benefits are used up, single mothers are returned to circumstances similar to those of the early twentieth century when state support was unavailable. Indeed, many earlier concerns are still salient today. In both periods, reformers worried that female headship and single motherhood were associated with poverty and occurred disproportionately among specific racial-ethnic groups. In 1900 (and sometimes even now), public discourse assumed that women were best off when they had a man to depend on.

Because household composition has a continuing significance for women's place in the political economy, this chapter explores the material conditions under which female household heads and single mothers lived in 1900. Although these two groups are often confused in popular imagery—and they do overlap considerably— they are not identical. Female household heads did not (and do not) necessarily have young children living with them, and single mothers did not (and do not) always head their own households. They both lack husbands, but the former survive independently.

It is useful to study these two groups together for several reasons. First, and most significant, there was and is considerable fluidity between them. For example, as state or federal support declines, some single mothers are not able to maintain their own households. They and their children can easily become hidden as census-defined "subfamilies," living in a household headed by a relative or friend. In a parallel manner, if a single mother acquires resources, such as by inheriting a house, farm, or family business or by entering a well-paid job, she might become an independent female household head. Second, from a contemporary standpoint, single mothers heading households have become a major focus of public policy, and they represent the intersection of these two groups. Finally, at the beginning of the twentieth century, female household heads and single mothers shared the experience of having few economic support structures.

Of course, there is a difficulty in focusing on the similarities and differences between female household heads and single mothers because they are not separate groups. I disentangle them by focusing on their living arrangements, using their necessity or ability to live independently as the key distinction. Hence I actually compare women who could claim household headship and mothers who headed families but lived as subfamilies within another's household.

I designate the first group of women "official household heads" because they were recorded as such following the 1900 census enumerator instructions. It is unclear whether these women also wanted to claim the identity of household head. A person was labeled as head of the family "whether a husband or father, widow or unmarried person of either sex" (Census Office 1900, 28), and so few wives with husbands present were considered heads. A family was defined as "a group of individuals who occupy jointly a dwelling place or part of a dwelling place" (ibid. 25). One person, living alone, could be considered a family for census purposes, allowing widows and other singles to be considered the household head. This aspect of the definition of family head is comparable to the late twentieth century one of a household head.[1]

I call the second group of women "hidden heads." These single mothers, whether divorced, separated, widowed, or never married, would be considered household heads if they were not living with other family members. In a certain sense they were potential household heads. However, defining them by what they might be obfuscates their status. In fact they were household heads whose status was hidden by the survival strategy of living with kin.

WOMEN-HEADED HOUSEHOLDS: ECONOMIC INDEPENDENCE OR A SCARCITY OF OPTIONS?

Women's intentions, socioeconomic coercion, and social policy were all involved in constructing official and hidden heads' social position. During the early twentieth century, the dual-spheres concept—namely, that a woman's place was in the home and a man's was in the labor force—and the idea of the family wage, or one income to support a whole family, were used to justify constricting women's job opportunities. These ideas rendered women's ability to stay home with their children and be supported by male kin, or perhaps labor in a family business or farm, the most desirable or credible situation. Yet there were practical limits to this economic *dependence.* Women were often pushed into independence when their husband died, deserted, or migrated for work, or if they had a child while unmarried. They were on their own if they lacked relatives they could rely on or if there were no state policies that provided economic support.

Using a late twentieth century feminist perspective, we easily assume that women's economic independence is valuable, and argue that finding a well-paid job for female household heads and single mothers is more important than finding a spouse. This is certainly the thrust of current social welfare policies that encourage women to be employed. However, we should not assume that jobs or economic independence were the objective of most female official or hidden household heads in 1900. Indeed, while young men on their own were considered to be starting out on life's journey, young women in the same position were considered "adrift" (Meyerowitz 1988). Nonetheless, in spite of this pressure, some of those women did choose to head their own households (Folbre 1991).

Thus, one goal of this chapter is to determine whether hidden headship was more possible or necessary for some women. Furthermore, in the absence of state or federal welfare policy, did another family completely support hidden household heads, or were these women also employed? Second, I explore the material conditions forcing or facilitating women's move out of someone else's household and into living independently.

I begin by describing how I located women who were official and hidden heads of households in 1900. The second and third sections contrast the individual characteristics of these two groups, and then describe the interplay of household and contextual characteristics in their lives. Because of continuing stereotypes, I pay particular attention to the differences among varying racial-ethnic and age groups of women. The fourth section explores both possible and actual economic survival strategies, then predicts which women chose gainful employment. Finally, to bring men into the picture, I compare official female heads' lives and strategies with those of male household heads.

LOCATING AND INVESTIGATING FEMALE HOUSEHOLD HEADS

In the 1900 census, enumerators recorded the name of the household head within a dwelling unit on the first line of the form, then listed each person in terms of their relationship to the head. The census definitions made it difficult for wives with a husband present to be considered a head of household. Indeed, only 0.6 percent of female official household heads had a spouse present, while 89 percent of male heads did. Nonetheless, fully 9.8 percent of all adult women were officially counted as household heads. Some of these women lived alone (21 percent), but the remainder resided in a wide variety of household structures. Some were unmarried or deserted mothers living with young children. Many others were widows, heading a family of grown children, or single women heading other types of extended family groups, perhaps composed of younger siblings. Census definitions of household relationships preclude knowing whether servants or employees were also household heads, since they were living in another person's home at the time of the enumeration. In contrast, the tiny number of women boarders who we know headed households were excluded precisely because they were not living independently.[2]

The hidden female household heads are much more difficult to locate than the official ones because they were not considered to be household heads, even though they headed subfamilies or family extensions within other households. The 1900 census categorized household interrelationships only in terms of people's connection to the main household head, clouding other relationships and keeping subfamilies statistically out of sight. In order to operationalize the concept of hidden heads, or single mothers living with kin, I looked for a combination of household and individual characteristics. I selected women who were daughters or other nonspousal relatives of the household head who (1) were either never married, divorced, married but spouse absent, or widowed, (2) had at least one surviving child, and (3) lived in households that had family extensions, including an individual with her or his own children. The records of women meeting these criteria were examined by hand to see if they appeared to be living with their own children in a household headed by someone else. Most of the women were hidden heads of subfamilies; I excluded those who were not. The resulting group includes all the hidden single mothers in the sample, based on Gordon's (1994) estimate that 20 percent of single mothers lived as subfamilies and Gordon and McLanahan's (1991) reports on the numbers of single-parent children in subfamilies.[3] Thus the hidden heads are well-represented, and their survival strategies can usefully be compared with those of female official household heads.

THE DEMOGRAPHY OF WOMEN HEADING EITHER HOUSEHOLDS OR SUBFAMILIES

Turn-of-the-century discussions on the need for widows' pensions leave the impression that women who headed households in 1900 were older and widowed, probably avoiding poverty by living with their families of origin, rather than the young single mother we now expect to see. Indeed there is some basis for the stereotype that the predominant route to women's household headship has changed in this fashion over the course of the twentieth century.

Today, women frequently become official household heads through divorce or unmarried pregnancy, while in 1900 the primary cause was widowhood. As Table 23 indicates, 77 percent of official and 55 percent of hidden household heads were widowed, in comparison to 12 percent among all adult women. Nonetheless, a full 12 percent of official household heads had never married and another 9 percent had an absent spouse who had either migrated in search of a job or had deserted the family. Divorce was rare at the turn of the century, but desertion was not uncommon. Only a minuscule 0.6 percent of women recorded as household heads were married with a spouse present, probably because of a husband's disability; in contrast, 55 percent of all adult women were married. Official household heads averaged 51 years old, and only 38 percent of them resided with children age 14 or younger, again supporting the stereotype of the older widow.

Nonetheless, a dichotomous then-and-now approach to history would be inaccurate. The hidden household heads of 1900 look a little more like our image of present-day official heads, even though 55 percent of them were also widowed. They were younger, averaging 37 years old. Almost one-third either were divorced or had an absent spouse, and another 15 percent were never married. Fully 86 percent of them lived with children under 15, and, as a partial outcome, their households were large, averaging nearly six people. The association of hidden headship with children suggests the social and economic difficulties faced by a woman living on her own, especially with young children present, in the early twentieth century.

In spite of these difficulties, many women who were official household heads also had children. Therefore I decided to compare the subset of official household heads living with children under the age of 15—the group most similar to our contemporary image of the female household head—to the hidden household heads. On most indicators, this group fell between hidden and all official household heads. They were significantly different from hidden heads on most dimensions except for their counties' geographic

TABLE 23. Characteristics of Women Heading Households and Hidden Heads, 1900

Variable	Official heads, all (n = 2,671)	Official heads, with children 0–14 (n = 1,023)	Hidden heads (n = 318)	All women age 15 or older (n = 31,665)
Individual characteristics				
Age (yr)	51***	45***	37	36
Literacy: Reads a language (%)	81*	75***	86	90
Marital status (%)	***	***		
Married	0.6	0.7	0	55
Widowed	77	79	55	12
Divorced	2	2	6	0.4
Spouse absent	9	13	24	2
Never married	12	6	15	31
Total	100.6	100.7	100	100.4
Race and nativity (%)				
White, 3rd+ gen.	44	40*	48	52
Black, 3rd+ gen.	17	24*	18	11
Immigrant	27***	22	17	19
2nd gen. immigrant	13*	14	17	19
Total	101	100	100	101
% with gainful employment	50***	57***	32	22
Household characteristics				
Avg. no. in family	3.2***	4.6***	5.9	4.7
Avg. no. of children ages 0–9	0.4***	1.1***	1.5	1.0
% with children ages 0–9	25***	65***	74	49
% with children ages 0–14	38***	100 (redundant)	86	60
% with extended family	26***	37***	100	26
% with boarders present	16*	15	12	10
Proportion of adults employed	.25***	.23***	.31	.29
County characteristics				
Urban vs. rural (%)	60***	50	45	51
Farm residence (%)	18***	23***	35	34
% of women who were immigrants	36***	30	29	35
Avg. women's manufacturing wage ($)	241*	230	231	241

TABLE 23. *Continued*

Variable	Official heads, all (n = 2,671)	Official heads, with children 0–14 (n = 1,023)	Hidden heads (n = 318)	All women age 15 or older (n = 31,665)
Region of residence (%)				
North Atlantic	31*	23	24	31
North Central	30	28	30	34
South Atlantic	14	20	17	14
South Central	19*	25	24	17
West	6	5	5	5
Total	100	101	100	101

Note: Asterisks indicate significance levels from appropriate χ^2 (marital status only) or t tests: $^*p \leq .05$; $^{**}p \leq .01$; $^{***}p \leq .001$. Column 1 significance levels indicate difference between all official heads and hidden heads. Column 2 significance levels indicate difference between official heads residing with any children (less than 15 years old) and hidden heads.

traits (as described in columns 2 and 3 of Table 23), even though both groups usually lived with children. In fact, in some ways they were more like official household heads since 79 percent of them were widows. Yet they were distinctive in that they had the highest rate of gainful employment and the lowest literacy rate, perhaps because they were slightly more likely (24 percent) to be black. In sum, living with children was not the defining difference between hidden and official household headship.

Despite some changes in the routes to official female headship since 1900, there are several continuities over the century in other attributes of female household heads. As we will see, their proportion among all women has risen only slightly, their rates of labor force participation tend to be high, and racial-ethnic background and/or immigrant generation often play a complex role in their lives.

To elaborate on the first point, the lack of a national social welfare policy did not make female-headed households rare in 1900. Almost 10 percent of all adult *women* were recorded as household heads and 12 percent of all *family households* were female-headed. By 1993, the latter figure had risen to 17.5 percent of family households (Andersen 1997), an increase of less than six percentage points. In spite of fears that providing support structures for female household heads would destabilize families and make it easier for men to leave (Gordon 1994), change over the century has not been nearly as dramatic as was predicted.

The second similarity is that, like today, women official household heads were more likely to be employed (50 percent) than were their married contemporaries (4 percent) or hidden heads (32 percent). The gap in labor force participation rates is much smaller now, although the exact difference is hard to judge because the reporting categories we use are different. Published data on *employment* now are recorded by marital or motherhood status, not household headship, while information on *headship* types focuses on income and poverty, not employment rates. Nonetheless, the data are informative. In 1992, among mothers of children younger than 18, 53 percent of never-married and 73 percent of ever-married (divorced, widowed, and spouse-absent) women were employed, with married women (whose spouse is present) falling in between, at 68 percent. When the presence of children is ignored, the difference among these three general groups is even narrower (ranging between 59 and 74 percent), although widows' employment rates then fall to 19 percent (U.S. Department of Labor Women's Bureau 1994).

Finally, in both periods the highest rates of women officially heading households were commonly found among people of color. In 1900, 11 percent of (third-generation or later) white, 18 percent of Latin American, and 18 percent of (third-generation or later) black women were official household heads. By 1993, 14 percent of white, 23 percent of Hispanic/Latino, and fully 47 percent of black households were female-headed (Andersen 1997). The greatest increase in headship rates over the century was among African Americans. Despite their relatively high female headship rates, however, women of color were largely ignored in the family policy debates early in the twentieth century. Discussions instead focused on immigrants, who were often described as if they were racial minorities who had arrived from strange places to land on U.S. shores.

Irish households were the most likely to record women as household heads (20 percent, versus 12 percent on average), reflecting the economic similarities between themselves and U.S.-born blacks, who often lived in the same urban neighborhoods during the 1800s. Just as important, the Irish migration pattern included a greater proportion of women, especially single women, than other groups. Irish women were more likely to remain single than were most immigrant women and, concomitantly, the Irish community was more likely than were other working-class immigrants or native-born residents to expect women to work continuously (Turbin 1992). Therefore it is no surprise that there were high percentages of Irish households headed by women.

The overall impression is less dramatic when we consider that only 13 percent of black and 11 percent of Irish adult women were official heads, compared to the average of 10 percent. Yet just 6 to 8 percent of women from most other racial-ethnic groups headed households in 1900. Especially low rates of women's official headship were found among Italian (4.2 percent) and Russian (3.7 percent) women, totaling 5 percent of their households. Italian women's low headship and high marriage rates were typical for groups whose migration was dominated by men, reducing the likelihood of an adult woman's living on her own (Cohen 1992). This explanation does not account for the Russian pattern. However, these two national-origin groups were the only ones to be composed almost entirely (90 percent or more) of immigrants and, in general, immigrant marriage rates were high in comparison to their second-generation children.

As Table 23 illustrates, the numerical majority of women who officially headed households in 1900 actually were native-born whites who had been in the United States for three generations or longer. Why, then, were immigrant women so socially visible as heads of households? First, they comprised the second largest group of official female household heads, followed by smaller numbers of third-generation blacks and U.S.-born children of immigrants. Second, while immigrants constituted only 19 percent of the female population, they accounted for 27 percent of the women officially heading households. Thus they were overrepresented. In addition, immigrants composed a larger proportion of the women official household heads (and of household heads with children) than of the more hidden subfamily heads. Looking only at immigrant single parents—who were at the intersection of hidden and official household heads—Gordon and McLanahan (1991) observed a similar pattern. All of these factors supported the interpretation, common at the time, that culture gave rise to certain women becoming acknowledged household heads.

The data suggest demographic reasons for the apparent cultural significance of immigration. Official household heads more rarely lived with extended family, at least in comparison to hidden heads. Hence, at least one cause of immigrant women's proportionately greater representation among official than hidden heads was that, as for most migrants, they had fewer kin to take them in. Second-generation immigrants and third-generation or later resident white women were more able to depend on family.

Another way to look at the relationship of culture to material conditions is by focusing on the women officially heading households, whose lives were socially visible and likely to be considered problematic. Among these, let us contrast the two groups sharing some cultural characteristics: immigrants and second-generation, U.S.-born nationality groups. Although their household size was similar (3.3 and 3.4 persons, respectively), their household composition was not. Among immigrant women who officially headed households, 20 percent lived with extended family, usually of a younger generation, and only 30 percent lived with children under age 10. Marital status was a factor in their household composition: 82 percent were widows (compared to 77 percent of all female household heads), 12 percent had married but had been deserted or divorced, and only 6 percent had never married. This suggests that immigrant women were buffered from early headship by their high marriage rates but propelled into later headship by widowhood and lack of extended family. (This pattern is also found among hidden heads, where 74 percent of immigrant women were widowed, in comparison to 55 percent of the whole group.) Immigrant women seem to have been the basis for the early twentieth century archetype of the female household head as an older widow. Immigrant men's hazardous blue-collar jobs and high early mortality rates undoubtedly increased immigrant women's widowhood rates. Indeed, immigration and female headship may both have been characteristic of working-class life, each compounding the other's effects.

Turning to second-generation immigrant women heading households, I found that 34 percent lived with extended family, either of the same or a younger generation, but fully 51 percent lived with children under 10. The higher presence of children was partly a function of age. Second-generation immigrants, at about 46 years old, were somewhat younger than the average female household head (age 51) and considerably younger than first-generation immigrant ones (age 55). There was also a difference in their marital status: 68 percent were widows, 14 percent were deserted or divorced, and fully 18 percent had never married. These women became household heads earlier through never marrying and being more willing or able to live with extended family, especially of the same generation. Their household context looked a bit more like that of present-day female household heads did immigrant women's homes. Despite some shared culture, the two immigrant generations had differing outcomes.

Geographic variations suggest additional material conditions associating immigration with female-headed households. As Table 23 shows, official female heads were most frequently found in urban areas, where families already living in crowded apartments might not have the space to take in a subfamily. It was in such areas that immigrants tended to reside. In contrast, hidden heads were more common in rural areas, where farm households might accommodate them. Whites and blacks were the most likely to live on farms in such rural areas. (Meanwhile, women official heads with children 14 or younger matched the national urban-rural split.) One result of these residential patterns was that hidden household heads were underrepresented in the North Atlantic region, which was highly urbanized and a common immigrant destination, but overrepresented in the South Central states.

In order to disentangle the complex contributions of national origin and race, economic opportunity available with urban residence, or household and marital characteristics to initiating women's official household headship, I use a multivariate approach, described in the next section.

Household and Contextual Conditions
Distinguishing Official from Hidden Heads

The significant material factors that forced or allowed some women to become official heads rather than remain hidden in subfamilies can be discovered using a statistical technique called logistic regression analysis, the results of which are shown in Appendix Table A.9. In this case, I use the technique to account for a woman's status as either an official or a hidden household head. To do so, I investigated four groups of possible explanatory factors, or independent variables, including a woman's individual and household characteristics, her sources of economic support, and the geographic context of her place of residence.

The individual characteristics I thought could explain women's form of headship were age, literacy, and racial-ethnic background. Older, literate women could be more able to live on their own. In addition, given their high absolute rates of female-headed households and cultural reputation for independence, one might think that black and Irish women would be less likely to be hidden heads, even after other material conditions often associated with race and ethnicity are taken into account. Because there were relatively few female household heads of any type in 1900, I divided the racial-ethnic variable into only five categories: white, black, Irish and German (the two largest ethnic groups), and all other national origins combined.

I examined household composition by measuring the number of household members in each of six groups: children (age 0 to 9), seniors (age 65 and over), female and male adolescents (ages 10 to 14), considered separately, and the two groups, single and married adult men (ages 15 to 64). These categories combine various aspects of social gender, marital status, and age, but each one has implications for women's employment possibilities. Children and seniors are often dependents, whose presence in the household would require extensive caregiving, while the other four groups could serve as alternative income-generating labor sources for an adult woman.

I considered four additional sources of economic support that might allow a woman to head her own household. One is homeownership, which is a good general indicator of social class and economic stability. In addition, it could facilitate home-based occupations such as taking in boarders. Indeed, the actual presence or absence of extended family and boarders, two types of nonfamily household residents, are included to represent a second source of economic support. Extended families were not economically beneficial during the nineteenth century. However, by the early twentieth century their presence did tend to reduce the proportion of dependents in a household by adding more income; ironically, at the same time, extended families had become a declining social form (Ruggles 1987). Finally, a woman might support herself through employment, and if she worked, I coded her job into one of seven broad occupational categories, expecting that any job, especially a high-status one, could facilitate official household headship.

The geographic measures are drawn from earlier chapters of this volume. They represent various aspects of a woman's location, particularly contextual information about residence in a town or city of at least 1,000 people, where women's work was most available, and measures of a county's economic environment, indicated by the average women's wage in manufacturing. Also considered are the region of the United States and the local county's racial and ethnic diversity, measured by the percentage of women who were black or the percentage of women who were immigrants or had foreign-born parents.

Overall, this analysis indicates which women were able to use the subfamily strategy and who survived independently in a time when there was no federal support for either of them. The four groups of variables just described explain fully 40 percent of the difference in type of headship (in a comparable OLS regression). Appendix Table A.9 provides all logistic regression coefficients and more easily interpretable changes in the average probability (.90) of being an official head for each significant variable. For example, among the individual factors, age is the only variable to affect type of headship. It increases the probability of being an official head (by .008 for each year or by .08 for each 10 years of age), as predicted.

Household composition factors explain the majority of the variation in type of headship, and several different significant variables were involved. First, the more family members of almost any kind who were present, or the larger the household size, the higher the probability of remaining a hidden head. This is consistent with the findings on age which, like household composition, is related to life-cycle stage. Older age is usually associated with reduced family size and, in this case, predicts official headship. In fact, when describing Massachusetts towns in 1880, Folbre (1991) argues that life cycle determined women's residential independence: relatively young (unmarried) women and relatively old widows were most likely to be "on their own." Second, those household members who might seek employment, such as adolescent women or adult men, and dependents who required care, such as young children or senior citizens, both inhibited official headship. This apparently contradictory finding suggests that women living in subfamilies had access to the earnings of others and caretaking responsibilities to perform, while official heads had fewer family resources and fewer dependents. Third, the presence of married men had the the largest impact (of any single variable) on women's type of headship. In providing support to hidden heads, they decreased the probability of a woman's official headship by fully $p = -.27$ (from $p = .90$ to only .62). Thus, striking a "patriarchal bargain" with a father, married uncle, or brother was the major route for single mothers to become subfamilies. Of course, the opposite factors, living in a small household and having no married men present, were associated with a woman's official headship.

Two additional measures were very important and facilitated (or were the outcome of) official headship—living in an urban area and holding a job. Overall, urban living had the second strongest effect on type of headship, regardless of whether a woman was an immigrant or not. Its effect reflects both the unavailability of housing for subfamilies and the accessibility of jobs for women. Furthermore, the only source of support that significantly predicts women's official headship is holding some type of working-class job, especially operative, service, or agricultural work. Neither the middle-class indicators of home ownership or professional-white collar employment nor the actual presence of boarders (to provide income) or of extended family (to provide child care or added income) seem to distinguish official from hidden heads.

Perhaps one of the most important findings is the irrelevance of race and ethnicity. Neither an individual's background nor the percentages of black or immigrant women in her county predicted who would be an official or hidden head. The apparent (zero order) association of official headship with women of color and some immigrant groups disappears when this multivariate approach is used. Once other variables are accounted for, there was no difference in the propensity of black, other racial-ethnic, or white women to elect independent official household headship over being hidden in a subfamily. (Gordon and McLanahan [1991] found this was also true in 1900 specifically for single parents.) Headship was not a cultural feature. Instead, a racial-ethnic group's rate of female official headship was associated with the significant material factors noted above: usual type of household composition, access to jobs, and urban residence. Undoubtedly, these same factors laid some of the foundation for the increasing numbers of official female-headed households over the course of the twentieth century: generally smaller family size, women's greater entrance into formal employment, and increased urban living.

ECONOMIC SUPPORT STRATEGIES

After learning about women's routes to official or hidden household headship in 1900, the next step is to compare their economic support strategies. We have already seen that the official household heads were more likely to be employed than hidden ones. Interestingly, this means that living as a subfamily within someone else's home did not necessarily allow hidden household heads to escape employment. Furthermore, net of other factors, official and hidden household heads were no different in their access to some resources such as home ownership, live-in boarders, or extended family members. We will now examine each group's income sources.

SOURCES OF INCOME

Just as they are today, women's economic opportunities at the beginning of the twentieth century were shaped by personal and family resources and by the economic possibilities located where they lived. However, their options were more limited by occupational segregation, the lack of part-time work or available child care, and rural-urban differences than they would be now. Women had four major economic resources in the pre-welfare state environment of 1900: obtaining gainful employment outside the home, creating home-based income-producing work (such as taking in boarders or doing industrial homework), supporting oneself through subsistence farming, or seeking extended family to join in their households and contribute income. Each approach could be used alone or in combination with others. Charity assistance was the only other resource, and it cannot be directly measured using census data. However, we know that such aid (like the difficult-to-measure industrial homework) was more available in cities, and urban residence serves as one proxy for such activities.

Panel A of Table 24 shows how official and hidden household heads used these four support strategies. Sometimes the women used multiple support sources, which I separated into mixtures that included paid employment and those that did not. There were significant differences between the two types of household heads. Most official household heads (68 percent) could rely on a single source of support or no visible support at all, while hidden heads generally relied on multiple sources (61 percent). In fact, only 39 percent of hidden heads were able to rely solely on their extended kin. One-third (33 percent) of them also reported jobs, and nearly a third lived with boarders or on a farm, which usually necessitated unreported, home-based work. In contrast, official household heads' primary income was from gainful employment, either alone (20 percent) or mixed with other sources (30 percent).

Once employed, official and hidden household heads had different occupational distributions, as shown in panel B of Table 24. Like all other women, they were especially concentrated in service work. However, hidden household heads' next most common job was manufacturing operative. Such work was plentiful in urban areas, especially for younger women, particularly if relatives could help with child care. Indeed, the larger families of hidden household heads probably needed their employment. In contrast, women officially heading households were almost

TABLE 24.   Income Sources of Women Official and Hidden Household Heads, 1900

A. INCOME SOURCES BY HEADSHIP TYPE (%)

Household headship type		Single sources			Combinations			
	None	Work	Board-ers	Farm	Extend-ed kin	Work + other	Non-work mix	Total
Official (n = 2,594)	30	20	5	2	11	30	1	99
Hidden (n = 301)	n/a				39	33	28	100

χ^2 result: significant at $p \leqslant .001$.

B. OCCUPATIONAL SECTORS OF GAINFULLY EMPLOYED WOMEN (%)

Household headship type			Occupational category					
	Profes-sional	Cler-ical	Craft	Opera-tive	Service	Agri-cul-ture	Un-classi-fiable	Total
Official (n = 1,330)	10	2	1	18	34	33	2	100
Hidden (n = 100)	5	5	1	29	41	18	1	100

χ^2 result: significant at $p \leqslant .001$.

C. PERCENTAGE OF WOMEN GAINFULLY EMPLOYED IN SPECIFIC JOBS, BY HOUSEHOLD HEADSHIP TYPE

Official household heads		Hidden heads	
Farmers, family	29	—	
Farm labor	4	Farm labor	8
—		Farm labor, family	10
Laborer, general	4	Laborer, general	5
Laundry work, hand	14	Laundry work, hand	12
Housekeeper, domestic	6	Housekeeper, domestic	11
Servant	6	Servant	12
Dressmaker	7	Dressmaker	10
Seamstress	2	Seamstress	4
Nurses, not specified	2	Nurses, not specified	5
—		Saleswomen	4
Teacher	1	Teacher	3
Landlord	5	—	
Other jobs	20	Other jobs	16
Total (n = 1,330)	100	Total (n = 100)	100

n/a, not applicable.

equally as likely to work in agricultural jobs as in service work. In some ways this occupational distribution appears contradictory, because the majority of official heads actually resided in urban areas yet worked in agriculture as well as in service jobs, while hidden heads most frequently lived in rural settings of less than 1,000 people.

In fact, there was a strong "back to the country" movement in this period as a solution to social problems (Brush 1997). Yet in rural settings, the opportunities for hidden heads, who were younger than official ones, could be limited to family farm labor on a male-owned farm. Such work generally went unreported when done by women. Older women in rural areas might inherit a farm, enabling both their official headship and recorded gainful employment as a farmer. Whether or not they themselves were working on the farm, their wealth was easily translated into recorded gainful employment. Indeed, as panel C of Table 24 indicates, 29 percent of employed official women heads were family farmers (owners) and only 4 percent were farm laborers, while none of the hidden heads were farmers and fully 18 percent of hidden heads were farm laborers.

Home ownership was the urban capital resource most comparable to farm ownership, but it did not play the same role in sustaining women's official headship. Although fully 5 percent of the official women heads were landlords who rented to others, homeownership showed a slight negative relationship with having lodgers ($r = -.10$). Rather than translating into gainful employment, the wealth of home ownership indicated a secure social class position, and for both official and hidden household heads it was associated with having no recorded occupation.

Surprisingly, 30 percent of the official household heads seemed to have no form of support. However, most of these women (74 percent) were living with immediate relatives other than extended kin. Indeed, 54 percent of their households had employed adults and a few (4 percent) had employed adolescents. Compared to other official household heads, these women were slightly older (56 years old versus 51) and more likely to be widowed (86 versus 77 percent). They were immigrants (39 versus 27 percent) and urban dwellers (71 versus 60 percent). Among these women, the

26 percent who lived alone closely matched the stereotyped portrait of the female household head in 1900. They were the most likely to be considered "worthy" for the philanthropic help that was an important source of cash and in-kind services during this time period (Brush 1997), and their city residence increased the probability they would receive this aid.

Gainful Employment

On the one hand, adult women's gainful employment was not encouraged in 1900; on the other hand it was the primary income strategy of official household heads. This apparent contradiction led me to ask what conditions forced or allowed official and hidden household heads to seek gainful employment at the beginning of the twentieth century.

In order effectively to answer this question, especially to judge the relative importance of many possible predictors, I performed another multivariate analysis. Once again, because the dependent variable I want to predict—whether a woman was employed or not—is dichotomous, logistic regression analysis is required. The results of this analysis are shown in Appendix Table A.10 and are described here. As in Appendix Table A.9, Table A.10 provides both the regression coefficients and significant changes in the probability of employment, this time from the average of .46 (or 46 percent) for the official and hidden household heads combined. Once again, explanatory factors are grouped into individual characteristics, household composition features, sources of support (other than work), and geographic variables.

Some specific measures, however, needed modification. Among the individual variables, I added whether or not a woman's household headship was official or hidden and if she was a widow, to help separate which of these two intertwined factors was more important. I also replaced the three national-origin groups with immigrant generation—first-generation immigrants versus U.S.-born women of foreign-born parents—since this factor also seemed intertwined with type of headship. The sources of support also had to be adjusted. A woman's own employment type was eliminated. If I had not done so, I would be using employment to predict employment—a futile exercise. This was replaced with a measure of the proportion of family members who were employed, excluding the woman head herself. Based on earlier results predicting employment for all women, it seemed likely that the greater proportion of economically active people, the greater the family need and the more likely an official or hidden female household head would be employed. I also added farm residence, which was a source of support that was likely to suppress recording women's work. There were no changes in either the household composition or geographic context variables.

Gainful employment was more difficult to predict than type of headship: all of the measures combined accounted for just 24 percent of the variation in who reported work (using a comparable OLS regression). Individual factors were the major determinant of women's employment. Among them the two most important measures were being a hidden head, which depressed the probability of work down to .20 (or 20 percent), and being black, which increased it up to .78 (or 78 percent). Importantly, the much-discussed individual characteristics of widowhood and immigrant status[4] were irrelevant in predicting a female household head's employment.

Household composition features, especially household size, were still influential in predicting employment. Official and hidden household heads recorded work when there were no other adults to do so. In contrast, the numbers of single and married men in the household greatly reduced women's probability of employment (to $p = .37$ and $p = .35$, respectively). Dependents had a variety of effects on women's work. There was no trade-off between women's employment and adolescents' employment. Even though under-enforced or nonexistent child labor laws would have allowed reliance on these children, decreasing women's employment rates, their residence had no effect. Nonetheless, the presence of both younger dependents and older senior citizens did reduce women's work probabilities (children, $p = .41$, and senior citizens, $p = .39$). This indirectly suggests that household composition factors changed women's economic options over their life course, requiring their presence at home in both early and later stages of life, although perhaps less so in the middle years.

Among the other sources of support, neither residence with extended family nor the proportion of the household employed mattered. Apparently it was the presence (or absence) of immediate family members that influenced the work decision of hidden and official household heads. However, higher employment probabilities did occur among women who had other income-generating resources: women living with boarders ($p = .55$) and older women living on farms both were more likely to record work. Thus, the effect of age was situational. Although the individual characteristic of being older generally reduced the probability of being employed (by 1.1 percent per year), older women living on farms were more likely to record work (increasing by 1.2 percent per year), as was suggested by our earlier findings. The effect of race also was situational, but it worked in the opposite direction. Although black women generally had higher employment rates than other household heads, black women living on farms had a low .24 average probability of reporting work. They were less likely than white women to live on family-owned farms that they might inherit, turning such ownership into the reported occupation of farmer (Schweninger 1990). In contrast to the multiple effects of farm ownership or residence, home ownership was a middle-class resource that usually decreased rather than increased the probability of employment ($p = .35$).

The geographic context variables had no independent effect on female household heads' work.[5] Indeed, the importance of the urban versus rural measure disappeared when I included farm residence as an economic support source. This upholds my contention that women's unreported farm work made women's urban employment rates appear usually high.

Since age was one of the most important predictors of gainful employment, I decided to see if the results would be different when I focused on younger official and hidden household heads, age 50 or less. Were they motivated to work by similar concerns? In general the answer is yes. Most of the explanatory factors had the same effects as before. The only difference was in the significance of some resources. For younger women, the presence of extended family facilitated work, but the presence of boarders or the residence of black women on farms were no longer significant factors. Apparently all female household heads relied on other people, but boarders were an important resource for the older group, while an extended family was important for the younger women, further illustrating the life-cycle effects previously noted.

GENDER DIFFERENCES

Up to this point, I have been contrasting the situation of two groups of women who did not have a spouse—official and hidden household heads. Now, to illustrate the gendered meaning of headship, I contrast two groups of official household heads— women and men. Their characteristics and economic resources are described in Table 25.

Female household heads were older than male household heads. In addition, their families were smaller and had fewer young children. These differences were partially due to women's later life stage—their families were more likely to be grown. However, women's household size was also related to their marital status. Most of the women were widowed and the rest had never been married, had been deserted, or were divorced. Being single reduced their household size, but it also was the precipitating factor forcing or facilitating their roles as household heads. In contrast, 89 percent of male household heads were married with their wives present.

While this may seem obvious, it actually helps us understand why some racial-ethnic groups had high rates of (official) female household headship. Among such groups, for one reason or another, women were less likely to be married. For example, only 52 percent of Irish or Latin American women and 56 percent of African-American women were married with their spouse present, in contrast to 61 percent among (third-generation) white women. These differences in marriage rates were not usually a reflection of cultural preference but were largely due to migration and immigration effects. One factor was the proportion of immigrants among each racial-ethnic group: the more immigrants, the lower the incidence of female-headed households. What are some of the reasons for this? First, immigrants were more likely to be married than their U.S.-born counterparts. A second factor was the female-

TABLE 25.   Characteristics of Households Headed by Women and by Men, 1900

Variable	Significance level	Household head Woman	Household head Man
Individual characteristics			
Age (yr)	***	51	43
Marital status (%)	***		
Widowed		77	5
Divorced		2	0.2
Spouse absent/deserted		9	1
Never married		12	6
Married, spouse present		0.6	89
Total		100.6	101.2
Household characteristics			
Avg. no. of family members	***	3.2	4.6
Avg. no. of children, 0–9 yr	***	0.4	1.2
Type of headship by race-ethnicity (%)	***		
Irish		20	80
Black, 3rd+ gen.		18	82
Latin American		18	82
British		13	87
German		12	88
French and English Canadian		12	88
White, 3rd+ gen.		11	89
Scandinavian		9	91
Eastern European		7	93
Russian		5	95
Italian		5	95
Sources of support			
Home ownership (%)	*	49	46
Extended family present (%)	***	26	19
Boarders present (%)	***	17	10
Urban residence (%)	***	60	46
Gainful employment of head (%)	***	50	96
Prestige of head's occupation	***	17	21

Note: Significance levels from appropriate *t* or χ^2 tests: *p ≤ .05; **p ≤ .01; ***p ≤ .001.

to-male ratio among migrants or immigrants. High rates of immigration among never-married Irish women increased their female headship rates, as did the separate migration of husbands or wives in search of employment among black and Latin American households. Such "disproportionately" female migration patterns did not occur among Scandinavian, Eastern European, Russian, or Italian households. Indeed, a comparable "excess" of men among Italians, who may also have been unmarried or waiting to raise money to send for their families, was not seen as problematic because it did not violate the norm of male headship.

Turning to their means of economic support, we see that half of the official female household heads were gainfully employed, but almost all the male household heads (96 percent) reported work. Women's jobs were slightly lower in prestige than men's and varied less (with standard deviations of 13 and 19, respectively), suggesting lower income. Thus, other income sources were necessary for both employed and nonemployed women. Women relied much more heavily on taking in boarders than did men. Even though female household heads were just slightly more likely to own their dwelling, their opportunity to take in boarders was enhanced by proportionately greater urban residence—areas where boarders were found more often. Not only did women take in boarders and lodgers, but their households were more likely to include extended family members, who could be additional sources of support. As mentioned earlier, one-third (31 percent) of female official household heads needed to use multiple income strategies in 1900. This economically desperate group may have been comparable to the one-third (36 percent) of current female-headed households who live in poverty (Andersen 1997, citing data for 1994). Life as a household head had different meanings for men and women.

DISCUSSION AND CONCLUSIONS

An important component in this analysis of women's household headship has been the inclusion of hidden household heads, that is, women living with their children as subfamilies in another household. They were often rural residents and as a result went unnoticed by early urban social reformers. However, hidden heads were one of the important source groups for female household heads. Ignoring them was a mistake because farm location (interacting with age) created different support options for each headship group. Older women living on farms often were official heads, recorded as farmers (although they might not work the land themselves), while the younger hidden household heads were less likely to record work when they lived there (even when actually doing so in the rural informal economy). Therefore, if we assume that early twentieth century families were more willing to support single mothers and their children than now, without noting that such families may have had the ability to do so because they also lived in low-population rural areas, we are misreading the lessons of the past.

Hidden heads are also important because they shared the obstacles facing female household heads—most notably, a dearth of economic support structures for women on their own. In 1900 it was difficult for a woman to live on her own with a family to maintain. The dual, or separate, spheres ideology served to discourage adult women's employment and made living in a male-headed household the most desirable option. Few women's jobs paid sufficiently well to provide for a family. There was little child care available (Gordon 1994), and the existing "baby farms" had poor reputations (Broder 1988), making jobs difficult to hold when women could not also care for their children. As a result, about one-third of female household heads and almost two-thirds of hidden heads used multiple income strategies and often incorporated some form of home-based support. Not surprisingly, such multiple strategies are still necessary for single mothers today, whether they are in low-wage employment or are welfare-reliant (Edin and Lein 1996). Combination survival strategies were not a matter of choice in either period but of narrowed economic options.

In a certain sense, hidden headship was an intermediate strategy between being married and being on one's own as a female household head. It is important to understand that the hidden household heads I have described, who were living as subfamilies, chose the way to be "hidden" that is most common today. At the beginning of the twentieth century, there were other ways to be a hidden household head. However, these strategies required making choices that are both less available and less palatable now. Some single mothers, whose extended families could not or would not help support them, faced the challenging political economy by using long-term placement of their children in institutions such as orphanages, children's homes, or foster care, while themselves entering gainful employment. Enumerators rarely counted women coerced into this survival strategy as official household heads, and they could not be included here as hidden heads because they did not appear to be mothers in the census data.

In 1900, two other intermediate economic survival strategies were possible for women with children, especially within urban areas. They could be employed as servants and have their housing provided as part of the job, or they could live as boarders and lodgers, essentially renting space in someone else's home. These residential opportunities multiplied between 1860 and 1900 (Folbre 1991). Such living arrangements provided important alternatives to life within the traditional patriarchal family and offered a range of residential independence that also reflected varying degrees of economic independence (Folbre 1991, 88). Of course, not all employers would house servants' children, and lodging did not come with child care. Census records tell us a good deal about women lodgers and boarders but have insufficient information to reveal which servants were comparable to hidden household heads.

Although boarders and lodgers lived in someone else's home, they were not hidden subfamilies, dependent on other relatives. Although they were apparently independent women, they usually were not designated as household heads either. The vast majority of women lodgers (78 percent) were considered single-person households, called "primaries" in the Public Use Sample. Most were young and never married, often having moved from a family farm in search of a job. In 1900, only 1 percent of women lodgers or boarders were designated as family heads, but fully 70 percent of this small group were employed—a rate higher than the comparable female official household heads (50 percent) or the young, unmarried boarders (64 percent). Among the women primaries, 17 percent were widowed, 6 percent had an absent spouse or had been deserted, and 1 percent were divorced. These previously married women, whose marital status and lack of visible extended family made them seem like nonboarding official household heads, shared a comparable average employment rate (47 percent) with them. Such high employment rates among women boarders and lodgers are not surprising, since they had few obvious other resources—no home or farm of their own, for example. In a symbiotic fashion, they often lived in the homes of widowed official household heads, providing them with an independent income.

These residential options declined rapidly after the turn of the century, leaving the hidden subfamily strategy as the major alternative to being a female household head. By 1910, large rooming houses replaced family-based boardinghouses and, by 1920, domestic day work predominated over live-in work (Katzman 1978). These changes made the intermediate status of simultaneously living on one's own and in another's household increasingly difficult to maintain. By mid-century, many single mothers and other women were forced or able to become official household heads due to diminishing extended families and the lower frequency of kin living nearby. Access to a wider range of jobs, achieved by declining occupational segregation and more child-care services, as well as increased urban living facilitated women's establishing their own households. Furthermore, ideological and political support for women's official headship was found in the feminist and welfare rights movements of the 1960s, which, among other concerns, sought to improve the lives of the increasing numbers of never-married mothers. Because of these trends, this chapter has focused on hidden and official heads in 1900.

There have been continuities and changes in the characteristics of hidden and official household heads. At the beginning of the twentieth century, official female household heads were differentiated from women living in subfamilies by their older age and smaller household size. They had fewer extended family members or young children present. Official household heads tended to be urban dwellers, probably because urban households were often too crowded to contain subfamilies. In addition, urban immigrants or migrants had fewer kin, forcing more women into headship in cities.

A repeated theme in discussions of women's household headship is its purported association with immigration and ethnicity early in the century or with race after the 1960s. Popular discussion assumed that some racial-ethnic groups were more likely than others to tolerate men's desertion of their wives. On the surface it appeared that African-American and some immigrant women were overrepresented among official household heads in 1900, but a more complex multivariate approach clearly showed this was due to the underlying material conditions. Race or ethnicity per se did not determine official or hidden headship. Instead the economic and social conditions experienced by some national-origin groups, especially their migration patterns and average age, explained their situation. Whether or not this was true at century's end, some welfare proposals attempting to eliminate support to immigrant noncitizens were still based on the fear of a connection between immigration and the creation of female-headed households.

What does the beginning of the twentieth century tell us about the economic support strategies of women without husbands who headed households or subfamilies? First, we saw that official household heads, especially those with children in the household, had high rates of employment. However, even hidden household heads also had higher employment rates than the average woman. Overall, being young or black increased the likelihood of employment, but the middle-class status reflected in home ownership, the responsibility associated with dependents, or the alternative workers found in the presence of adult men decreased that probability. Some of these variables, such as age and the presence of young children, currently retain the same effects on official heads' work as they did in 1900, while being black now decreases instead of increases the likelihood of their employment (Browne 1997). According to Browne (1997), this change is associated with two factors that had little influence a century ago. The first is long-term welfare support, which was unavailable in 1900, while the second is education, especially dropping out of high school, which had limited effect on black women's jobs in the turn-of-the-century segregated economy. At the time, urban residence had no effect on female household heads' employment when all other factors were held constant, but farm residence was an important geographic factor. Today urban labor market characteristics do affect single mother's employment (Edin and Lein 1997).

In combination, these findings suggest that any reduction in contemporary federal support for official female household heads might not force them into hidden household headship. First, urban and suburban zoning regulations or occupancy limits in public housing could hamper the ability of subfamilies to join another household and might instead render them homeless. Second, few households provide the kind of subsistence that farm living once did. Third, in the last few decades, the increased availability of child care outside of the home and the decline in average family size have reduced the reliance of official female household heads on co-resident relatives. Indeed, in 1990, only 8.3 percent of all households contained extended family,[6] while in 1900 about 16 percent of all households did. Finally, cultural norms now stress the value of women's economic independence. Indeed, Gordon and McLanahan (1991) argue that single-parent children are currently more likely to live with an official household head rather than in a subfamily, owing to the current culture of independent living and not because of the changes in marital patterns associated with single parenthood (for example, widowhood in 1900 versus contemporary divorces or never marrying). Indeed, those female relatives who might help out female household heads are increasingly likely to hold jobs themselves, reflecting the positive value placed on women's economic autonomy in the late twentieth century. In fact, when an official female household head returns to subfamily status, her new household head might be her mother or grandmother, merely doubling up female-headed households.

Hence, having jobs available with which official (or hidden) household heads could support themselves remains a paramount concern at the turn of this new century as it was a century ago. Indeed, the most recent positive stereotype of a single mother is now the "welfare heroine" who is a model worker (Michel 1999). However, the late twentieth century growth of traditional "women's jobs," especially in the service sector, has not always provided sufficient income, leaving female household heads caught between a rock and a hard place and in pursuit of multiple income strategies.

7   Regional Segregation

Geography as a Context for Work

TWO TYPES of geographic disparity in labor market opportunities—those according to region and by population density—have caught the attention of researchers and workers alike. Geographic differences in employment rates are not so much due to physical terrain as they are to the economic, social, and demographic features of a specific area. In this way, place of residence sets a context that expands or limits a person's work possibilities—a fact of life that was as true at the beginning of the twentieth century as it is today.

Labor market disparities among regions occur because places tend to experience economic development at different points in time, resulting in uneven opportunities. At the beginning of the twentieth century, rapid growth in manufacturing and heavy industry was especially concentrated in the Northeast and Midwest. This growth was the subject of unionization drives, investigative journalists' reports, labor bureau studies, and social welfare concerns. More recently, in the 1970s, another surge in economic restructuring occurred when the corporate search for cheaper production costs resulted in a decline in U.S. industrial manufacturing, coupled with an expansion of the service sector. This process turned some of the busy northeastern and Midwestern centers of the U.S. economy into areas dubbed the rust belt, while new job growth was taking place in the sun-belt cities of the South and Southwest. Ironically, the regions most noted for their industrial growth at the beginning of the century had become the ones undergoing deindustrialization.

The second, and related, labor market disparity is encountered among areas of varying population density. Population density per se is not the force that shapes employment patterns; instead it is the other factors associated with it. Business growth creates a

190

demand for labor and, throughout most of the twentieth century, firms tried to locate near abundant sources of labor or production materials. At the same time, workers were drawn to those primarily urban jobs. In 1900, urbanization was the major social phenomenon, fed by high rates of immigration as well as by internal migration from rural farms. Although urban growth had gone on for some time, 53 percent of the U.S. population still lived in rural areas of 1,000 or fewer people. Hence, economic studies of the early twentieth century tended until recently to concentrate on individual cities, such as Boston, New York, Philadelphia, or Chicago; on particular racial-ethnic groups, especially the Irish, Italians, Jews, or African Americans; or on industries, like textiles, rather than examining national patterns.

Beginning after World War II, and supported by Veterans' Administration and Federal Housing Authority policy, a new residential pattern of suburbanization began to supplement the pattern of urbanization as people sought houses with some green space around them. The initial assumption was that jobs would remain in cities, but eventually corporations followed people to the suburbs, particularly attracted by increased percentages of women living there who chose to enter the labor force. Indeed, by the 1980s so many people and jobs had moved to the suburbs that social scientists were concerned over the potential mismatch between the skills of the often poor central-city residents and the jobs available to them locally (Wilson 1987). At the same time, employers also moved to the South in search of cheaper labor.

Throughout the twentieth century, such changing flows of labor supply, combined with corporate economic restructuring, fed shifts in both urban and regional development, interconnecting these two geographic patterns of employment change. Indeed, urban growth was the major route to higher regional rates of women's employment, but even in the early part of the century it could not have been the only factor. For example, although the North Atlantic and South Atlantic regions had very different proportions of their population living in urban areas in 1900— 77 percent and 28 percent, respectively—they had equally high women's employment rates (26 percent).

This chapter directly addresses how geographic location—defined as region and degree of urbanization—structured individual women's economic lives in 1900. It draws together various threads of discussion about the geographic, or contextual, effects on women's employment that are woven throughout this volume. Most significantly, I show that the employment opportunities associated with any location did not affect women in a uniform fashion. They varied in their impact on the work of married and single women as well as on women of varying racial-ethnic groups. Indeed, stereotypes about the employment patterns of any particular racial-ethnic group of women often held only for a single region or city, while a national comparison shows that another location could change a group's employment rates. Such associations of geographic location with women's employment rates remain a contemporary concern.

This chapter also explores which aspects of regions or cities provided employment opportunities or created barriers to them. How did the availability of manufacturing or agricultural work shape the demand for women's labor in different locations? How did the varying geographic distributions of racial-ethnic groups create different pools of female labor supply? The answers require looking at the societal level rather than at individual workers. Data about counties' economic and social features, such as number of manufacturing firms, manufacturing wages, number and size of farms, population density, and ethnic mix, illustrate how place of residence could set a context for work opportunities. In 1900, women living in the Northeast or urban areas had definite employment advantages. What were those advantageous conditions, and are they the same as the ones found today in the sun belt?

REGIONAL AND URBAN OPPORTUNITIES FOR WOMEN

Women who earned an income in 1900 usually were gainfully employed or taking in boarders. Table 26 shows the rates of women engaged in either of these economic pursuits and how region or urban versus rural location was associated with such work. The urban areas of the time included towns and cities of

TABLE 26   Geographic Differences in Individual Women's Economic
Opportunities, Age 15 or Older, 1900

Region or density	Total	Gainful employment*				Living with boarders*
		Manufac- turing	Domes- tic	Agri- culture	White collar	
Region (%)						
North Atlantic	26.1	10.6	8.0	0.4	4.6	11.6
(n = 9,713)						
South Atlantic	25.9	4.8	8.8	8.3	2.1	10.3
(n = 4,316)						
North Central	17.0	5.3	5.5	1.2	4.1	9.6
(n = 10,734)						
South Central	20.6	2.4	6.4	9.5	1.2	8.6
(n = 5,353)						
West	18.5	5.0	5.0	1.6	4.8	13.3
(n = 1,549)						
Population density (%)						
Urban	27.3	9.8	9.5	0.2	5.4	12.7
(n = 15,373)						
Rural	15.8	2.7	4.1	6.5	1.6	7.9
(n = 16,029)						
Total (%)†	21.7	6.3	6.8	3.4	3.5	10.3
(n = 31,665)						

*Analysis of variance F-statistics indicate that regional differences and urban-rural differences in each of the six columns are significant at $p < .001$.

†The total number of women across rural and urban areas is slightly less (n = 31,402) than the number across regions because of missing information on size of place.

1,000 people or more. These population centers may seem smaller than what we would now consider urban, but the contrast is really with rural areas of less than 1,000 people. The regions, however, as shown in Figure 1, remain comparable to the present ones.

Turning first to overall gainful employment, Table 26 (column 1) reveals that women's highest work rates—approximately 26 percent—were shared by North Atlantic and South Atlantic residents, while other regions were below the national average of 21.7 percent. This suggests that the often discussed North-South division in women's employment opportunities, based on the early growth of New England manufacturing, was no longer significant

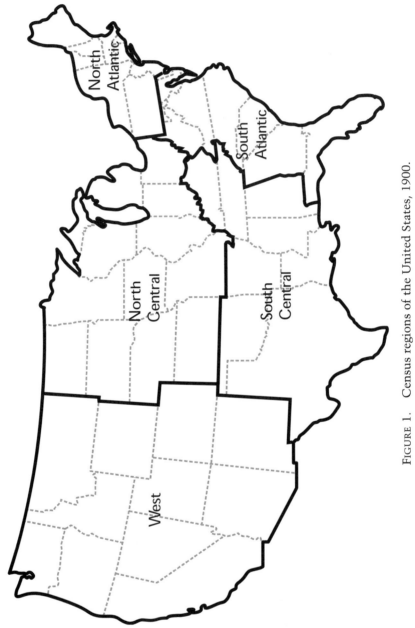

FIGURE 1. Census regions of the United States, 1900.

and that instead, the division was between the entire eastern seaboard and the remainder of the United States.

Such East-West differences appear to be related to the availability of jobs. The North Atlantic region had a higher percentage of adult women working in manufacturing jobs than any other area (Table 26, column 2), probably because many textile and garment firms were located in the Northeast. Manufacturing in other regions drew more on a male labor force. As Figure 2 illustrates, counties with a female manufacturing labor force of 25.4 percent or more were located primarily in the North Atlantic and South Atlantic regions.

Domestic service, women's most typical work in 1900, was significantly more common in the North and South Atlantic regions than elsewhere (Table 26, column 3), although the gap between the Atlantic Coast and other regions was not great. Meanwhile, the South Atlantic and South Central regions had considerably higher rates of women's recorded agricultural work than other areas (column 4). Neither the West nor the North Central region had high rates for these three traditional forms of women's work, thus fostering an East-West split in employment patterns. Only in the small but growing niche of white-collar work (column 5) did women in these two regions reach employment rates comparable to those in the North Atlantic.

In some ways, this dearth of women's employment, especially in the North Central region, seems odd. There was no East-West division in the distribution of groups whose adult women were most likely to seek work. Blacks were fairly evenly dispersed across the South, at 29 percent of the South Central and 33 percent of the South Atlantic region's population, while averaging only 2 percent in the North. First- and second-generation immigrant groups, among whom women were also frequently employed, especially when single, comprised 49 percent of the North Central region's population and 53 percent in the North Atlantic, but only 7 to 10 percent of the population in the two southern regions. These were southern and northern demographic patterns, not East-West ones.

One East-West difference did occur, at least in the North, and that was in the degree of urbanization. In the North Atlantic

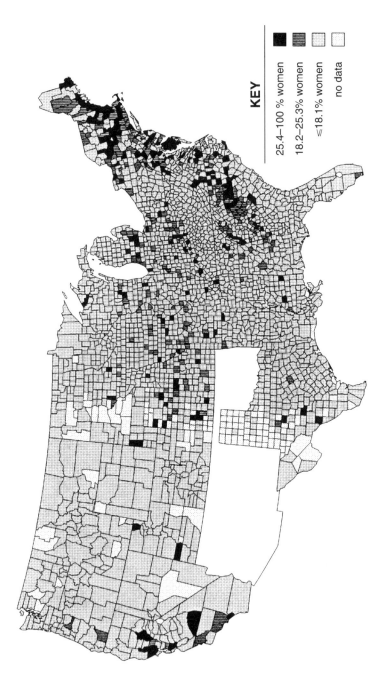

KEY

■	25.4–100 % women
▦	18.2–25.3% women
▧	≤18.1% women
□	no data

FIGURE 2. Women as a percentage of manufacturing wage earners, by county, 1900. This map is based on women age 16 or older, while census individual-level analyses are for women age 15 or older. The map is still a good approximation. Arizona, New Mexico, and Oklahoma are in the census data analyses, but are not included in the map data for 1900. The map was generated from data and software contained on the compact disk *Great American History Machine* (College Park, MD: University of Maryland, Academic Software Development Group, 1995).

region, 77 percent of the population lived in urban areas, compared to 46 percent in the North Central region and 47 percent
in the West. In the South there was no East-West gap because the
rates of urbanization generally were low: 28 percent in the South
Atlantic and 23 percent in the South Central region. The result-
ant North-South urbanization gap might have created a North-
South disparity in women's employment, but the high recorded
work rates of black women, who lived primarily in the South and
worked especially in agricultural work, overrode the North-South
differences on both the Atlantic seaboard and in the central
regions. On the other hand, first- and second-generation immigrant women's employment rates did not override the North
Atlantic-North Central gap in urban-based jobs. Why? First, there
was insufficient women's manufacturing or domestic employment in the North Central region to close the gap—the area was
not as urban as the North Atlantic region, and many of its firms
were engaged in male-dominated heavy manufacturing work,
rather than in textiles or garment production. Second, farm work
was rarely recorded for white or first- and second-generation
immigrant women, as it was for black women, but many more
immigrant or ethnic women lived in rural areas in the North
Central region (46 percent) than did so in the North Atlantic
region (12 percent).

I turn last to taking in boarders (Table 26, column 6), which
also was a source of income produced through women's labor. As
with other opportunities, the North Atlantic region offered good
conditions for this work, resulting in 11.6 percent of all adult
women living with boarders. Boarders tended to be immigrants
or rural-to-urban migrants, and both of these were abundant in
this region. Once again, rates for the South Atlantic region were
statistically similar to those for the North Atlantic.

Nonetheless, living with boarders was most common among
women residing in the West. The West was relatively newly set-
tled, both through migration and immigration, and often by men
who were alone and needed housing. On average, there were 1.5
men to every woman living in this region. Men went west to
homestead, ranch, or mine, seeking economic opportunity before
starting or bringing their families with them, and creating male-

to-female ratios as high as 1.7:1 in rural areas. A second factor was that the West shared comparable percentages of first-generation immigrants with the North Atlantic (33 and 31, respectively). Some immigrants went westward by migrating from the East, and others, like the Chinese, arrived directly on the Pacific Coast. In sum, the difference found in women's gainful employment rates between the eastern seaboard and the remainder of the country was supplemented by a bicoastal-central division in access to boarders. Neither of the central regions had as large an immigrant population (24 and 4 percent, respectively) as the West or the North Atlantic, reducing their numbers of potential boarders. In addition, the South Central region had fewer rural migrants to cities than the neighboring Atlantic or Pacific coastal areas, resulting in the smallest urban population of any region (23 percent) and the largest farms.

All told, the effects of *population density* were predictable: urban areas had higher rates of both women's gainful employment and taking in boarders than did rural ones. In contrast, the *regional* patterns in women's work were surprising. First, in spite of differences in their rates of urbanization or their characteristic forms of women's work, the North and South Atlantic regions had fairly similar overall women's employment rates. Second, the North Central region had persistently low women's employment rates, presenting an interesting conundrum that is partially explained by the racial-ethnic demography of the regions. Black women, living primarily in the South, were the most likely to report agricultural work and thus raised South Atlantic employment rates, while first- and second-generation immigrant women in the North Central region rarely reported farm work, keeping women's employment rates down in this predominantly rural area. Even so, the North Central-North Atlantic employment difference might have been mitigated if more female-dominated manufacturing work had been available in the North Central states. This kind of demographic explanation raises an interesting question: Did the same regional and rural-urban variations in women's employment rates hold for all racial-ethnic groups?

Differing Regional and Urban Employment for Black, White, and Other Racial-Ethnic Women

Studies of the early twentieth century often note that, within cities or within the Northeast, women of different racial-ethnic backgrounds also had different employment rates. Although such variations in women's employment *within* regions have been amply described, especially for the Northeast, little systematic attention has been paid to national variation *across* regions in the employment rates of women from any single racial-ethnic group. That is, do different regional economic possibilities set a context that allows group members to have high rates of women's employment in one region but restricts them in another? This question was rarely asked partly because detailed ethnic case studies focused on only one city at a time and partly because groups were assumed to reside primarily in one region or another. Yet in 1900, women of most racial-ethnic groups actually resided in at least two of the five regions identified in the census. The exceptions are groups with little representation in the sample and who therefore appear to have lived predominantly in one region—Italians in the North Atlantic region, and Asians and Native Americans in the West.

It was initially assumed by some researchers that a few cultural groups, such as the Irish, French Canadians, or African Americans, held beliefs that were very supportive of women's paid work simply because their employment rates were high, while others, like Italians, were assumed to be culturally opposed to it. Such studies were written when social history focused on the individual or micro-level case studies, while recent research is more nationally comparative.

Now, other determinants are recognized as equally or more important, such as the average economic needs of the group, women's skills, or the type of women's work that was seen as desirable by a particular group. As an example of the latter, young, single Italian women were unlikely to do much servant work, away from Italian male protection, but would do jobs ranging from factory outwork in their homes to farm and field tasks when the family worked together. Thus, cultural opposition rarely prohibited all types of women's earning, but it might restrict the range of "permissible" jobs. These restrictions could raise or lower a group's rate of female employment more in some geographic locations than in others.

Indeed, the data show that geography and its economic correlates did shape women's employment opportunities, no matter what the cultural preferences might have been. Overall, eleven of the racial-ethnic groups considered here had significantly different women's employment rates across the regions of the United States and/or between rural and urban areas. Those groups whose rates did not vary also could not vary, because they were geographically concentrated. Location undoubtedly influenced which groups took in boarders as well, but there were too few women in the census sample doing this work to study them simultaneously according to racial-ethnic group and geography.

Regional location or urban-rural residence, while important to almost all racial-ethnic groups, primarily affected single women and not the employment of wives living with their husbands. Even geography did little to override the importance of marital status. As described in Chapter 3, married women's employment rates averaged 4.3 percent and were less than 5 percent among most first- and second-generation immigrant women and all white women (third-generation immigrant or later). Only married women of color reported high gainful employment rates, at 23 percent of black, 18 percent of Asian, and 9 percent of Native American wives. Region of residence affected wives' employment in the aggregate. Their work rates were 10 and 8 percent in the South Atlantic and South Central regions, but only 3 and 2 percent in the North Atlantic and North Central regions, respectively. These differences actually reflected the regional distributions of demographic groups, especially the greater number of blacks in the South, rather than different economic opportunities for wives. We know this was true because only one of the individual racial-ethnic groups showed any significant differences in married women's employment rates by region. The exception was white wives, whose 1.7 percent employment rate in the North Central region was significantly lower than their 3.5 percent rate in the South Atlantic—a very small difference at that. In sum, families of any racial-ethnic group either needed wives' employment or they avoided it, but opportunity for wives' paid employment did not vary much by region.

Urban-rural differences in wives' overall employment were less than 1 percent—smaller than the variation by region—and, once again, there were few employment differences among married women of the same ethnicity. These included some small significant differences for Russian wives, who reported higher work in rural areas (3 versus 0 percent), and for white wives, who held more employment in urban than in rural areas (3 and 2 percent, respectively). However, the only large effects were found among black wives, who reported 30 percent employment in urban areas and 20 percent in rural ones. In general, urban residence did not greatly change the work opportunities for wives except among African Americans.

In contrast, the influence of geography on the employment of single women from various racial-ethnic groups was substantial. This group of "singles" actually included a diversity of women who had never married or were widowed, divorced, or separated, but their work patterns represented a sharp contrast to those of wives. Single women's average rates of employment went from a low of 26 or 31 percent among Native American and Latin American women, respectively, to a high of 64 percent among French Canadian, Russian and black women. These figures, as shown in Table 27, confirm the racial-ethnic variation in work patterns that is often discussed for this period.

More consequential is that, for ten of the fourteen racial-ethnic groups, single women had employment rates that varied significantly, depending on the region where they resided. The most consistent difference occurred between higher rates of employment in the North Atlantic region and lower rates in the North Central region. This is the same East-West pattern I found at the national level, and it occurred for white women and almost all national-origin groups, at least when they had representation in both northern regions, while black women were largely unaffected by this phenomenon. In addition, there were few North-South employment differences except among the three groups having some representation in both locations: whites and the two

TABLE 27. Geographic Variation in Percentage of Single Women Gainfully Employed, by Racial-Ethnic Group, Age 15 or Older, 1900

Race or ethnicity	Region					Population density		Overall gainful employment (single women)
	North Atlantic	South Atlantic	North Central	South Central	West	Rural	Urban	
White*** (n = 7,149)	40	31	31	23	34	25	41	33
Black***(D) (n = 1,706)	68	65	52	64	83	61	69	64
Irish*** (n = 1,614)	59	25	47	37	46	34	57	54
British*** (n = 679)	49	22	34	25	31	29	45	40
Scandinavian*** (n = 398)	80	—†	42	—	46	28	67	48
German*** (n = 1,662)	53	41	44	25	19	30	50	45
Eastern European*** (n = 196)	69	—	42	14	—	19	63	52
Russian*** (n = 98)	76	—	32	—	—	21	71	64
Italian (n = 55)	50	—	—	—	—	29	53	50

TABLE 27. *Continued*

Race or ethnicity	Region					Population density		Overall gainful employment (single women)
	North Atlantic	South Atlantic	North Central	South Central	West	Rural	Urban	
French Canadian**(R)/***(D) (n = 152)	70	—	57	—	—	30	71	64
English Canadian*** (n = 412)	62	—	40	—	58	37	58	52
Latin American*(R)/***(D) (n = 66)	71	33	—	18	56	8	46	31
Asian (n = 6)	67 (n = 3)	—	—	0 (n = 1)	50 (n = 2)	50 (n = 2)	50 (n = 4)	50
Native American (n = 33)	—	—	0	50	41	28	—	26
Total*** (n = 14,306)	50	43	37	37	37	32	50	42

Note: Significance levels from analysis of variance F-statistics: $^*p \leq .05$; $^{**}p \leq .01$; $^{***}p \leq .001$. "(R)" indicates significance for region differences and "(D)" indicates significance for rural-urban, or density, differences. If no letter is indicated, the same level of significance holds for region and density differences of that racial-ethnic group.

The total number of women for each racial-ethnic group is based on the five regions. Totals may be slightly lower for rural-urban distributions since the size of place was not always recorded in the census Public Use Sample, but the region was almost always known.

†Dashes indicate that fewer than five women of the racial-ethnic group resided in that particular geographic area (in our sample) and the resulting percentages would be too unreliable to report. An exception is made in the case of Asian women, since following the rule of five would result in no reportable data on them. Their percentages should be interpreted with caution.

largest, oldest ethnic groups. The North Atlantic employment rates of both Irish and white women were significantly higher than in either southern region, while the North Central rates of German and white women's employment were higher than in the South Central region.

Within rural and within urban areas, single women's employment patterns varied considerably by racial-ethnic group, as Table 27 (columns 6 and 7) illustrates. In rural areas, on average, 32 percent of single women reported employment, but the rates ranged from a low of 8 percent among Latin Americans to a high of 61 percent among blacks. In urban areas, on average fully 50 percent of single women were employed, starting at 41 percent among white women (if we discount the lack of employment among the small numbers of urban Native American women) and rising to 71 percent for Russian and French Canadians.

More important for exploring the power of geographic contextual effects is the fact that single women of most racial-ethnic groups had higher urban than rural employment. The only exceptions were Asian and Native American women, whose higher rural employment reflects their agricultural concentration but can only be taken as suggestive because of the small number of cases. In general, cities offered women more diverse employment opportunities than rural places. The effect of urban living was strongest for single Latin American women, whose low rural employment rates increased almost sixfold in cities. They went from rarely recorded farm and other agricultural work to frequent employment as servants. They had more work opportunities, but occupationally segregated ones. Urban living also increased Eastern European and Russian women's work by more than threefold and Scandinavian and French Canadian women's work rates by more than twofold.

Interestingly, the city effect was relatively small for single black women. But they already reported far more work in rural settings (61 percent) than women of other groups, perhaps nearing some ceiling effect, so that cities could increase their employment by only 8 percent. Similarly, married black women had both the highest rural and urban employment rates (20 and 30 percent, respectively) among wives. Black women, whose families may have most needed their employment, maximized all opportunities in both settings and made work compatible with marriage to the greatest extent possible. The city effect was comparatively unimportant to other married women, who rarely reported work. Instead, cities helped maximize work opportunities and sharply increased employment rates for most single women because of an increased demand for their labor and decreased social disapproval of their recording work.

Consequently, geography had fairly systematic effects on the employment patterns of women from most racial-ethnic groups, and cultural preferences were shaped by or adapted to the regional or urban job offerings. In order to understand what it was about urban life that increased employment rates, or about the North Central area that decreased women's recorded work, we need to shift our focus away from the experiences of individual women.

County-Level Differences
in Economic Opportunities

By turning to aggregate data on counties, we learn about location-related features that shaped the work context. Data for counties, available through the Inter-University Consortium for Political and Social Research (ICPSR), provide some limited information about the labor supply and demand features of whole geographic areas in the United States during 1900. These counties can be organized into regions, just as individual women were for earlier analyses.

Many factors shaped demand for labor, although only some of these can be directly measured. Population density is an indirect indicator of early nineteenth century labor demand that is useful because it serves as a proxy for economic development. Cities were job centers offering more women's employment in manufacturing, domestic, and white-collar work than the rural areas. Two other available indicators more specifically measure the differences within that growing urban industrial economy. The first is average firm size: larger firms needed more employees, although they might not necessarily employ women. The second is average county manufacturing wages for women. Paying higher

TABLE 28.   County-Level Differences in Labor Demand and Supply Factors by Region, 1900

Factor	Region					
	North Atlantic	South Atlantic	North Central	South Central	West	Avg.
Population density (per square mile)	497	77	56	34	34	87
Manufacturing wages ($)	252	178	222	217	291	223
Firm size (no. of employees)	10.9	8.7	4.5	4.6	4.7	5.9
Farm size (acres)	96.5	117.1	201.4	2,980.9	457.9	924.5
% Black women	1.4	35.3	1.3	24.2	0.4	13.6
% 1st- or 2nd-gen. immigrant women	33.7	2.5	39.6	6.8	39.8	23.6
No. of counties (for density)*	225	509	1,031	740	291	

Note: Each factor row (excluding No. of counties) represents an analysis of variance. All F-statistics were significant at $p \le .001$.

*There are slight differences in the county sample size per region, depending on the missing data for each measure. Large sample reductions occur only for county-level women's average manufacturing wages in the South Atlantic, North Central, and South Central regions, where only 366, 887, and 422 counties, respectively, reported this measure.

wages to women indicated a need to attract labor: more women workers were sought, and there was labor demand.

Table 28 shows how the counties within each geographic region varied on these measures. North Atlantic counties were by far the most densely populated, with an average of 497 people per square mile, compared to fewer than 77 people for each of the other regions' counties. In addition, North Atlantic counties had the largest business firms, and they paid women's wages that were higher than anywhere else except in the West (where few women resided). Thus, there was considerable demand for women's labor in the North Atlantic region. South Atlantic counties also had relatively large firms, but the average county manufacturing wages paid to women were considerably lower than elsewhere—a feature that was still true later in the century and that helped foster sunbelt job growth, as northern businesses moved south to reduce wage costs. As might be expected from the results among individual women, North Central counties measured significantly lower than North Atlantic ones on all three demand indicators. Furthermore, the North and South Central regions were not distinguished from each other on any of them.

In contrast to the effects of these urban and industrial demand measures, which were associated with increased women's employment, rural work in agriculture could diminish women's recorded employment because their farm labor often went uncounted (see Chapter 2). Thus the number or size of farms in a county could, ironically, be considered demand-reducing factors. However, the only significant regional difference in these two factors was that farms in South Central counties were tremendous in size, in contrast to those in the rest of the nation. In particular, Texas farms (or ranches) averaged over 8,800 acres. These large ranches primarily were concentrated in a few counties, but they tended to push up this region's average. Such large farms might have required housekeeping work for resident employees and certainly increased the distance to the nearest town, leading me to expect a reduction in women's off-farm employment in the South Central region. This dampening effect also occurred in the western states, where farms tended to be over 400 acres, while farms in the North and South Atlantic and North Central regions generally were 200 acres or less in size.

There are two potential measures of women's labor supply in a county available in ICPSR data for 1900. These are the county percentages of black women or first- and second-generation immigrant women. Because both groups were among the most likely to seek employment, counties with large percentages of either one would have a substantial supply of women's labor. Although a large supply of workers does not guarantee the existence of jobs, it is plausible that women's gainful employment rates would be higher in such areas. Table 28 shows that the population of South Atlantic counties averaged 35 percent black women and the South Central region averaged 24 percent, with negligible rates elsewhere. Meanwhile, the county populations of the North Atlantic, North Central, and western regions averaged between 34 and 40 percent first- and second-generation immigrant women, with less than 7 percent elsewhere. These figures indicate a considerable female labor supply in every region. However, this supply was differentiated: each region tended to have large percentages of either black or first- and second-generation immigrant women, but never of both. The early twentieth century predated the great migration of blacks to the North, and indeed, only 22 percent of black women had even moved from the state in which they were born, in contrast to 28 percent of white women.

On the whole, the differences shown in Table 28 seem to suggest that labor demand differentiated the counties of each region more than did labor supply. To test this hypothesis I used the statistical technique of ordinary least squares regression to predict the percentage of women employed in each county. The predictive variables I included were the two county-level labor supply factors (percentages of black women and of first- and second-generation immigrant women), the four county-level demand factors (percent urban, average female manufacturing wages, firm size, and farm size), and additional controls for region. The results (not shown) indicated that the general demand factor of urbanization was the single major predictor of women's recorded paid work. Because the more specific demand factors—farm size, firm size, and women's manufacturing wages—were not significant, other aspects of economic development must have been the source of women's employment advantage in cities. One factor, for example, was that cities offered less unpaid work in a family farm or business, in which women's labor contributions were seen merely as an extension of their roles as wives and daughters. Instead, cities offered women considerably more full-time paid work than did rural areas. In addition, some urban-based industries, such as garment and textile work or domestic service, drew heavily on a female work force.

Among women workers themselves, the only statistically important supply factor was the percentage of black women, and its effect was about half that of urbanization (judged by comparing standardized beta coefficients of .07 and .14, respectively). Although black women's labor supply was statistically important, first- and second-generation immigrant women's was not. In sum, demand was indeed more important than supply in predicting women's work.

Nonetheless, even when these supply and demand factors are taken into account, North Central counties still had significantly lower women's employment rates than North Atlantic ones. In fact, this regional impact was somewhat stronger than that of labor supply (beta = −.10). Earlier I suggested that this regional effect could be due to the different levels of urbanization but, since that factor is already controlled for in the regression, features I was unable to measure at a county level must cause the difference. As suggested by the analysis of individual women's work, that cause was the different industrial composition of the two Northern regions—the North Central region had less of the kinds of manufacturing in garment and textile work that helped draw women into the North Atlantic labor force.

CONCLUSIONS

Three main geographic-contextual factors shaped the national variation in women's gainful employment in 1900. Degree of urbanization, also measured as county population density, was the most important of these influences, creating opportunities for single women to leave family-based farm work and enter factory, domestic, clerical, or craft work. However, because occupational sex and race segregation were both higher in urban than in rural areas, the increased availability of paid work in cities was accompanied by increased separation of men and women's tasks and of white from black women's work.

The second important influence was region. At the county level, living in the North Central area reduced the employment rates for all women. At an individual level, women of most racial-ethnic groups also exhibited regional variations in their work rates, illustrating that cultural preferences for a particular form of women's work were often molded by the opportunities available. "Culture," as revealed in employment patterns, was not a constant but varied by region and degree of urbanization.

Finally, as a variable, race acted contextually. Higher percentages of black women in a county were associated with increased women's employment rates. The same effect was found within and outside of the South, but it is not surprising, as both married and single black women had the highest employment rates when looked at from an individual level. However, I had expected that large percentages of immigrant women would have the same aggregate or contextual effect, and they did not. Perhaps the reluctance of *married* first- and second-generation immigrant women to record paid employment, in contrast to that of married black women, reduced the apparent labor supply of the former more than the latter.

Indeed, there was one constant effect that we have seen in other chapters as well—being married usually dampened women's employment rates, and, with the exception of black women, married women's employment remained fairly unaffected by geography.

In combination, the three contextual effects and the fixed effect of marriage meant there were two groups of women with little geographic variation in their employment patterns: single black women *and* married white or first- and second-generation immigrant women. Single black women's consistently high rates of employment were based on economic need. The census did not collect information on income for this period, but black families' household heads held jobs of lower status than other groups, averaging prestige scores of 12, compared to the national figure of 22. Furthermore, the jobs black women could obtain were unlikely to pay well, both because of their concentration in the agricultural South and and because of their own comparatively low literacy rates (55 percent versus the national female average of 90 percent). Indeed, black residential segregation in the South substituted for occupational segregation by race in this period. Although they were often excluded from manufacturing jobs, when they did such work, black women also found they lived in counties where it paid less than anywhere else ($207 per year, when the national average was $239). Thus, high rates of employment among black women reflected many forms of racism and exclusion.

White and (non-Asian) first- and second-generation immigrant wives represented another extreme, with consistently low rates of employment. In their case, they found it difficult to combine work and family because most paid employment was full-time and outside of the home. Most white women (61 percent) lived in rural areas and had little access to paid work. For others, the only paid part-time work available was home-based: factory outwork, hand laundry work, or taking in boarders. With larger families than today (averaging 4.7 persons) and little available child care, it was difficult for women to leave their homes for the kind of employment that would be recorded. Their low rates of employment also represented exclusion, but primarily based on patriarchy.

Even now, at the beginning of the twenty-first century, with more child care, more part-time paid work, and less family-based unpaid agricultural work, geography still influences women's employment. The location effect is still a function of labor demand, but labor supply factors have changed and have some effect, too (Jones and Rosenfeld 1989). As noted in Chapter 3, differences among married and single women are rarely important now, as neither marriage nor motherhood prevents women's employment (Goldin 1990). Although labor markets with higher proportions of married women meant women had lower proportions of the jobs, this effect declined between 1950 and 1980 (Jones and Rosenfeld 1989). Indeed, by the 1970s, inflation and the erosion of men's wages meant that most families needed two earners (Kodras and Padavic 1993), further increasing the supply of women workers.

Around World War II, demand also increased for women workers, since the occupations that were growing were traditional women's jobs (Oppenheimer 1976). Another major shift in labor demand occurred in the 1970s as rapid industrial restructuring occurred, characterized by the relocation of many manufacturing industries and an escalation of service employment. While in 1900, urbanization and the loss of agriculture were spurs to women's employment, in the 1970s employment for women grew in small to midsize cities and in suburbs.

In 1900, manufacturing work was most available for women in the North Atlantic, but by mid-century (1920–1970) it was also located in the South Atlantic and South Central regions (Kodras and Padavic 1993). By 1980, manufacturing firms were taking advantage of declining agricultural opportunities in the small towns of the rural South to hire more women at low wages. In addition, they increased female employment through the shifting industrial concentrations in western metropolitan areas, such as California's Silicon Valley, in which canneries disappeared, to be replaced by microprocessor firms, often leaving unchanged the race and sex segregation within the manufacturing sector. At the same time, women's manufacturing jobs were declining in the North Atlantic region. This shift has been described as a transfer of work to the sun belt. Indeed, Jones and Rosenfeld (1989) found that residence in the South increased women's share of employment.

Women's white-collar work, which was rare in 1900 and was clustered in the North Atlantic and North Central regions, expanded over the century. Kodras and Padavic (1993) show that women's work in the nonprofessional services exhibited little geographic variation during the 1970s, but women's professional work, which previously had concentrated in university towns, state capitals, and large metropolitan areas, became more widely diffused, showing considerable growth in many East Coast cities. Comparably, Jones and Rosenfeld (1989) have shown that labor markets with government or public administration jobs also had higher rates of women's employment.

There is no doubt that geographic setting continuously affects women's job opportunity, although there are few permanent links between location and occupation, especially for manufacturing. The services and nonprofessional white-collar jobs are more likely to be evenly distributed geographically.

8 Epilogue

CONTEMPORARY DISCUSSIONS about globalization of the economy or global interdependency often start with "as the United States becomes more diverse. . . ." This recent discourse too handily dismisses old realities, including the fact that diversity has always been an integral part of U.S. society. We could easily call the time around 1900 a period of diversity as well, although the old images of assimilation and the mythical melting pot have a strong hold on the public imagination. Immigration was as serious a public issue a century ago, with 14 percent of the population foreign born, as it is now, with about 9 percent foreign born. Indeed, the number of immigrants residing in the United States has risen only recently from a century low of 9.6 million in 1970 to 25.2 million in 1998, creating new parallels between 1900 and 2000. Only the immigrant groups' countries of origin have changed. Many of the public issues are similar. In fact, there was the same hostility toward the Chinese in the nineteenth century as there might be toward the so-called "Asian gangs" today. Immigrant groups like the Jews and Irish were once considered to be "nonwhite" in the same way that Latinos of all hues are now thought of as "people of color" (Brodkin 1998; Ignatiev 1995). In 1900, public schools insisted on teaching in English, not unlike the current advocates of the English-only movement.

As world systems theorists and international development theorists agree, migration within countries and immigration between them have both gone on for quite some time and are likely to continue. What is unusual is immigrants' maintaining transnational connections through strong bidirectional contacts and travel between the United States and the countries of origin. Indeed, many transnational communities have been created, especially with the countries of Latin America and the Caribbean (Acosta-Belén and Bose 2000). We should therefore expect continued racial-ethnic diversity among women (and men) well into the twenty-first century's political economy. In fact, the 2000 census recognized some of this diversity by adding several biracial categories and allowing for other multiracial ones in their racial-ethnic background question.

The increase in contemporary immigration, facilitated by the Immigration Acts of 1965 and 1976, is related to the increased globalization of the U.S. economy. Like immigration, globalization reached its previous peak between 1900 and 1910. Indeed, the world's economies were equally as interconnected then as now. According to Uchitelle (1998), trade and foreign investment, which are key measures of global integration, have only recently attained the higher levels they had before two world wars and the global Great Depression dismantled many of the previous global connections. He writes, "foreign direct investment as a percentage of the world's total output reached 9 percent in 1913; in the mid-1990s it was 10.1 percent, up from 4.4 percent in 1960." Thus, in a second sense, there are parallels between the beginning and the end of the twentieth century. Yet, while globalization itself is not new, its forms have changed. Globalization is no longer structured by the maneuvers of colonial governments but by the activities of transnational corporations.

As a result, there have been changes in the internal U.S. economic landscape over the century. The economic significance of agriculture had declined considerably by mid-century, and the importance of heavy industry began its decline in the 1970s, reducing the number of blue-collar employment opportunities that did not require higher education. Many manufacturing jobs have moved directly to their new source of labor—in developing countries. One result is a parallel structure in the gendered division of labor within the United States and in many developing countries. For example, immigrant women are still likely to work in the textile industry (either through home subcontracting or in small shops), but they also work in light industry such as electronics and computer assembly, similar to jobs held by other women in their countries of origin. Immigrant women's labor has also been integrated into the expanding service economy. Indeed, the fact that so many immigrant women still work in domestic service or child care has recently been referred to as "the international division of reproductive labor" (Parreñas 2000). It is household labor such as theirs that frees other women to enter the paid labor force.

Regional diversity in the U.S. economic structure remains as important a theme in 2000 as it was in 1900, even if the regions where job growth is concentrated have changed. Such geographically based opportunities have always been a combined function of industrial location and racial-ethnic group distributions across the regions. Therefore, it is not surprising that Frey and DeVol (2000) expect one of the driving demographic forces in the early twenty-first century to be this new wave of immigration. It is already creating metropolitan areas of diversity and ethnic concentrations in California and the West, in contrast to the heartland, which is less diverse. Although the specific regions of immigrant concentration may have changed, even in 1900 there were regions of the country with relatively few foreign-born persons.

Although the "traditional family" was never as widespread as ideology would have it, families too have changed over the century. Desertion is relatively uncommon now, but divorce rates have been increasing gradually for over one hundred years. The median age at which women marry had attained what was considered a high point of 21.9 years in 1900, but it then declined until 1970, and gradually increased again to reach a new peak of 24.4 years in the 1990s. As a consequence of this change, about 53 percent of adult women are married now, compared to 61 percent in 1900. There are fewer extended families (8 percent) than there were in 1900 (16 percent), but there are more blended families, step-families, female-headed households, gay and lesbian couples, and cohabiting relationships. Concomitantly, the impact of household context and marital status on women's employment has been muted, and employment is now determined more by a woman's own education and her family's need for multiple earners.

The need for multiple income strategies is not new. In 1900, the second earner was likely to be an adult son, daughter, or other relative, rather than the wife of the household head. At that time, with more family enterprises and farms than now, wives did considerable subsistence work that helped generate family income but gave married women only an "invisible wage": their work was hidden by men's self-employment. By the middle of the twentieth century this type of work had achieved a name, the "two-person single career," but then the census counted it as a job only when a spouse contributed 15 hours or more per week to the family business. Indeed, at an international level, the United Nations is still struggling with how best to count women's unpaid production of household goods or other home-based work in their System of National Accounts, and the International Labor Organization is trying to decide how to count subsistence agriculture effectively in their International Standard Classification of Occupations.

In the United States, the nature of work has changed, and labor market shifts have meant that women's economic contributions are more visible now than they were one hundred years ago. The expansion of service and clerical work and the growth of paid part-time jobs drew women into counted employment. Today, fully 60 percent of all women are employed, but this does not mean that equity has been achieved. Occupational sex segregation has been reduced but not eradicated: in 1996 only 55 percent of all employed women work full-time year-round, and their median annual earnings were 74 percent of men's (Briefing Paper 1998). Unfortunately, two-thirds of the growth in women's wages since 1980 has been due to the decline in men's real wages. So we still need further progress for both women and men in the current U.S. political economy.

Finally, although not an explicit subject of this book, it is important to note that women have not been mere victims of the political economy they face but have been active architects of their own opportunities. Women's labor organizations and feminist alliances as well as groups emphasizing more general social issues have had several periods of resurgence throughout the century and should be expected to continue to do so in the future. I anticipate that their quests for equity will continue to influence the productive lives of women, no matter what strategies they use.

Appendix

Supplementary Tables

APPENDIX TABLE A.1.   Logistic Regression Predicting Boarders' Presence Among Wives and Female Household Heads, Ages 15–64, 1900

Variable	b	Probability of boarders present	
		Overall	Unit change
Individual characteristics			
Female head, has job	.747***	.21	.10
Female head, no job	.422***	.16	.05
Age	.002		
Ethnicity			
Italian	.785***	.21	.10
Eastern European	.621***	.19	.08
Russian	.639***	.19	.08
French Canadian	.480*	.17	.06
Scandinavian	.351*	.15	.04
German	−.225*	.09	−.02
Irish	−.153		
British	−.166		
English Canadian	−.045		
Latin American	−.489		
Social class			
Proportion employed	−.438*	.07	−.04
Home ownership	−.216***	.09	−.02
Male head's occupation (vs. agriculture)			
Professional	.374***	.15	.04
Clerical and sales	−.093		
Operative or laborer	.216*	.13	.02
Craft	−.061		
Service	.288		
Unclassified work	.251		
Unemployed	−.225		

(continued)

Appendix Table A.1.   *Continued*

Variable	b	Probability of boarders present Overall	Probability of boarders present Unit change
Household composition			
No. of children, 0–9 yr	−.098***	.10	−.01
No. of adolescents, 10–14 yr	−.153***	.10	−.01
No. of adults, 15–64 yr	−.055*	.10	−.01
No. of seniors, 65+ yr	−.284**	.08	−.03
Geographic context			
Urban (vs. rural)	.349***	.15	.04
Avg. women's manufacturing wage	.001		
% Immigrant women in county	.002		
Constant	−2.157***		
No. of households	15,411		
Overall % correct	89.0%		
Regression χ^2	15,471***		
Avg. probability of boarder presence		.11	

*p ≤.05; **p ≤.01; ***p ≤ .001. Probabilities were not calculated when variables did not significantly affect the presence or absence of boarders.

APPENDIX TABLE A.2. Logistic Regression of Gainful Employment on Class, Racial-Ethnic, and Gender Structure Variables for Women of Seven Racial-Ethnic Groups, Ages 15–64, 1900

Variable	White b (SE)	Black b (SE)	Irish b (SE)	German b (SE)	Eastern European b (SE)	Russian b (SE)	French Canadian b (SE)
Class and economic structures							
Reads a language/literacy	-.413* (.164)	-.178 (.122)	.204 (.353)	.452 (.499)	.341 (.676)	2.923 (1.640)	1.027 (.803)
Head's occupation							
Professional or manager	.207 (.125)	-.524 (.494)	-1.174*** (.331)	.460 (.293)	.224 (1.049)	-5.134* (2.229)	-.098 (1.519)
Clerical and sales	.451** (.160)	.253 (.714)	-.307 (.396)	.183 (.402)	.850 (1.541)	.946 (2.294)	1.022 (1.655)
Craft	.545*** (.118)	-.085 (.329)	-.286 (.322)	1.081*** (.267)	.813 (.968)	-.045 (2.387)	-.547 (1.007)
Operative and laborer	.616*** (.114)	.318* (.161)	-.122 (.266)	.785** (.269)	.828 (.888)	-.617 (2.288)	.809 (.951)
Service	.449* (.192)	.735** (.254)	.131 (.355)	1.488*** (.387)	1.248 (1.379)	no cases	-1.325 (1.878)
Unclassified	.406 (.284)	.325 (.868)	-.202 (.522)	.392 (.506)	-5.692 (28.229)	-10.871* (4.711)	12.797 (99.638)
Unemployed	.880*** (.132)	.521 (.296)	.214 (.277)	1.203*** (.285)	1.104 (1.086)	3.153 (2.573)	1.908 (1.433)
Woman respondent is household head	1.432*** (.128)	2.673*** (.254)	-.166 (.310)	1.271*** (.303)	.935 (1.149)	-.755 (2.912)	-.611 (1.310)

(continued)

APPENDIX TABLE A.2. *Continued*

Variable	White b (SE)	Black b (SE)	Irish b (SE)	German b (SE)	Eastern European b (SE)	Russian b (SE)	French Canadian b (SE)
Class and economic structures *(continued)*							
Proportion employed in household	2.973*** (.220)	4.337*** (.383)	.343 (.409)	1.185** (.415)	-1.976 (1.463)	.065 (3.369)	-1.294 (2.147)
Boarders present	.362*** (.094)	.243 (.174)	.015 (.205)	.189 (.196)	1.443* (.744)	-4.263* (2.043)	.214 (.630)
Extended family present	-.105 (.075)	-.107 (.132)	.348* (.149)	.040 (.151)	-.333 (.570)	.856 (1.471)	-.122 (.579)
Servants present	-.631*** (.143)	-1.076 (.825)	.110 (.377)	-.564 (.359)	-.778 (1.178)	-5.901* (2.793)	-7.323 (35.754)
Avg. women's manufacturing wages	-.001* (.001)	.000 (.001)	.003 (.002)	.004* (.002)	.006 (.005)	-.026 (.016)	.002 (.011)
Avg. firm size	.001 (.005)	.002 (.008)	.023 (.012)	-.001 (.011)	.021 (.046)	.174 (.119)	.154** (.058)
Racial-ethnic structures							
2nd-gen. immigrant	omitted	omitted	.314 (.194)	-.285 (.160)	-1.053 (.600)	-7.647** (2.656)	-.300 (.588)
County ethnic mix	.005* (.002)	.001 (.006)	.013** (.005)	.014*** (.004)	-.021 (.018)	-.046 (.042)	-.030 (.026)
% Black women in county	.006* (.003)	.025*** (.003)	-.007 (.019)	.023 (.013)	-.278* (.112)	.287 (.341)	.197 (.224)
% Other race in county	.024 (.040)	.223* (.091)	-.841** (.338)	.009 (.110)	-3.218* (1.585)	3.890 (22.343)	3.883 (2.328)

APPENDIX TABLE A.2. *Continued*

Variable	White b (SE)	Black b (SE)	Irish b (SE)	German b (SE)	Eastern European b (SE)	Russian b (SE)	French Canadian b (SE)
Racial-ethnic structures (*continued*)							
South Atlantic	-.120 (.143)	-.082 (.410)	-.423 (.586)	.116 (.491)	1.064 (32.855)	-16.754 (48.850)	no cases
North Central	-.227** (.086)	-.456 (.379)	-.196 (.179)	-.080 (.152)	-.048 (.574)	-4.299* (1.846)	2.141* (1.046)
South Central	-.453** (.139)	-.271 (.395)	.066 (.559)	-.839 (.470)	3.559 (2.391)	-3.079 (164.467)	-15.727 (52.198)
West	-.148 (.174)	-.252 (.893)	.514 (.370)	-1.718** (.599)	4.529 (2.462)	-4.239 (73.231)	-3.447 (25.982)
Gender structures							
Married	-3.010*** (.105)	-1.619*** (.148)	-3.423*** (.244)	-3.770*** (.225)	-3.950*** (.715)	-11.650*** (3.157)	-4.284*** (.777)
Age	.003 (.003)	-.007 (.005)	-.023** (.007)	-.033*** (.007)	-.039 (.025)	-.214** (.080)	-.021 (.028)
Household composition							
No. of children, ages 0–9	.037 (.034)	.146*** (.044)	-.227** (.080)	.078 (.065)	-.411* (.201)	-.462 (.446)	-.504 (.267)
No. of seniors, age 65+	.380*** (.078)	.634*** (.172)	-.066 (.159)	.293* (.144)	-.227 (.739)	-2.326 (1.354)	-.334 (1.255)
No. of male adolescents, ages 10–14	.018 (.061)	-.079 (.094)	.089 (.132)	-.081 (.121)	.961** (.321)	-.207 (1.103)	-.053 (.448)

(*continued*)

APPENDIX TABLE A.2. *Continued*

Variable	White b (SE)	Black b (SE)	Irish b (SE)	German b (SE)	Eastern European b (SE)	Russian b (SE)	French Canadian b (SE)
Gender structures (*continued*)							
Household composition (*continued*)							
No. of female adolescents, ages 10–14	.124* (.062)	.050 (.088)	−.014 (.143)	.239* (.115)	.572 (.369)	2.983* (1.520)	.687 (.467)
No. of single men, ages 15–64	−.313*** (.043)	−.458*** (.078)	−.286*** (.070)	−.327*** (.079)	−.322 (.305)	−1.274 (.883)	−.149 (.268)
No. of single women, ages 15–64	.065 (.037)	−.019 (.071)	.188** (.067)	.054 (.061)	.567 (.338)	.791 (.814)	.898* (.376)
Urban (vs. rural) residence	.269** (.083)	.584*** (.156)	.224 (.247)	.043 (.197)	1.634 (.859)	omitted†	.787 (1.003)
Constant	−1.756*** (.266)	−2.459*** (.530)	−1.579* (.710)	−2.493*** (.729)	−.348 (1.793)	18.373** (6.428)	−1.761 (2.800)
Overall % correct	87.4%	78.6%	82.6%	88.2%	91.6%	95.2%	89.9%
No. of women	12,013	2,244	2,144	3,156	440	250	286

*$p \leq .05$; **$p \leq .01$; ***$p \leq .001$.
†Omitted due to multicolinearity with various heads' occupations.

APPENDIX TABLE A.3.   Logistic Regression of Gainful Employment on Class, Racial-Ethnic, and Gender Structure Variables for White, Black, Irish, and German Non-wives, Ages 15–64, 1900

Variable	White b (SE)	Black b (SE)	Irish b (SE)	German b (SE)
Class and economic structures				
Reads a language/literacy	−.282	−.089	.100	.485
	(.183)	(.184)	(.366)	(.561)
Head's occupation				
Professional or manager	.196	−.044	−1.050**	.337
	(.137)	(.701)	(.342)	(.310)
Clerical and sales	.552**	.215	−.145	.348
	(.177)	(1.115)	(.430)	(.430)
Craft	.583***	−1.450*	−.090	1.057***
	(.125)	(.659)	(.343)	(.286)
Operative and laborer	.604***	.286	.123	.727*
	(.129)	(.252)	(.279)	(.290)
Service	.524**	.881**	.309	1.726***
	(.203)	(.330)	(.377)	(.446)
Unclassified	.454	6.113	−.235	.437
	(.313)	(36.659)	(.525)	(.531)
Unemployed	.838***	.498	.271	1.114***
	(.137)	(.353)	(.281)	(.295)
Woman is the household head	1.478***	2.957***	.004	1.422***
	(.135)	(.306)	(.321)	(.322)
Proportion employed in household	2.885***	4.946***	.310	1.216**
	(.231)	(.510)	(.417)	(.427)
Boarders present	.299**	.715**	−.092	.194
	(.102)	(.253)	(.212)	(.211)
Extended family present	−.088	.001	.251	.129
	(.080)	(.184)	(.158)	(.162)
Servants present	−.727***	−10.557	.219	−.553
	(.154)	(13.796)	(.390)	(.384)
Avg. women's manufacturing wages	−.001	−.000	.003	.004
	(.001)	(.001)	(.002)	(.002)
Avg. firm size	.001	.008	.026*	−.000
	(.006)	(.012)	(.013)	(.012)

(continued)

APPENDIX TABLE A.3.   *Continued*

Variable	White b (SE)	Black b (SE)	Irish b (SE)	German b (SE)
Racial ethnic structures				
2nd-gen. immigrant	omitted	omitted	.442* (.213)	−.243 (.178)
County immigrant mix	.005* (.002)	.007 (.008)	.013** (.005)	.014*** (.004)
% Black women in county	.003 (.003)	.025*** (.004)	−.010 (.019)	.007 (.014)
% Other races in county	.044 (.044)	1.560* (.785)	−1.044** (.366)	.027 (.119)
South Atlantic	−.113 (.154)	.172 (.536)	−.382 (.585)	.352 (.531)
North Central	−.219* (.093)	−.316 (.492)	−.237 (.187)	−.073 (.164)
South Central	−.441** (.149)	−.028 (.514)	.098 (.563)	−.431 (.492)
West	−.238 (.187)	.880 (1.379)	.670 (.406)	−1.772** (.619)
Gender structures				
Married	−2.663*** (.347)	−1.404** (.466)	−1.176* (.504)	−7.165 (5.277)
Age	.001 (.003)	−.013 (.008)	−.023** (.008)	−.040*** (.008)
No. of children, 0–9 yr	.074* (.034)	.151** (.058)	−.158* (.082)	.102 (.070)
No. of seniors, 65+ yr	.343*** (.081)	.591** (.211)	−.052 (.160)	.288 (.150)
No. of single men, 15–64 yr	−.307*** (.045)	−.485*** (.098)	−.302*** (.072)	−.365*** (.082)
No. of single women, 15–64 yr	.060 (.040)	−.039 (.092)	.179** (.069)	.075 (.063)
Urban (vs. rural) residence	.294*** (.089)	.180 (.219)	.227 (.254)	.152 (.210)
Constant	−1.836*** (.287)	−2.903*** (.713)	−1.523* (.736)	−2.455*** (.800)
Overall % correct	72.5%	78.6%	67.3%	71.4%
No. of non-wives	5,035	1,052	1,067	1,215

*$p \le .05$; **$p \le .01$; ***$p \le .001$.

APPENDIX TABLE A.4.   Census Occupations Employing at Least 1 Percent of Working Women, Organized into Nine Occupational Groups, by Race and National Origin, Age 15 or Older, 1900†

Occupational category and occupational title†	Race or national-origin group													
	White	Black	Irish	British	Scandinavian	German	Eastern European	Russian	Italian	French Canadian	English Canadian	Latin American	Asian	Native American
Professional and technical‡	**15.1**	**1.4**	**8.7**	**16.2**	**4.7**	**6.8**	**0.9**	**3.1**	**0**	**0.9**	**7.2**	**9.5**	**0**	**13.3**
Teacher	10	1	6	9	3	3				1	4	5		
Musician/music teacher	1	+	+	1	1	+		3						
Banker or broker	+	+	+	1		+					+			
Landlord	1	+	+	2		2					+	5		13
Managers, officials, proprietors‡	**1.3**	**0.1**	**1.0**	**1.7**	**0.5**	**1.1**	**1.8**	**3.1**	**0**	**0**	**0.5**	**0**	**0**	**0**
Manufacturers and officials	+	+	+					3						
Clerical‡	**5.6**	**0.2**	**5.8**	**7.4**	**3.1**	**4.6**	**1.8**	**6.3**	**0**	**9.3**	**7.7**	**0**	**0**	**0**
Clerk/copyist	2	+	2	2	2	2		3		8	2			
Clerk, shipping										1				
Stenographer	2	+	2	2	1	1		2			3			
Bookkeeper/accountant	2		2	3	+	1	+	2		1	2			
Sales‡	**3.9**	**0.1**	**4.2**	**2.7**	**0.5**	**5.1**	**4.5**	**1.6**	**0**	**0.9**	**4.1**	**0**	**14.3**	**0**
Saleswomen	3		3	2		4	5	2		1	3			
Huckster/peddler		+											14	
Service‡	**33.8**	**50.6**	**45.0**	**38.9**	**67.9**	**42.2**	**42.7**	**18.8**	**14.3**	**26.2**	**48.0**	**61.9**	**14.3**	**13.3**
Janitors	+	+	+	+	+	1								
Laundry work, hand	2	18	4	2	6	4	5		3	2	2	14		13
Nurse, training unspecified	4	1	2	6	2	1				1	13			

(continued)

APPENDIX TABLE A.4.   *Continued*

Occupational category and occupational title†	Race or national-origin group													
	White	Black	Irish	Brit-ish	Scan-dina-vian	Ger-man	East-ern Euro-pean	Rus-sian	Ital-ian	French Cana-dian	Eng-lish Cana-dian	Latin Amer-ican	Asian	Native Amer-ican
Service‡ (continued)														
Servant	16	28	30	17	51	28	29	16	3	10	21	38	14	
Waiter/waitress	+	+	+	+	+	+	2			3	2			
Boardinghouse keeper	1	+	1	1	1	+	+			5	2			
Housekeeper/steward	2	+	2	3	3	1		3	3	2	2			
Housekeeper, domestic resident	8	2	5	8	3	4	7	3	6	4	5	10		
Craft‡	**1.6**	**0**	**3.1**	**2.0**	**2.6**	**6.2**	**7.3**	**3.1**	**0**	**3.7**	**2.3**	**0**	**0**	**0**
Harness/saddle maker			+			+	+			1				
Gold and silver worker			+			1				1				
Jewelry manufacturing						+				1				
Bookbinder	+		+	+		1					+			
Tailoress/tailor	+		2	+	3	4	7	3		1	2			
Operative‡	**21.6**	**1.6**	**25.2**	**25.7**	**14.5**	**27.1**	**30.0**	**50.0**	**57.1**	**53.3**	**22.2**	**14.3**	**0**	**0**
Packer/shipper	+		+	+		+	+		3	3	+			
Canner/preserver						+	+		3					
Confectioner	+		+			+			3					
Metal worker	+		+	+		1		2	6		2			
Boot/shoe operative	+		1	+		+				4	2			
Box maker, paper	+		+	+		+		3		1				
Box maker, not specified	+		+	1		+								

APPENDIX TABLE A.4.   *Continued*

Occupational category and occupational title†	Race or national-origin group													
	White	Black	Irish	British	Scandinavian	German	Eastern European	Russian	Italian	French Canadian	English Canadian	Latin American	Asian	Native American
Operative‡ *(continued)*														
Paper mill operative	+		+			+	+			1	2			
Cotton mill operative	2		2	2		+	4		3	23	1			
Knitting mill operative	+		+	1		+	+			1	+			
Silk mill operative	+		+	+		1	+	2		3				
Woolen mill operative	+		1	1	+	+			3	4	1			
Worsted mill operative	+			+			2							
Other textiles operative	+		2	3		+	+		3	6	1			
Dressmaker	7	+	6	6	6	8	4	6	11	5	8			
Milliner	3	+	1	3	1	2	2	2		1	2			
Hat/cap maker	+		+			+	3							
Seamstress	3	+	2	1	1	3	5	11	3	1	2	14		
Shirt/collar/cuff maker	+		+	+	+	+	2	5	3	3	+			
Lace/embroidery maker	+		+	+				2						
Artificial flower maker								2	3					
Button maker						+			3	1	+			
Sewing machine operator	+					+			6		+			
Textile worker, not specified	+		+	+	2	1	2	8	3					
Rubber factory operative			1			+					+			
Tobacco/cigar operator	+		+	+		1	2	6			+			

(continued)

APPENDIX TABLE A.4.   *Continued*

Occupational category and occupational title†	Race or national-origin group													
	White	Black	Irish	British	Scandinavian	German	Eastern European	Russian	Italian	French Canadian	English Canadian	Latin American	Asian	Native American
Laborer‡	**1.7**	**6.6**	**2.1**	**0.7**	**1.0**	**1.0**	**3.6**	**0**	**11.4**	**1.9**	**1.4**	**4.8**	**28.6**	**26.6**
Laborer, general	1	6	1	+	+	+	+		6		+	5	29	
Steam railroad laborer		+							3					
Fishermen														13
Hunters														13
Agriculture‡	**14.6**	**39.2**	**2.0**	**3.7**	**4.7**	**3.7**	**5.4**	**4.7**	**5.7**	**0.9**	**5.0**	**4.8**	**42.9**	**46.7**
Farm/plantation labor	2	15	+	+	+	+	+	2	3		+		29	27
Farm labor, family	3	17	+		1	+	2	3			1			7
Farmer or planter	10	5	2	3	3	3	2				4	5	14	13
Florist or nurserymen	+								3					
Unspecified/uncodable‡	**0.8**	**0.2**	**2.9**	**1.0**	**0.5**	**2.1**	**1.8**	**9.3**	**11.4**	**1.9**	**1.8**	**4.8**	**0**	**0**
Total percentage	**100**	**100**	**100**	**100**	**100**	**99.9**	**99.8**	**99.9**	**99.9**	**99.0**	**100.2**	**100.1**	**100.1**	**99.9**
No. of employed women	2,566	1,481	908	296	193	805	110	64	35	107	221	21	7	15
No. of occupations with any women	115	34	78	63	34	80	34	22	22	30	45	8	5	7
No. of occupations with ≥1% women	21	9	22	23	17	22	16	22	22	30	23	8	5	7
Occupational prestige score	28	12	23	29	17	22	17	22	14	16	23	15	8	12

Appendix Table A.4. *Continued*

Note: In all cases, except for Asians, χ² values comparing male and female complete occupational distributions are significantly different at *p* ≤ .001.

Plus signs (+) indicate that women hold these jobs, but the percentage is less than 1 percent.

†Occupations listed under each of the nine occupational groupings are those in which at least one racial-ethnic group has at least 1 percent of its employed women. For these occupations the percentage of employed women are rounded to the nearest whole number. There are other jobs in each category, but no group of women reached the 1 percent threshold to be included in this table. For groups with the fewest employed women, especially Asians and Latin Americans, the range of jobs could be wider if the census sample were larger and contained more women from each group. In these two cases the figures should be regarded as conservative estimates.

‡The percentages of women in each of the nine categories (plus unspecified or uncodable jobs) are rounded to the nearest tenth of a percentage point to give more precision to these category totals. The category totals include all occupations within that category, not just the occupations listed here.

APPENDIX TABLE A.5.   Logistic Regression of Servant-Employer
Racial-Ethnic Group Match on Employer, Servant, and Geographic
Variables for Female Servants, Individual Level, 1900

| | | | Probability of match | |
| | | | | Unit |
Variable	b	SE	Overall	change
Household head's characteristics				
Prestige score (in 1950 codes, 0–100)	−.014***	.004	.357	−.003
Speaks English (1 = yes)	−9.358	70.047		
Immigrant (1 = yes)	.421	.281		
2nd-gen. immigrant (1 = yes)	.106	.281		
Black (1 = yes)	18.706	32.794		
Female servant's characteristics				
Speaks English	−.887†	.539	.190	−.170
Immigrant	−2.058***	.277	.060	−.300
2nd-gen. immigrant	−2.372***	.306	.050	−.310
Black	−11.376	9.711		
Geographic/contextual variables				
Density (in 1,000s)	.019	.015		
South Atlantic (vs. North Atlantic)	−.569	.761		
South Central (vs. North Atlantic)	−1.651†	.857	.100	−.260
North Central (vs. North Atlantic)	−.286	.256		
West (vs. North Atlantic)	−.303	.637		
% Immigrant women in county	−.008	.006		
% Black women in county	.034	.026		
Interaction: South by % Black women	.010	.037		
Avg. women's manufacturing wages	−.005*	.003	.359	−.001
Constant	13.440	70.049		
No. of female servants	655			
Overall % correct	81%			
Avg. probability of match			.360	

Note: The dependent variable = 1 when servant matches employer on race-ethnicity,
measured in 13 categories; no match = 0.
*p ≤ .05; **p ≤ .01; ***p ≤ .001; †p ≤ .10.

Appendix Table A.6.   Logistic Regression of Presence or Absence of Live-in Servants (Both Genders) on Household and Geographic Characteristics, All Households, 1900

Variable	b	SE	Probability of servant Overall	Unit change
Household head's status				
Professional/manager	1.627***	.101	.218	.166
Clerical/sales	.767***	.141	.106	.054
Craft	−.466**	.151	.033	−.019
Operative/laborer	−.837***	.149	.023	−.029
Service	.346	.218		
Unclassified	1.096***	.218	.141	.089
Unemployed	.551**	.199	.087	.035
Women is head	.252†	.135	.066	.014
Native-born white of native-born parents (1 = yes)	.586***	.079	.090	.038
Household composition				
Proportion employed	−1.012***	.219	.020	−.032
Number of single adult women, 15–64 yr	−.047	.051		
Number female adolescents, 10–14 yr	−.094	.076		
Number of children, 0–9 yr	−.065*	.030	.049	−.003
Extended family present (1 = yes)	.153***	.025	.060	.008
Geographic context				
Density (in 1,000s)	−.009	.006		
South Atlantic (vs. North Atlantic)	.303	.191		
South Central (vs. North Atlantic)	−.158	.182		
North Central (vs. North Atlantic)	−.407***	.088	.035	−.016
West (vs. North Atlantic)	−.758***	.188	.025	−.027
% Immigrant women in county	.015***	.002	.053	.001
% Black women in county	.064***	.016	.055	.003
Interaction: South by % Black women	−.063***	.016	.049	−.003
Avg. women's manufacturing wages	.000	.001		
Constant	−3.903***	.222		
No. of households	18,396			
Overall % correct	95%			
Avg. probability of live-in servants			.052	

Note: The excluded occupational category is agriculture.
*$p \leq .05$; **$p \leq .01$; ***$p \leq .001$; †$p \leq .10$; overall regression significant at $p \leq .001$.

APPENDIX TABLE A.7.   Which Servants Work in Which Households?
Logistic Regression of Black vs. Ethnic Female Live-in Servants
on Household and Geographic Characteristics

	Black vs. ethnic		Probability of black servant	
Variable	b	SE	Overall	Unit change
Household head's characteristics				
Prestige score (in 1950s codes, 0–100)	−.018**	.006	.246	−.003
Black	6.689	14.928		
Irish	−1.459†	.763	.072	−.178
German	−1.155*	.535	.090	−.160
Other national origins	−.987*	.470	.110	−.140
Household characteristics				
No. of employed relatives	−.455†	.266	.170	−.080
No. of single adult women, 15–64 yr	.386*	.186	.322	.072
No. of female adolescents, 10–14 yr	−.545	.410		
No. of children, 0–9 yr	.040	.142		
Geographic/contextual variables				
Density (in 1,000s)	.082	.121		
South Atlantic (vs. North Atlantic)	2.207*	1.096	.752	.502
South Central (vs. North Atlantic)	2.119*	.907	.735	.485
North Central (vs. North Atlantic)	.309	.396		
West (vs. North Atlantic)	−.777	1.104		
% Immigrant women in county	−.038***	.010	.243	−.007
% Black women in county	−.036	.034		
Interaction: South by % Black women	.089*	.037	.267	.017
Interaction: Density by % Immigrant women	−.000	.002		
Avg. women's manufacturing wage	.011*	.004	.252	.002
Constant	−1.518	1.281		
No. of black and ethnic servants	490			
Overall % correct	88%			
Avg. probability for blacks			.250	

Note: Dependent variable code: 1 = servant is black; 0 = servant is first- or second-generation immigrant.

*p ≤ .05; **p ≤ .01; ***p ≤ .001; †p ≤ .10.

APPENDIX TABLE A.8.   Which Servants Work in Which Households?
Logistic Regression of Black vs. White Female Live-in Servants
on Household and Geographic Characteristics

Variable	Black vs. 3rd-gen. white		Probability of black servant	
	b	SE	Overall	Unit change
Household head's characteristics				
Prestige score (in 1950s codes, 0–100)	.011†	.006	.352	.002
Black	8.729	15.333		
Irish	−.757	.821		
German	.197	.560		
Other national origins	−.244	.511		
Household characteristics				
No. of employed relatives	−.186	.247		
No. of single adult women, 15–64 yr	.765***	.207	.524	.174
No. of female adolescents, 10–14 yr	−.440	.410		
No. of children, 0–9 yr	.165	.130		
Geographic/contextual variables				
Density (in 1,000s)	−.017	.101		
South Atlantic (vs. North Atlantic)	1.731*	.767	.753	.403
South Central (vs. North Atlantic)	1.726*	.698	.752	.402
North Central (vs. North Atlantic)	−.468	.425		
West (vs. North Atlantic)	−1.836	1.243		
% Immigrant women in county	.018†	.011	.354	.004
% Black women in county	.127†	.072	.379	.029
Interaction: South by % black women	−.077	.073		
Interaction: Density by % immigrant women	.000	.001		
Avg. women's manufacturing wage	.008*	.003	.352	.002
Constant	−4.876	1.063		
No. of black and white servants	322			
Overall % correct	79%			
Avg. probability for blacks			.350	

Note: Dependent variable code: 1 = servant is black; 0 = servant is third-generation or later white.
    *$p \le .05$; **$p \le .01$; ***$p \le .001$; †$p \le .10$.

APPENDIX TABLE A.9.   Logistic Regression Predicting Women's Official vs. Hidden Headship

| | | | Probability of official headship | |
Variable	b	SE	Overall	Unit change
Individual characteristics				
Age	.087***	.008	.903	.008
Reads a language/literacy	−.410	.377		
Black (3rd+ gen.)	.136	.421		
Irish	.488	.380		
German	−.387	.328		
Other racial-ethnic groups	.336	.322		
Household composition				
No. of children, 0–9 yr	−.337***	.101	.859	−.036
No. of female adolescents, 10–14 yr	−.419*	.185	.849	−.046
No. of male adolescents, 10–14 yr	−.043	.185		
No. of single adult men, 15–64 yr	−.286*	.114	.865	−.030
No. of married adult men, 15–64 yr	−1.646***	.235	.622	−.273
No. of seniors, 65+ yr	−.572**	.198	.828	−.067
Sources of support				
Home ownership	.234	.229		
Extended family present	−10.685	10.049		
Boarders present	.481	.311		
Employment (vs. no job)				
Professional/manager	1.010	.566		
Clerical/sales	.203	.789		
Craft	1.227	1.377		
Operative/Laborer	.762*	.354	.948	.053
Service	.718*	.310	.946	.051
Agriculture	2.560***	.449	.928	.033
Unclassifiable work	9.814	75.073		
Geographic/contextual variables				
Urban (vs. rural)	1.317***	.261	.970	.075
South Atlantic (vs. North Atlantic)	−.243	.486		
South Central (vs. North Atlantic)	−.140	.426		
North Central (vs. North Atlantic)	.031	.270		
West (vs. North Atlantic)	.544	.543		
% Immigrant women in county	−.005	.006		
% Black women in county	.001	.009		
Avg. women's manufacturing wage	−.001	.002		
Constant	8.215	10.079		
No. of official and hidden heads	2,446			
Overall % correct (logit)	93.5%			
r^2 (for comparable OLS regression)	.40			
Avg. probability of official headship			.895	

*$p \leq .05$; **$p \leq .01$; ***$p \leq .001$.

APPENDIX TABLE A.10.   Logistic Regression Predicting Gainful
Employment of Official and Hidden Household Heads

Variable	b	SE	Probability of employment Overall	Unit change
Individual characteristics				
Hidden head (vs. official head)	−1.209***	.204	.200	−.256
Age	−.045***	.005	.445	−.011
Widow	−.093	.118		
Reads a language/literacy	.039	.162		
Black (3rd+ gen.)	1.434***	.221	.779	.323
Immigrant (1st gen.)	−.082	.135		
2nd-gen. immigrant	.024	.024		
Household composition				
No. of children, 0–9 yr	−.178**	.059	.412	−.044
No. of female adolescents, 10–14 yr	.200	.105		
No. of male adolescents, 10–14 yr	.130	.103		
No. of single adult men, 15–64 yr	−.374***	.068	.366	−.090
No. of married adult men, 15–64 yr	−.434*	.200	.352	−.104
No. of seniors, 65+ yr	−.291*	.128	.385	−.071
Sources of support				
Home ownership	−.440***	.110	.351	−.109
Farm resident	−.575	.473		
Interaction: Farm by age	.050***	.009	.468	.012
Interaction: Farm by black	−.933*	.385	.242	−.214
Extended family present	.202	.123		
Boarders present	.386**	.128	.552	.096
Proportion of household employed	.109	.241		
Geographic context				
Urban (vs. rural)	.206	.136		
South Atlantic (vs. North Atlantic)	.012	.248		
South Central (vs. North Atlantic)	−.081	.217		
North Central (vs. North Atlantic)	.051	.125		
West (vs. North Atlantic)	.012	.213		
% Immigrant women in county	−.001	.003		
% Black women in county	.008	.005		
Avg. women's manufacturing wages	.000	.001		
Constant	1.915***	.407		
No. of official and hidden heads	2,458			
Overall % correct (logistic regression)	72.5%			
r² (comparable OLS regression)	.24			
Avg. probability of gainful employment			.456	

*p ≤ .05; **p ≤ .01; ***p ≤ .001.

Notes

CHAPTER TWO

1. Estimates from later in the century show a fluctuating pattern in the amount of such homework, which declined from 7.2 to 2.3 percent of all workers between 1960 and 1980. At the same time, it also shifted from being predominantly farm work to being predominantly urban work (Silver 1989).

2. If we include women age 15 or older, the overall percentage employed would be slightly lower (21.9 percent).

3. This result is similar to rates calculated using other gender-equity–based measures, which reestimated women's employment in 1900 at 48.8 percent (Ciancanelli 1983) or a probable rate of 48.6 percent (Bose 1987).

4. Using fewer census points and more conservative estimation methods that attempt to project current employment definitions back in time, Goldin (1990) estimates that the low point for married women's labor force participation was somewhere between 1880 and 1920.

5. Unfortunately, it is not possible to include uncounted factory work here, since the manufacturers' reports are aggregated by county of residence and cannot be separated according to the ethnicity of the workers.

6. The value is just barely significant at $p \leq .05$ for a one-tailed test, but not for the more appropriate two-tailed tests.

7. Still, the correlation between the reported and recounted employment rates of the ten ethnic groups, blacks, and whites is high and positive at $r = .84$, $p \leq .001$.

CHAPTER SIX

1. Today, household heads also may or may not live with other family members, but published reports often distinguish family household heads as one subgroup of these. In the 1900 census, several groups of people were not counted as household heads. Persons living in a lodging house and having no other home were considered part of a class of "individuals living without families" (Census Office 1900, 25) or "primaries." Institutionalized persons or employees living in group quarters at their place of work also were considered primaries.

2. It is impossible to judge whether servants or other employees who were recorded as part of their employer's household might themselves have

been household heads. Their relationship to the head was considered to be "servant" or "employee." Among the 1,233 women boarders in the sample, only 21 percent were wives or children of another boarder. Most women boarders were not attached to men but were either never married (60 percent), widowed (13 percent), or married to an absent spouse, who often had deserted them (5 percent). Only ten women boarders (1 percent) were considered family heads, and I chose to exclude this small number from the sample of official heads.

3. Gordon and McLanahan (1991) report 559 children ages 0 to 14 living with one parent in a subfamily in 1900 and estimate that 80 percent (or 447) of these were in female-headed subfamilies. In my sample, fully 654 children ages 0 to 14 lived with hidden household heads (or in female single-parent subfamilies). Using Gordon's 1994 estimate that 20 percent of single mothers lived as subfamilies, I assume that since 1,023 of the official female household heads were single mothers of children ages 0 to 14, then an additional 256 women should be hidden heads. In fact, 272 of the hidden heads had children in this age bracket. I have uncovered slightly more hidden female household heads (318) than were previously estimated for this sample primarily by including those with older children.

4. Ethnicity was not significant, whether it was measured specifically in the three categories of Irish, German, and other ethnic groups or was measured more generally as first- or second-generation immigrant, as is done in Appendix Table A.10.

5. Other regressions, not shown, indicate that the interaction between the Southern region and counties with high percentages of black women did produce higher gainful employment rates.

6. This figure was calculated using the Integrated PUMS census data (Ruggles and Sobek 1995).

References

Abel, Marjorie, and Nancy Folbre. 1990. "A Methodology for Revising Estimates: Female Market Participation in the U.S. Before 1940." *Historical Methods* 23: 167–76.

Abramovitz, Mimi. 1988. *Regulating the Lives of Women: Social Welfare Policy from Colonial Times to the Present.* Boston: South End Press.

Acosta-Belén, Edna, and Christine E. Bose. 2000. "U.S. Latina and Latin American Feminisms: Hemispheric Encounters." *Signs: The Journal of Women in Culture and Society* 25, no. 4 (summer): 1113–19.

Almquist, Elizabeth. 1987. "Labor Market Gender Inequality in Minority Groups." *Gender & Society* 1 (December): 400–14.

Amott, Teresa, and Julie Matthaei. 1991. *Race, Gender and Work: A Multicultural Economic History of Women in the United States.* Boston: South End Press. [Revised edition also available, 1996.]

Andersen, Margaret L. 1997. *Thinking About Women: Sociological Perspectives on Sex and Gender.* 4th ed. Boston: Allyn and Bacon.

Anderson, Karen. 1987. "A History of Women's Work in the United States." In *Women Working,* edited by Shirley Harkess and Ann Stromberg. 2nd ed. Palo Alto, Calif.: Mayfield.

Anderson, Margo J. 1988. *The American Census: A Social History.* New Haven, Conn.: Yale University Press.

Baca Zinn, Maxine. 1989. "Family, Race, and Poverty in the Eighties." *Signs: The Journal of Women in Culture and Society* 14, no. 4: 856–74.

Bakan, Abigail, and Daiva K. Stasiulis. 1995. "Making the Match: Domestic Placement Agencies and the Racialization of Women's Household Work." *Signs: The Journal of Women in Culture and Society* 20, no. 2: 303–35.

Baron, Ava. 1991. *Work Engendered: Toward a New History of American Labor.* Ithaca, N.Y.: Cornell University Press.

Beller, Andrea H. 1984. "Trends in Occupational Segregation by Sex and Race, 1960–1981." In *Sex Segregation in the Workplace: Trends, Explanations, Remedies,* edited by Barbara F. Reskin, 11–26. Washington, D.C.: National Academy Press.

Benería, Lourdes. 1982. "Accounting for Women's Work." In *Women and Development: The Sexual Division of Labor in Rural Societies,* edited by Lourdes Benería, 119–147. New York: Praeger.

Benería, Lourdes. 1992. "The Mexican Debt Crisis: Restructuring the Economy and the Household." In *Unequal Burden: Economic Crises, Persistent*

Poverty, and Women's Work, edited by Lourdes Benería and Shelley Feldman, 83–104. Boulder, CO: Westview.

Benson, Susan Porter. 1986. *Counter Cultures: Saleswomen, Managers, and Customers in American Department Stores: 1890–1940.* Urbana: University of Illinois Press.

Berheide, Catherine White. 1992. "Women Still 'Stuck' in Low-Level Jobs." *Women in Public Services: A Bulletin for the Center for Women in Government* 3 (fall). Albany: Center for Women in Government, State University of New York.

Bernstein, Rachel Amelia. 1984. "Boarding-house Keepers and Brothel Keepers in New York City, 1880–1910." Ph.D. diss. Rutgers University.

Bielby, William T., and James N. Baron. 1984. "A Woman's Place Is with Other Women: Sex Segregation Within Organizations." In *Sex Segregation in the Workplace: Trends, Explanations, Remedies,* edited by Barbara F. Reskin, 27–55. Washington, D.C.: National Academy Press.

Bielby, William T., and James N. Baron. 1986. "Men and Women at Work: Sex Segregation and Statistical Discrimination." *American Journal of Sociology* 91: 759–799.

Bielby, William T., and James N. Baron. 1987. "Undoing Discrimination: Job Integration and Comparable Worth." In *Ingredients for Women's Employment Policy,* edited by Christine Bose and Glenna Spitze, 211–29. Albany: State University of New York Press.

Blackwelder, Julia Kirk. 1997. *Now Hiring: The Feminization of Work in the United States, 1900–1995.* College Station: Texas A & M University Press.

Bonacich, Edna, and Ivan Light. 1988. *Immigrant Entrepreneurs: Koreans in Los Angeles, 1965–1982.* Berkeley: University of California Press.

Bonachich, Edna, Ivan Light, and Charles Choy Wong. 1977. "Koreans in Small Business." *Society* 14: 54–59.

Boris, Eileen. 1994. *Home to Work: Motherhood and the Politics of Industrial Homework in the United States.* New York: Cambridge University Press.

Boris, Eileen, and Cynthia R. Daniels. 1989. *Homework: Historical and Contemporary Perspectives on Paid Labor at Home.* Urbana: University of Illinois Press.

Bose, Christine E. 1984. "Household Resources and U.S. Women's Work: Factors Affecting Gainful Employment at the Turn of the Century." *American Sociological Review* 49 (August): 474–90.

Bose, Christine E. 1987. "Devaluing Women's Work: The Undercount of Women's Employment in 1900 and 1980." In *Hidden Aspects of Women's Work,* edited by Christine Bose, Roslyn Feldberg, and Natalie Sokoloff, 95–115. New York: Praeger.

Bridges, William P. 1982. "The Sexual Segregation of Occupations: Theories of Labor Stratification in Industry." *American Journal of Sociology* 88, no. 2: 270–95.

Briefing Paper. 1998. "Stall in Women's Real Wage Growth Slows Progress in Closing Wage Gap." Washington, D.C.: Institute for Women's Policy Research.

Broder, Sherri. 1988. "Child Care or Child Neglect? Baby Farming in Late Nineteenth Century Philadelphia." *Gender & Society* 2: 128–48.

Brodkin, Karen. 1998. *How Jews Became White Folks and What That Says About Race in America.* New Brunswick, N.J.: Rutgers University Press.

Browne, Irene. 1997. "Explaining the Black-White Gap in Labor Force Participation Among Women Heading Households." *American Sociological Review* 62: 236–52.

Brush, Lisa D. 1997. "Worthy Widows, Welfare Cheats: Proper Womanhood in Expert Needs Talk About Single Mothers in the United States, 1900 to 1988." *Gender & Society* 11, no. 6 (December): 720–46.

Bureau of Labor Statistics. 1997. "Labor Force Statistics from the Current Population Survey." URL: www.bls.gov/news.release/work.t01.htm

Carlson, Susan M. 1992. "Trends in Race/Sex Occupational Inequality: Conceptual and Measurement Issues." *Social Problems* 39, no. 3: 268–87.

Census Office. 1900. *Twelfth Census of the United States: Instructions to Enumerators.* Washington, D.C.: U.S. Government Printing Office.

Chang, Grace. 1996. "Women's Work and the Politics of Latina Immigration." *Radical America* 26, no. 2: 5–20.

Charles, Maria, and David B. Grusky. 1995. "Models for Describing the Underlying Structure of Sex Segregation." *American Journal of Sociology* 100, no. 4: 931–71.

Ciancanelli, Penelope. 1983. "Women's Transition to Wage Labor: A Critique of Labor Force Statistics and Reestimation of the Labor Force Participation of Married Women from 1900 to 1930." Ph.D. diss., New School for Social Research.

Clark-Lewis, Elizabeth. 1994. *Living In, Living Out: African American Domestics in Washington, DC.* Washington, D.C.: Smithsonian Institution Press.

Cobble, Dorothy Sue. 1991. *Dishing It Out: Waitresses and Their Unions in the Twentieth Century.* Urbana: University of Illinois Press.

Cohen, Miriam. 1992. *Workshop to Office: Two Generations of Italian Women in New York City, 1900–1950.* Ithaca, N.Y.: Cornell University Press.

Cohen, Rina. 1991. "Women of Color in White Households: Coping Strategies of Live-in Domestic Workers." *Qualitative Sociology* 14, no. 2: 197–215.

Conk, Margo Anderson. 1978. "Occupational Classification in the United States Census: 1870–1940." *Journal of Interdisciplinary History* 9, no. 1 (summer): 111–30.

Conk, Margo Anderson. 1981. "Accuracy, Efficiency and Bias: The Interpretation of Women's Work in the U.S. Census of Occupations, 1890–1940." *Historical Methods* 14 (spring): 65–72.

Coontz, Stephanie. 2000. *The Way We Never Were: American Families and the Nostalgia Trap.* New York: Basic Books.

Cotter, David A., JoAnn DeFiore, Joan M. Hermsen, Brenda Marsteller Kowalewski, and Reeve Vanneman. 1997. "All Women Benefit: The Macro-Level Effect of Occupational Integration on Gender Earnings Equality." *American Sociological Review* 62: 714–34.

Davies, Marjorie W. 1974. "Women's Place Is at the Typewriter: The Feminization of the Clerical Work Force." *Radical America* 8: 1–28.

Davies, Marjorie W. 1982. *Women's Place Is at the Typewriter: Office Work and Office Workers, 1870–1930.* Philadelphia: Temple University Press.

Deacon, Deasley. 1985. "Political Arithmetic: The Nineteenth-Century Australian Census and the Construction of the Dependent Woman." *Signs: The Journal of Women in Culture and Society* 11 (autumn): 27–47.

DeGrazia, Raffaele. 1982. "Clandestine Employment: A Problem of Our Times." In *The Underground Economy in the United States and Abroad,* edited by Vito Tanzi, 29–44. Lexington, Mass.: Lexington Books/D. C. Heath.

DeVault, Ileen A. 1990. *Sons and Daughters of Labor: Class and Clerical Work in Turn-of-the-Century Pittsburgh.* Ithaca, N.Y.: Cornell University Press.

Dublin, Thomas. 1994. *Transforming Women's Work: New England Lives in the Industrial Revolution.* Ithaca, N.Y.: Cornell University Press.

Duncan, Otis Dudley, and Beverly Duncan. 1955. "A Methodological Analysis of Segregation Indices." *American Sociological Review* 20: 200–17.

Durand, John D. 1968. *The Labor Force in the United States, 1890–1960.* New York: Gordon and Breach.

Durand, John D. 1975. *The Labor Force in Economic Development: A Comparison of International Census Data, 1946–66.* Princeton, N.J.: Princeton University Press.

Edin, Kathryn, and Laura Lein. 1997. "Work, Welfare, and Single Mothers' Economic Survival Strategies." *American Sociological Review* 62: 253–66.

England, Paula. 1981. "Assessing Trends in Occupational Sex Segregation, 1900–1976." In *Sociological Perspectives on Labor Markets,* edited by Ivar Berg, 273–95. New York: Academic Press.

England, Paula. 1993. *Theory on Gender/Feminism on Theory.* New York: Aldine de Gruyter.

England, Paula, Karen Christopher, and Lori L. Reid. 1999. "Gender, Ethnicity, and Wages." In *Latinas and African American Women at Work: Race, Gender, and Economic Inequality,* edited by Irene Browne, 139–82. New York: Russell Sage Foundation.

England, Paula, and Lori McCreary. 1987. "Gender Inequality in Paid Employment." In *Analyzing Gender: A Handbook of Social Science Research,* edited by Beth B. Hess and Myra Marx Ferree, 286–320. Newbury Park, Calif.: Sage Publications.

Ewen, Elizabeth. 1985. *Immigrant Women in the Land of Dollars: Life and Culture on the Lower East Side, 1890–1925.* New York: Monthly Review Press.

Feige, Edgar L. 1996. "Overseas Holdings of U.S. Currency and the Underground Economy." In *Exploring the Underground Economy: Studies of Illegal and Unreported Activity,* edited by Susan Pozo, 5–62. Kalamazoo, Mich.: W. E. Upjohn Institute for Employment Research.

Folbre, Nancy. 1991. "Women on Their Own: Residential Independence in Massachusetts in 1880." *Continuity and Change* 6: 87–105.

Folbre, Nancy. 1993. "Women's Informal Market Work in Massachusetts, 1875–1920." *Social Science History* 17: 135–60.

Folbre, Nancy, and Marjorie Abel. 1989. "Women's Work and Women's Households: Gender Bias in the U.S. Census." *Social Research* 56: 545–70.

Fossett, Mark, Omer R. Galle, and Jeffrey A. Burr. 1989. "Racial Occupational Inequality, 1940–1980: A Research Note on the Impact of the Changing Regional Distribution of the Black Population." *Social Forces* 68, no. 2: 415–27.

Frader, Laura L. 1998. "Bringing Political Economy Back in: Gender, Culture, Race, and Class in Labor History." *Social Science History* 22 (spring): 7–18.

Frey, William H., and Ross C. DeVol. 2000. "America's Demography in the New Century: Aging Baby Boomers and New Immigrants as Major Players." Milkin Institute Report. URL: www.milken-inst.org/pdf/frey.pdf

Friedman-Kasaba, Kathie. 1996. *Memories of Migration: Gender, Ethnicity, and Work in the Lives of Jewish and Italian Women in New York, 1870–1924.* Albany: State University of New York Press.

Gimenez, Martha. 1990. "The Dialectics of Waged and Unwaged Work: Waged Work, Domestic Labor, and Household Survival in the United States." In *Work Without Wages: Domestic Labor and Self-Employment Within Capitalism,* edited by Jane L. Collins and Martha Gimenez, 25–45. Albany: State University of New York Press.

Glazer, Nona Y. 1993. *Women's Paid and Unpaid Labor: The Work Transfer in Health Care and Retailing.* Philadelphia: Temple University Press.

Glenn, Evelyn Nakano. 1980. "The Dialectics of Wage Work: Japanese-American Women and Domestic Service, 1905–1940." *Feminist Studies* 6: 432–71.

Glenn, Evelyn Nakano. 1986. *Issei, Nisei, War Bride: Three Generations of Japanese American Women in Domestic Service.* Philadelphia: Temple University Press.

Glenn, Evelyn Nakano. 1987. "Racial Ethnic Women's Labor: The Intersection of Race, Gender, and Class Oppression." In *Hidden Aspects of Women's Work,* edited by Christine E. Bose, Roslyn Feldberg, and Natalie Sokoloff, 46–73. New York: Praeger.

Glenn, Evelyn Nakano. 1992. "From Servitude to Service Work: Historical Continuities in the Racial Division of Paid Reproductive Labor." *Signs: The Journal of Women in Culture and Society* 18: 1–43.

Glenn, Susan A. 1990. *Daughters of the Shtetl: Life and Labor in an Immigrant Generation.* Ithaca, N.Y.: Cornell University Press.

Goldin, Claudia. 1990. *Understanding the Gender Gap: An Economic History of American Women.* New York: Oxford University Press.

Gordon, Linda. 1994. *Pitied, But Not Entitled: Single Mothers and the History of Welfare 1890–1935.* New York: Macmillan.

Gordon, Linda, and Sara McLanahan. 1991. "Single Parenthood in 1900." *Journal of Family History* 16: 97–116.

Graham, Steven N. 1980. *1900 Public Use Sample: User's Handbook* (draft version). Seattle: University of Washington Center for Studies in Demography and Ecology.

Great American History Machine. 1995. Academic Software Development Group. College Park: University of Maryland.

Gross, Edward. 1968. "Plus ça change: The Sexual Segregation of Occupations Over Time." *Social Problems* 16: 198–208.

Hartmann, Heidi, and Julie Whittaker. 1998. "Briefing Paper: Stall in Women's Real Wage Growth Slows Progress in Closing Wage Gap." Washington, D.C.: Institute for Women's Policy Research.

Hewitt, Nancy A. 1991. "Politicizing Domesticity: Anglo, Black, and Latin Women in Tampa's Progressive Movements." In *Gender, Class, Race and Reform in the Progressive Era,* edited by Noralee Frankel and Nancy S. Dye, 24–41. Lexington: University Press of Kentucky.

Hill, Joseph A. 1929. *Women in Gainful Occupations: 1870 to 1920.* Washington, D.C.: U.S. Government Printing Office. Reprint, New York: Johnson Reprint Corporation, 1972.

Hill Collins, Patricia. 1990. *Black Feminist Thought: Knowledge, Consciousness, and the Politics of Empowerment.* Boston: Unwin Hyman.

Hill Collins, Patricia. 1993. "Toward a New Vision: Race, Class, and Gender as Categories of Analysis and Connection." *Race, Sex, & Class* 1: 24–45.

Hodson, Randy, and Teresa A. Sullivan. 1990. *The Social Organization of Work.* Belmont, Calif.: Wadsworth.

Hondagneu-Sotelo, Pierrette. 1994. "Regulating the Unregulated? Domestic Workers' Social Networks." *Social Problems* 41 (February): 50–64.

Ichioka, Yuji. 1988. *The Issei: The World of the First Generation Japanese Immigrants, 1885–1924.* New York: Free Press.

Ignatiev, Noel. 1995. *How the Irish Became White.* New York: Routledge.

Jacobs, Jerry. 1989. "Long-Term Trends in Occupational Segregation by Sex." *American Journal of Sociology* 95: 160–73.

Jacobsen, Joyce P. 1994. "Trends in Work Force Sex Segregation, 1960–1990." *Social Science Quarterly* 75, no. 1: 204–11.

Jaffee, A. J. 1956. "Trends in the Participation of Women in the Working Force." *Monthly Labor Review* 79 (May): 559–67.

Jensen, Joan. 1980. "Cloth, Butter, and Boarders: Women's Household Production for the Market." *Review of Political Economics* 12 (summer): 14–24.

Jones, Jacqueline. 1985. *Labor of Love, Labor of Sorrow: Black Women, Work, and the Family from Slavery to the Present*. New York: Basic Books.

Jones, Jo Ann, and Rachel A. Rosenfeld. 1989. "Women's Occupations and Local Labor Markets: 1950 to 1980." *Social Forces* 67, no. 3: 666–92.

Katz, William Loren. 1987. *The Black West*. N.p.: Ethrac Publications. Reprint, New York: Simon and Schuster, 1996.

Katzman, David M. 1978. *Seven Days a Week: Women and Domestic Service in Industrializing America*. New York: Oxford University Press.

Kennedy, Susan Estabrook. 1979. *If All We Did Was to Weep at Home: A History of White Working Class Women in America*. Bloomington: Indiana University Press.

Kessler-Harris, Alice. 1982. *Out to Work: A History of Wage-Earning Women in the United States*. New York: Oxford University Press.

Kilbourne, Barbara, Paula England, and Kurt Beron. 1994. "Effects of Individual, Occupational, and Industrial Characteristics on Earnings: Intersections of Race and Gender." *Social Forces* 72, no. 4: 1149–76.

King, Mary C. 1992. "Occupational Segregation by Race and Sex, 1940–88." *Monthly Labor Review* 115: 30–37.

Kodras, Janet E., and Irene Padavic. 1993. "Economic Restructuring and Women's Sectoral Employment in the 1970s: A Spatial Investigation Across 380 U.S. Labor Market Areas." *Social Science Quarterly* 74: 1–27.

Kunzel, Regina G. 1994. "White Neurosis, Black Pathology: Constructing Out-of-Wedlock Pregnancy in the Wartime and Postwar United States." In *Not June Cleaver: Women and Gender in Postwar America, 1945–1960*, edited by Joanne Meyerowitz, 304–31. Philadelphia: Temple University Press.

Lamphere, Louise. 1987. *From Working Daughters to Working Mothers: Immigrant Women in a New England Industrial Community*. Ithaca, N.Y.: Cornell University Press.

Logan, John R. 1997. "White Ethnics in the New York Economy, 1920–1960." Working Paper No. 112. New York: Russell Sage Foundation.

Long, Clarence. 1958. *The Labor Force Under Changing Income and Employment, 1890 to 1950*. New York: National Bureau of Economic Research.

Macdonald, Cameron Lynne. 1996. "Shadow Mothers: Nannies, *Au Pairs*, and Invisible Work." In *Working in the Service Society*, edited by Cameron Lynne Macdonald and Carmen Sirianni, 244–63. Philadelphia: Temple University Press.

Mason, Karen Oppenheim, and Barbara Laslett. 1983. "Women's Work in the American West: Los Angeles, 1880–1900, and Its Contrast with Essex County, Massachusetts, in 1880." Research Report No. 83-41. Ann Arbor: Population Studies Center, University of Michigan.

Massey, Douglas, and Zoltan L. Hajnal. 1995. "The Changing Geographic Structure of Black-White Segregation in the United States." *Social Science Quarterly* 76, no. 3: 527–42.

Matthaei, Julie. 1982. *An Economic History of Women in America: Women's Work, the Sexual Division of Labor, and the Development of Capitalism.* New York: Schocken Books.

McLaughlin, Virginia Yans. 1973. "Patterns of Work and Family Organization: Buffalo's Italians." In *The American Family in Social-Historical Perspective,* edited by Michael Gordon, 2nd ed., 136–51. New York: St. Martin's Press.

Meyerowitz, Joanne J. 1988. *Women Adrift: Independent Wage Earners in Chicago, 1880–1930.* Chicago: University of Chicago Press.

Michel, Sonya. 1999. *Children's Interests/Mothers' Rights: The Shaping of America's Child Care Policy.* New Haven, Conn.: Yale University Press.

Milkman, Ruth. 1987. *Gender at Work: The Dynamics of Job Segregation by Sex During World War II.* Urbana: University of Illinois Press.

Milkman, Ruth. 1998. "The Macrosociology of Paid Domestic Labor." *Work and Occupations* 25, no. 4: 483–510.

Mink, Gwendolyn. 1995. *The Wages of Motherhood: Inequality in the Welfare State, 1917–1942.* Ithaca, N.Y.: Cornell University Press.

Model, Suzanne. 1993. "The Ethnic Niche and the Structure of Opportunity: Immigrants and Minorities in New York City." In *The "Underclass" Debate,* edited by Michael B. Katz, 161–93. Princeton, N.J.: Princeton University Press.

Modell, John, and Tamara Hareven. 1973. "Urbanization and the Malleable Household: An Examination of Boarding and Lodging in American Families." *Journal of Marriage and the Family* 35: 467–79.

Molefsky, Barry. 1982. "America's Underground Economy." In *The Underground Economy in the United States and Abroad,* edited by Vito Tanzi, 47–67. Lexington, Mass.: Lexington Books/D. C. Heath.

Morawska, Ewa. 1996. *Insecure Prosperity: Small-Town Jews in Industrial America, 1890–1940.* Princeton, N.J.: Princeton University Press.

Napierski-Prancl, Michelle. 1998. "From Domestic Servant to Service Firm Employee: An Investigation into the Occupational Restructuring of the Job of Maid." Ph.D. diss. State University of New York at Albany.

Odem, Mary E. 1995. *Delinquent Daughters: Protecting and Policing Adolescent Female Sexuality in the United States, 1885–1920.* Chapel Hill: University of North Carolina Press.

Oppenheimer, Valerie Kincade. 1976 [1970]. *The Female Labor Force in the United States: Demographic and Economic Factors Governing Its Growth and Changing Composition.* Westport, Conn.: Greenwood Press.

Palmer, Phyllis. 1983. "The Racial Feminization of Poverty: Women of Color as Portents of the Future for All Women." *Women's Studies Quarterly* 11, no. 3 (fall): 4–6.

Palmer, Phyllis. 1989. *Domesticity and Dirt: Housewives and Domestic Servants in the United States, 1920–1945.* Philadelphia: Temple University Press.

Parreñas, Rhacel Salazar. 2000. "Migrant Filipina Domestic Workers and the International Division of Reproductive Labor." *Gender & Society* 14, no. 4 (August): 560–81.

Pearce, Diana M. 1978. "The Feminization of Poverty: Women, Work, and Welfare." *Urban and Social Change Review* 11 (winter): 28–36.

Pleck, Elizabeth H. 1978. "A Mother's Wages: Income Earning among Italian and Black Women, 1896–1911." In *The American Family in Social-Historical Perspective*, edited by Michael Gordon, 2nd ed., 490–510. New York: St. Martin's Press.

Portes, Alejandro, and Leif Jensen. 1987. "What's an Ethnic Enclave? The Case for Conceptual Clarity." *American Sociological Review* 52: 768–71.

Portes, Alejandro, and Robert D. Manning. 1986. "The Immigrant Enclave: Theory and Empirical Examples." In *Comparative Ethnic Relations*, edited by Susan Olzak and Joanne Nagel, 47–68. New York: Academic Press.

Research-in-Brief. N.d. "Increasing Working Mothers' Earnings: The Importance of Race, Family and Job Characteristics." Washington, D.C.: Institute for Women's Policy Research.

Reskin, Barbara F. 1984. *Sex Segregation in the Work place: Trends, Explanations, and Remedies*. Washington, D.C.: National Academy Press.

Reskin, Barbara F. 1999. "Occupational Segregation by Race and Ethnicity among Women Workers." In *Latinas and African American Women at Work: Race, Gender, and Economic Inequality*, edited by Irene Browne, 183–204. New York: Russell Sage Foundation.

Reskin, Barbara F., and Naomi Cassirer. 1996. "Occupational Segregation by Gender, Race, and Ethnicity." *Sociological Focus* 29, no. 3: 231–43.

Reskin, Barbara F., and Heidi I. Hartmann. 1986. *Women's Work, Men's Work: Sex Segregation on the Job*. Washington, D.C.: National Academy Press.

Reskin, Barbara F., and Irene Padavic. 1994. *Women and Men at Work*. Thousand Oaks, Calif.: Pine Forge Press.

Reskin, Barbara F., and Patricia A. Roos. 1990. *Job Queues, Gender Queues: Explaining Women's Inroads into Male Occupations*. Philadelphia: Temple University Press.

Rollins, Judith. 1985. *Between Women: Domestics and Their Employers*. Philadelphia: Temple University Press.

Romero, Mary. 1988. *Maid in the U.S.A.* New York: Routledge.

Rothstein, Frances Abrahamer. 1995. "Gender and Multiple Income Strategies in Rural Mexico: A Twenty-Year Perspective." In *Women in the Latin American Development Process: From Structural Subordination to Empowerment*, edited by Christine E. Bose and Edna Acosta-Belén, 167–93. Philadelphia: Temple University Press.

Ruggles, Steven. 1987. *Prolonged Connections: The Rise of the Extended Family in Nineteenth-Century England and America*. Madison: University of Wisconsin Press.

Ruggles, Steven, and Matthew Sobek. 1995. Integrated Public Use Microdata Series, Version 1.0. Minneapolis: Social History Research Laboratory, University of Minnesota.

Sanders, Jimy M., and Victor Nee. 1987. "Limits of Ethnic Solidarity in the Enclave Economy." *American Sociological Review* 52: 745–67.

Sassler, Sharon. 2000. "Learning to be an 'American Lady'? Ethnic Variation in Daughters' Pursuits in the Early 1900s." *Gender & Society* 14, no. 1: 184–209.

Sassler, Sharon, and Michael J. White. 1997. "Ethnicity, Gender, and Social Mobility in 1910." *Social Science History* 21, no. 3: 321–57.

Schweninger, Loren. 1990. *Black Property Owners in the South 1790–1915.* Urbana: University of Illinois Press.

Silver, Hilary. 1989. "The Demand for Homework: Evidence from the U.S. Census." In *Homework: Historical and Contemporary Perspectives on Paid Labor at Home,* edited by Eileen Boris and Cynthia R. Daniels, 103–29. Urbana: University of Illinois Press.

Smuts, Robert W. 1960. "The Female Labor Force: A Case Study in the Interpretation of Historical Statistics." *Journal of the American Statistical Association* 55 (March): 71–79.

Sobek, Matthew J. 1997. "A Century of Work: Gender, Labor Force Participation, and Occupational Attainment in the United States, 1880–1990." Ph.D. diss., University of Minnesota.

Sobek, Matthew J. 1999. "Occupational Segregation Indices, 1850–1990." Unpublished table, available from author (personal communication).

Sokoloff, Natalie. 1980. *Between Money and Love: The Dialectics of Women's Home and Market Work.* New York: Praeger.

Sokoloff, Natalie J. 1992. *Black Women and White Women in the Professions: Occupational Segregation by Race and Gender, 1960–1980.* New York: Routledge.

Solinger, Rickie. 1992. *Wake Up Little Susie: Single Pregnancy and Race Before Roe v. Wade.* New York: Routledge.

Sullivan, Mark. 1926. *Our Times: The United States, 1900–1925.* Vol. 1. *The Turn of the Century.* New York: Charles Scribner's Sons.

Sutherland, Daniel E. 1981. *Americans and Their Servants: Domestic Service in the United States from 1800 to 1920.* Baton Rouge: Louisiana State University Press.

Tentler, Leslie Woodcock. 1979. *Wage-Earning Women: Industrial Work and Family Life in the U.S., 1900–1930.* New York: Oxford University Press.

Treiman, Donald J., and Heidi Hartmann. 1981. *Women, Work, and Wages: Equal Pay for Jobs of Equal Value.* Washington, D.C.: National Academy Press.

Turbin, Carole. 1992. *Working Women of Collar City: Gender, Class, and Community in Troy, New York, 1864–86.* Urbana: University of Illinois Press.

Turbin, Carole. 1995. "Domestic Service Revisited: Private Household Workers and Employers in a Shifting Economic Environment." *International Labor and Working-Class History* 47: 91–100.

Uchitelle, Louis. 1998. "Some Economic Interplay Comes Nearly Full Circle." *New York Times*, 30 April.

United Nations. 1995. *The World's Women 1995: Trends and Statistics.* Social Statistics and Indicators Series K, No. 12, Sales no. E.95.XVII.2. New York: United Nations.

United States Bureau of the Census. 1995. *Statistical Abstract of the United States: 1995*, 115th ed. Washington, D.C.: U.S. Census Bureau.

United States Department of Labor, Women's Bureau. 1994. *1993 Handbook on Women Workers: Trends and Issues.* Washington, D.C.: U.S. Government Printing Office.

Wallace, Michael, and Chin-fen Chang. 1990. "Barriers to Women's Employment: Economic Segmentation in American Manufacturing, 1950–1980." In *Research in Stratification and Mobility*, vol. 9, edited by Arne Kalleberg, 337–61.

Ward, Kathryn. 1990. *Women Workers and Global Restructuring.* Ithaca, N.Y.: ILR Press.

Ward, Kathryn B., and Jean Larson Pyle. 1995. "Gender, Industrialization, Transnational Corporations and Development: An Overview of the Trends and Patterns." In *Women in the Latin American Development Process: From Structural Subordination to Empowerment*, edited by Christine E. Bose and Edna Acosta-Belén, 37–64. Philadelphia: Temple University Press.

Washington, Mary L. 1996. "Constructing the Substance of Race. Part II. Racial Classifications in the US Censuses of 1850 to 1920." Paper presented at the annual meeting of the Social Science History Association, New Orleans, October.

Watkins, Susan Cotts. 1994. *After Ellis Island: Newcomers and Natives in the 1910 Census.* New York: Russell Sage Foundation.

West, Candace, and Don H. Zimmerman. 1987. "Doing Gender." *Gender & Society* 1: 125–51.

Wharton, Amy. 1986. "Industrial Structure and Gender Segregation in Blue-Collar Occupations." *Social Forces* 64, no. 4: 1025–31.

Wilder, Laura Ingalls. 1953. *Little House on the Prairie.* New York: Harper.

Wilkie, Jane Riblett. 1985. "The Decline of Occupational Segregation Between Black and White Women." *Research in Race and Ethnic Relations* 4: 67–89.

Wilson, Kenneth L., and Portes, Alejandro. 1980. "Immigrant Enclaves: An Analysis of the Labor Market Experiences of Cubans in Miami." *American Journal of Sociology* 86: 305–19.

Wilson, William Julius. 1987. *The Truly Disadvantaged: The Inner City, the Underclass, and Public Policy.* Chicago: University of Chicago Press.

Wright, Carroll C. 1900. *The History and Growth of the United States Census.* Washington, D.C.: U.S. Government Printing Office.

Wright, Mareena McKinley. 1995. "'I Never Did Any Fieldwork, but I Milked an Awful Lot of Cows!' Using Rural Women's Experience to Reconceptualize Models of Work." *Gender & Society* 9 (April): 216–35.

Wyly, Elvin. 1996. "IPUMS and the Feminization of the Clerical Labor Force, 1880–1920." Paper presented at the annual meeting of the Social Science History Association, New Orleans, October.

Xu, Wu, and Ann Leffler. 1992. "Gender and Race Effects on Occupational Prestige, Segregation, and Earnings." *Gender & Society* 6 (September): 376–92.

Yezierska, Anzia. 1925. *Bread Givers.* New York: Persea Books. Reprint, 1975, with introduction by Alice Kessler Harris.

Yung, Judy. 1995. *Unbound Feet: A Social History of Chinese Women in San Francisco.* Berkeley: University of California Press.

Zhou, Min. 1992. *Chinatown: The Economic Potential of an Urban Enclave.* Philadelphia: Temple University Press.

Zhou, Min, and John R. Logan. 1989. "Returns on Human Capital in Ethnic Enclaves: New York City's Chinatown." *American Sociological Review* 54, no. 5: 809–20.

Zunz, Olivier. 1982. *The Changing Face of Inequality: Urbanization, Industrial Development, and Immigrants to Detroit, 1880–1920.* Chicago: University of Chicago Press.

Index

African Americans: and cultural position on women's work, 199; in 1900 Census, 15; northward migration of, 9, 56, 88, 121, 123, 158–59

African-American women: as agricultural workers, 97; and domestic work, 88, 100, 129, 138, 142; and farm work, 44, 88; gainful employment rates for, 60, 75, 76, 209–10; headship rates for, 67, 168; and home-based work, 41–47; and literacy rates, 95; and marital status, 204–5; non-wives among, 81; objection to cult of domesticity, 31; rural employment rates, 202, 204–5; and taking in boarders, 46; urban employment rates, 202, 204–5

age: and female headship, 174, 181–82; and gainful employment, 78; and occupational segregation, 126; and taking in boarders, 48

agricultural economy, 8, 9; at turn of century, 19

agricultural workers, 19; distribution of, 97, 99; and social class, 71

artisan occupations. *See* craft occupations

Asian immigrants, 16–17, 56; West Coast migration of, 9. *See also under individual ethnic groups*

Asian-Indian women, as cashiers, 99

Asian women: as agricultural workers, 97; and low literacy rates, 95; in nontraditional occupations, 104; and occupational diversity, 94; rural employment rates for, 203, 204

Australian census: of 1871, 30; of 1881, 30, 40

blacks. *See* African Americans

blue-collar occupations, 19–20; reduction in, 214; sex/race segregation in, 120–21; and social class, 71; specialization in, 97; at turn of century, 19

boarders, taking in, 4, 24, 27, 35, 45–50, 77; and female headship, 181–82; regional distribution of, 197–98; social class and, 64; as uncounted work, 26–27, 29, 38–39, 45; in urban vs. rural areas, 198; variables, 47–50

boarding, as intermediate survival strategy, 186

bookkeeping-cashier-accountant, 55; distribution of, 99

British census (1851, 1861), 30

British immigrants, 16

British women: as domestic workers, 142; and farm work, 44; as school teachers, 94; as service workers, 96; and white-collar work, 95

Canadians. *See* English Canadians; French Canadians

Caribbean immigrants. *See* Latin American immigrants

cashier, present-day distribution of, 99

casual workers, 27

Caucasian women. *See* white women

Census Bureau. *See* U.S. Census Bureau

census definitions, 25–33

child care, 4; by elderly, 79; and female headship, 189; present-day, 215; as self-employment, 27

Chinese Exclusion Act of 1882, 56, 104

Chinese immigrants, 16, 56, 213; in 1900 Census, 15

Chinese women, as cashiers, 99

citizenship, and domestic work, 131